Lecture Notes in Computer Science 6309

Mong Li Lee   Jeffrey Xu Yu
Zohra Bellahsène   Rainer Unland (Eds.)

Database and XML Technologies

7th International
XML Database Symposium, XSym 2010
Singapore, September 17, 2010
Proceedings

Volume Editors

Mong Li Lee
National University of Singapore
School of Computing
Singapore 117417, Republic of Singapore
E-mail: leeml@comp.nus.edu.sg

Jeffrey Xu Yu
The Chinese University of Hong Kong
Department of Systems Engineering and Engineering Management
Shatin, N.T., Hong Kong
E-mail: yu@se.cuhk.edu.hk

Zohra Bellahsène
Université Montpellier II
LIRMM UMR 5506 CNRS
34392 Montpellier, France
E-mail: bella@lirmm.fr

Rainer Unland
University of Duisburg-Essen
Institute for Computer Science and Business Information Systems (ICB)
45117 Essen, Germany
E-mail: rainer.unland@icb.uni-due.de

Library of Congress Control Number: 2010933595

CR Subject Classification (1998): H.2, H.3, E.1, H.2.8, H.4, F.2

LNCS Sublibrary: SL 3 – Information Systems and Application, incl. Internet/Web and HCI

ISSN	0302-9743
ISBN-10	3-642-15683-5 Springer Berlin Heidelberg New York
ISBN-13	978-3-642-15683-0 Springer Berlin Heidelberg New York

springer.com

Printed in Germany

Typesetting: Camera-ready by author, data conversion by Scientific Publishing Services, Chennai, India
Printed on acid-free paper 06/3180

Preface

Since its first edition in 2003, the XML Database Symposium series (XSym) has been a forum for academics, practitioners, users and vendors, allowing all to discuss the use of and synergy between database management systems and XML. The symposia have provided many opportunities for timely discussions on a broad range of topics pertaining to the theory and practice of XML data management and its applications. XSym 2010 continued this XSym tradition with a program consisting of 11 papers and a keynote shared with the 36th International Conference on Very Large Data Bases (VLDB 2010). We received 20 paper submissions, out of which 8 papers were accepted as full papers, and 3 as short papers. Each submitted paper underwent a rigorous and careful review by four referees.

The contributions in these proceedings are a fine sample of the current research in XML query processing, including XPath satisfiability, approximate joins, pattern matching, linear index construction for trees, dynamic labeling, and XQuery update translation based on schema. The papers focus on recent advances in detecting functional dependencies, modeling complex XML twig pattern output, promoting semantics capability of XML keys, and searchable compression of Microsoft office documents. In addition, we include a paper that shares lessons learned from real XML database development.

The organizers would like to express their gratitude to the authors, for submitting their work, and to the Program Committee, for providing very thorough evaluations of the submitted papers and for the discussions that followed under significant time constraints. We also would like to thank the invited keynote speaker, Prof. M. Tamer Özsu, for the challenging and thought-provoking contribution. Finally, we are also grateful to Microsoft and Michael Rys for their generous sponsorship, Andrei Voronkov and other contributors for the EasyChair conference management system, and the local organizers for their efforts in making XSym 2010 a pleasant and successful event. Finally, we would also like to thank Alfred Hofmann and his great team from Springer for their support and cooperation in putting this volume together.

July 2010

Mong Li Lee
Jeffrey Xu Yu
Zohra Bellahsene
Rainer Unland

Organization

Steering Committee

Zohra Bellahsene	LIRMM-CNRS/University Montpellier 2 (France)
Ela Hunt	University of Strathclyde (UK)
Michael Rys	Microsoft (USA)
Rainer Unland	University of Duisburg-Essen (Germany)

Program Co-chairs

Mong Li Lee	National University of Singapore (Singapore)
Jeffrey Xu Yu	Chinese University of Hong Kong (China)

International Program Committee

Bernd Amann	Université Paris 6 (France)
Veronique Benzaken	Université Paris-Sud (France)
Sourav S. Bhowmick	Nanyang Technological University (Singapore)
Stéphane Bressan	National University of Singapore (Singapore)
Chee Yong Chan	National University of Singapore (Singapore)
Yi Chen	Arizona State University (USA)
Minos Garofalakis	Technical University of Crete (Greece)
Giorgio Ghelli	Università di Pisa (Italy)
Torsten Grust	Universität Tübingen (Germany)
Giovanna Guerrini	Università di Genova (Italy)
H.V. Jagadish	University of Michigan (USA)
Yaron Kanza	Technion Israel Institute of Technology (Israel)
Raghav Kaushik	Microsoft Research (USA)
Jiaheng Lu	Renmin University of China (China)
Murali Mani	Worcester Polytechnic Institute (USA)
Peter McBrien	Imperial College - London (UK)
Atsuyuki Morishima	University of Tsukuba (Japan)
Tadeusz Pankowski	Poznan University of Technology (Poland)
Prakash Ramanan	Wichita State University (USA)
Pierre Senellart	Télécom ParisTech (France)
Jerome Simeon	IBM Research (USA)
Martin Theobald	Max-Planck-Institut für Informatik (Germany)
Wee Hyong Tok	Microsoft (China)

Vasilis Vassalos	Athens University of Economics and Business (Greece)
Yuqing Wu	Indiana University (USA)
Ni Yuan	IBM (China)
Xiaofang Zhou	University of Queensland (Australia)

External Reviewers

Pantelis Aravogliadis
Federico Cavalieri
Vassilis Christophides
Pierre Genevhès
Frangçoise Gire
Mirian Halfeld-Ferrari.

Table of Contents

Keynote Address

XML Query Processing

XML Update and Applications

XML Modeling

Distributed XML Query Processing
(Extended Abstract)

M. Tamer Özsu and Patrick Kling

Cheriton School of Computer Science, University of Waterloo
{tozsu,pkling}@cs.uwaterloo.ca

Over the past decade, XML has become a commonly used format for storing and exchanging data in a wide variety of systems. Due to this widespread use, the problem of effectively and efficiently managing XML collections has attracted significant attention in both the research community and in commercial products. One can claim that the centralized management and querying of XML data (i.e., data residing in one system) is now a well understood problem. Unfortunately, centralized techniques are limited in their scalability when presented with large collections and heavy query workloads. In relational database systems, scalability challenges have been successfully addressed by partitioning data collections and processing queries in parallel in a distributed system [1]. Our work is focused on similarly exploiting distribution in the context of XML. While there are some similarities between the way relational database systems can be distributed and the opportunities for distributing XML database systems, the significant differences in both data and query models make it impossible to directly apply relational techniques to XML. Therefore, new solutions need to be developed to distribute XML database systems.

Due to XML's tree structure it is possible to partition a collection by cutting individual document edges in an unconstrained fashion [2–4]. While this approach yields a very flexible distribution model, it does not offer a concise specification of how the data are fragmented, which has been shown to be an important asset for optimizing distributed query evaluation [5–9]. For our work, we have, therefore, chosen a distribution model that is based on schema characteristics and query operators (similar to relational distribution models): horizontal fragmentation based on selection (with predicates represented as tree patterns), vertical fragmentation based on projection (placing each element type in exactly one fragment), and hybrid fragmentation based on a concatenation of both operators.

Based on this distribution model, we have aimed to develop a complete framework for managing a distributed XML collection with particular focus on evaluating and optimizing queries (which we represent as tree patterns) over this collection. While this problem is large and complex, we can break it down into steps that we tackle independently:

Fragmentation algorithms. We primarily use distribution to improve the performance and scalability of query evaluation. Our experiments have shown that the performance impact of distribution is highly dependent on how we distribute our collection. Whereas a suitable distribution schema generally yields a significant improvement in performance when compared to centralized query evaluation, choosing a poorly suited distribution schema may lead to decreased performance. We solve this problem by defining fragmentation algorithms that take workload information into account. Whereas in the case of horizontal fragmentation this can be

M.L. Lee et al. (Eds.): XSym 2010, LNCS 6309, pp. 1–2, 2010.

achieved by adapting relational techniques based on minterm predicates, for vertical fragmentation, we have developed a greedy fragmentation algorithm based on a cost model for distributed query evaluation.

Localization and pruning. When evaluating a query, it is often not necessary to access all fragments of a distributed collection. By restricting query evaluation to the relevant fragments, we can decrease inter-query interference and improve performance. In order to take advantage of this, we have devised a number of localization techniques that, for a given query, identify the set of relevant fragments and generate a sub-query for each of them. In many cases, we can further prune this set of fragments by exploiting characteristics of the distribution schema that allow us to reason about the content of certain fragments without accessing then.

Optimizing distributed query execution. Once we have generated a sub-query for each relevant fragment, we need to define a distributed execution plan that determines how sub-query results are combined to the overall query result. In the case of vertical fragmentation, the naïve strategy is to evaluate all sub-queries independently and then join their results together. While this approach maximizes parallelism, it often yields very large intermediate results, a large portion of which is subsequently discarded. To solve this, we have devised a technique for exploiting the selectivity of one sub-query in order to reduce the cost of evaluating another, while incurring only a small parallelism penalty. Based on a cost model, we apply this technique wherever beneficial, yielding a significant improvement in overall query performance.

References

1. Özsu, M.T., Valduriez, P.: Principles of distributed database systems, 2nd edn. (1999)
2. Abiteboul, S., Benjelloun, O., Milo, T.: The Active XML project: an overview. VLDB Journal 17(5) (2008)
3. Buneman, P., Cong, G., Fan, W., Kementsietsidis, A.: Using partial evaluation in distributed query evaluation. In: Proc. of VLDB (2006)
4. Cong, G., Fan, W., Kementsietsidis, A.: Distributed query evaluation with performance guarantees. In: Proc. of ACM SIGMOD (2007)
5. Bremer, J.-M., Gertz, M.: On distributing XML repositories. In: Proc. of WebDB (2003)
6. Kling, P., Özsu, M.T., Daudjee, K.: Optimizing distributed XML queries through localization and pruning. University of Waterloo, Tech. Rep. CS-2009-13 (2009), `http://www.cs.uwaterloo.ca/research/tr/2009/CS-2009-13.pdf`
7. Andrade, A., Ruberg, G., Baião, F.A., Braganholo, V.P., Mattoso, M.: Efficiently processing XML queries over fragmented repositories with PartiX. In: Grust, T., Höpfner, H., Illarramendi, A., Jablonski, S., Mesiti, M., Müller, S., Patranjan, P.-L., Sattler, K.-U., Spiliopoulou, M., Wijsen, J. (eds.) EDBT 2006. LNCS, vol. 4254, pp. 150–163. Springer, Heidelberg (2006)
8. Ma, H., Schewe, K.-D.: Fragmentation of XML documents. In: Proc. of SBBD (2003)
9. Ma, H., Schewe, K.-D.: Heuristic horizontal XML fragmentation. In: Proc. of CAiSE (2005)

Approximate Joins for XML Using g-String*

Fei Li, Hongzhi Wang, Cheng Zhang, Liang Hao, Jianzhong Li, and Hong Gao

The School of Computer Science and Technology, Harbin Institute of Technology
lifei.cscs@163.com, wangzh@hit.edu.cn, domisol891018@hotmail.com,
hl8807@126.com, lijzh@hit.edu.cn, honggao@hit.edu.cn

Abstract. When integrating XML documents from autonomous databases, exact joins often fail for the data items representing the same real world object may not be exactly the same. Thus the join must be approximate. Tree-edit-distance-based join methods have high join quality but low efficiency. Comparatively, other methods with higher efficiency cannot perform the join as effectively as tree edit distance does.

To keep the balance between efficiency and effectiveness, in this paper, we propose a novel method to approximately join XML documents. In our method, trees are transformed to g-strings with each entry a tiny subtree. Then the distance between two trees is evaluated as the g-string distance between their corresponding g-strings. To make the g-string based join method scale to large XML databases, we propose the g-bag distance as the lower bound of the g-string distance. With g-bag distance, only a very small part of g-string distance need to be computed directly. Thus the whole join process can be done very efficiently. We theoretically analyze the properties of the g-string distance. Experiments with synthetic and various real world data confirm the effectiveness and efficiency of our method and suggest that our technique is both scalable and useful.

1 Introduction

For the ability to represent data from a wide variety of sources, XML is rapidly emerging as the new standard for data representation and exchange on the web. Given the flexibility of XML model, data in autonomous sources representing the same object may not be exactly the same. Thus the join must be approximate.

XML documents are often modeled as ordered labeled trees. A widely-used method to evaluate the similarity between trees is the tree edit distance [12]. It is effective for identifying similar trees but computationally expensive. The known fastest algorithm [5] still needs $O(n^3)$ runtime, where n is the tree size.

* Supported by the National Science Foundation of China (No 60703012, 60773063), the NSFC-RGC of China(No. 60831160525), National Grant of Fundamental Research 973 Program of China (No.2006CB303000), National Grant of High Technology 863 Program of China (No. 2009AA01Z149), Key Program of the National Natural Science Foundation of China (No. 60933001), National Postdoctor Foundtaion of China (No. 20090450126), Development Program for Outstanding Young Teachers in Harbin Institute of Technology (no. HITQNJS.2009.052).

M.L. Lee et al. (Eds.): XSym 2010, LNCS 6309, pp. 3–17, 2010.

Since it is difficult to improve the efficiency significantly by optimizing the tree edit algorithm independently, some transformations are often adopted. Trees are transformed into other data structures whose similarity are easier to evaluate.

Set (multi-set) is a data structure whose similarity can be evaluated effectively. *pq*-gram and Hashing tree [13] are set-based methods. They transform trees into sets and use Jaccard Coefficient or other metric between the sets to evaluate the similarity between trees. However, since trees are hierarchical data, they contain two kinds of information: label information and structure information. Existing set-based methods cannot properly describe the label and structure information at the same time. As a result, even in their own experiments, their join quality is lower than that using the tree edit distance.

String is a relatively simple data structure which contains order for structure as well as content information in each entry. In order to perform the join effectively and efficiently, in this paper, each tree is transformed into a *g*-string with each entry a tiny subtree. We use the *g*-string distance between *g*-strings to evaluate the distance between trees. The *g*-string distance can be computed in $O(n^2)$ time instead of $O(n^3)$ of computing the tree edit distance. Unlike set-based methods, experiments on various real world data show that our method has a higher join quality than the tree edit distance.

For fast join XML documents among large databases, we further transform *g*-strings into *g*-bags and use the *g*-bag distance as the lower bound of *g*-string distance. With the application of some well-known techniques (e.g. sort-merge and hash join), all the *g*-bag distance can be computed without nested-loop. Therefore, the lower bounds can be computed very efficiently. In most cases, by using *g*-bag distance, the *g*-string distance needs to be computed only on a small share of tree pairs. Thus the overall join process is performed efficiently.

In summary, the main contributions of this paper include:

- We present the *g*-string distance to evaluate the distance between trees. As we know, it is the first string-based similarity measure between trees. Experiments show that the join quality based on *g*-string distance is higher than that using the unit tree edit distance or set-based methods.
- We propose the *g*-bag distance as the lower bound of *g*-string distance. With this lower bound, only a small share of tree pairs need to be compared directly during the whole join process. As a result, our method can be nearly as efficient as the most efficient set-based method.
- Extensive experiments on various real-world XML databases (Municipality, SwissProt, Treebank and DBLP) confirm the analytical results and suggest that our technique is both scalable and useful.

The rest of the paper is organized as follows. In Section 2, related work is discussed. In Section 3, background knowledge is introduced. We propose *g*-string distance to evaluate the similarity between trees and analyze its properties theoretically in Section 4. In Section 5, we present the *g*-bag distance as the lower bound of *g*-string distance and give an efficient XML join algorithm. We test the efficiency and effectiveness of our method experimentally in Section 6. In Section 7, we draw the conclusions and point to future work.

2 Related Work

Most papers that compare XML documents model the XML data as ordered, labeled trees. A well known distance function for trees is the tree edit distance. Tai [12] presented the first algorithm for computing tree edit distance in time $O(n^6)$. Zhang and Shasha [17] improved this result to a worst-case $O(n^4)$ running time. Klein [9] improved this result to $O(n^3 \log n)$. A recent development by Demaine [5] describes an algorithm running in $O(n^3)$ time.

Obviously, the tree edit distance computation is expensive and does not scale to large tree sets. Therefore, many of the previous work transform trees into other data structures whose similarities are easier to evaluate. Set (multi-set) is a kind of data structure whose similarity is evaluated effectively. In the method of pq-gram [2], each tree is transformed into a set of pq-grams, a small subtree in a specific shape. By such transformation, the similarity between trees can be evaluated in time $O(n \log n)$. The latest set-transformation based method is presented in [13]. In that method, each tree is transformed into a set of pivots which contains the lowest communal ancestor information for node pairs. Other set based methods like histogram [8] and binary branch distance [16] give lower bounds for tree edit distance to accelerate the join process.

Compared with set-based methods, string-based methods are preliminary. In [7], XML documents are transformed into their preorder and postorder traversal sequences. Then the maximum of the string edit distance of the two sequences is used as the lower bound of tree edit distance. Unfortunately, previous works only use the string edit distance to estimate lower bounds of tree edit distance. To the best of our knowledge, none of the previous work use the similarity between strings to evaluate the similarity between trees directly.

3 Preliminary

Tree Edit Distance: Given two trees T_1 and T_2, the *tree edit distance* $TD(T_1, T_2)$ between T_1 and T_2 is the minimum number of edit operations (1.relabel a node. 2.delete a node. 3.insert a node) to transform one tree into another [12].

Approximate XML Join: Given two XML document sets, F_1 and F_2, the approximate join between F_1 and F_2 is the set $\{(T_i, T_j)|(T_i, T_j) \in F_1 \times F_2, sim(T_i, T_j)\}$, where $sim(T_i, T_j)$ is true only when T_i and T_j are evaluated similar using a predefined tree similarity evaluation.

Example 1. Figure 1(a) shows two XML document sets F_1 and F_2. Suppose the predefined similarity evaluation is tree edit distance [12] lower than 2. Only (T_1, T_3) and (T_2, T_4) fit that evaluation. So the join result is $\{(T_1, T_3), (T_2, T_4)\}$.

Euler Traversal: The Euler Traversal $Euler(T)$ of a tree T is the depth-first traversal on T beginning from the root and ending at the root where each node $v \in T$ is traversed twice in opposite direction. e.g. Figure 1(b) shows the Euler Traversal of T_1 in Figure 1(a).

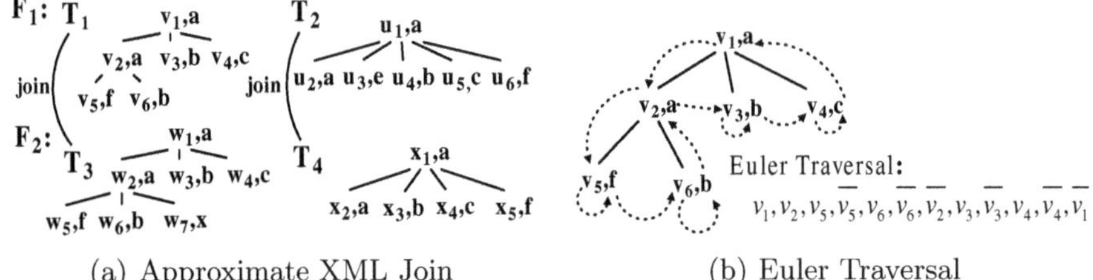

(a) Approximate XML Join (b) Euler Traversal

Fig. 1. Preliminary

String Alignment Distance: Given two strings s_1 and s_2, the string alignment distance $DistA(s_1, s_2)$ is the minimum number of string alignment operations (1.delete a character. 2.insert a character) to transform s_1 to s_2 [10].

4 The *g*-String Distance

4.1 *g*-String and *g*-String Distance

In this subsection, we define g-string and g-string distance. Intuitively, a g-string is a string with each entry a tiny subtree in a specific shape. The benefit of using this kind of string to represent trees is shown intuitively as follows:

1. The order of tiny subtrees describes the tree global structure information.
2. Each tiny subtree itself describes the tree local structure information.
3. The label information of a tree is described in each tiny subtree. Since each subtree is very small, the node label is hardly to be over emphasized.

Definition 1 (Sibling Subtree). *Let T be a tree and v be a node of T. The sibling subtree $T(v)$ of v consists of v as the root and all v's children as leaves. v is called the center node of $T(v)$.*

Definition 2 (g-Extended Sibling Subtree). *Given a sibling tree $T(v)$, its extended sibling subtree is a 2-level tree generated by adding dummy nodes: If v has no child, g dummy nodes are added to v. If v has one or more children, $g-1$ dummy nodes are added before the first and after the last child of v respectively. The g-extended sibling tree centered at v is denoted by $T_g^{ext}(v)$.*

Example 2. Figure 2(a) shows all the sibling subtrees of T_1. $T_1(v_2)$, $T_1(v_3)$, $T_1(v_4)$ in Figure 2(a) are extended into 2-extended sibling trees in Figure 2(b).

Definition 3 (g-MinTree). *Let v be a node of a tree T. A g-mintree of v is a subtree of $T_g^{ext}(v)$ with v as root and g consequent children of v as leaves.*

Definition 4 (g-Substring). *Given a g-extended sibling tree $T_g^{ext}(v)$, the g-substring s_v of v is a sequence S with each entry a g-mintree of $T_g^{ext}(v)$, where $\forall t_1, t_2 \in S$, t_1 is before t_2 iff the first leave in t_1 is left to first leave in t_2.*

(a) All the sibling subtrees in T_1 (b) Some 2-extended sibling subtrees

Fig. 2. Sibling Subtrees and Extended Sibling Subtrees

Definition 5 (g-String). *For a tree T, its g-string is a string $s^g(T){=}s_{v_1}s_{v_2}\cdots s_{v_n}$, where each s_{v_i} is the g-substring of v_i and $v_1,v_2,\cdots,v_n$ is the list of nodes in the order of the Euler Traversal of T.*

Theorem 1. *Let T be a tree with n nodes including l leaf nodes and i non-leaf nodes where $n = l + i$. The length of $s^g(T)$ is $4l + 2gi - 2$.*

Definition 6 (g-String Distance). *For $g > 1$, the g-string distance $\Delta^g(T_1, T_2)$ between two trees T_1 and T_2 is defined as follows:*

$$\Delta^g(T_1, T_2) = \frac{|DistA(s^g(T_1), s^g(T_2))|}{|s^g(T_1)| + |s^g(T_2)|}$$

Example 3. Figure 3(a) shows the 2-substring of v_2 in T_1. The 2-strings $s^g(T_1)$ and $s^g(T_3)$ of T_1 and T_3 are shown in Figure 3(b). The string alignment distance between them is 8. The sum length of $s^g(T_1)$ and $s^g(T_3)$ is 48. Thus the 2-string distance between T_1 and T_3 is $8/48 = 0.1667$.

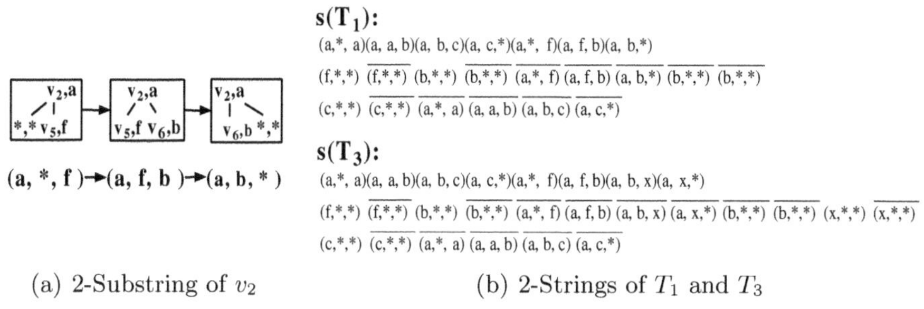

(a, *, f)→(a, f, b)→(a, b, *)
s(T1):
(a,*, a)(a, a, b)(a, b, c)(a, c,*)(a,*, f)(a, f, b)(a, b,*)
(f,*,*) (f,*,*) (b,*,*) (b,*,*) (a,*, f) (a, f, b) (a, b,*) (b,*,*) (b,*,*)
(c,*,*) (c,*,*) (a,*, a) (a, a, b) (a, b, c) (a, c,*)
s(T3):
(a,*, a)(a, a, b)(a, b, c)(a, c,*)(a,*, f)(a, f, b)(a, b, x)(a, x,*)
(f,*,*) (f,*,*) (b,*,*) (b,*,*) (a,*, f) (a, f, b) (a, b, x) (a, x,*) (b,*,*) (b,*,*) (x,*,*) (x,*,*)
(c,*,*) (c,*,*) (a,*, a) (a, a, b) (a, b, c) (a, c,*)

(a) 2-Substring of v_2 (b) 2-Strings of T_1 and T_3

Fig. 3. g-Substring and g-String

Theorem 2. *The g-string distance between a pair of trees is 0 if and only if the two trees are exactly the same. That is: $\Delta^g(T_1, T_2) = 0 \Leftrightarrow T_1 = T_2$.*

4.2 Algorithms for the g-String Computation

The core of our algorithms is the generation of g-string. Algorithm 1-3 transform a tree into its g-string. For efficient transformation, a shift reg: *base*, is used in the algorithms to store the base of the current g-mintree. The operation shift($base$,el) returns $base$ with its oldest element dequeued and el enqueue. For example, shift((a,b,c),x) returns (b,c,x). The center of the current g-mintree is stored in r. The operation $r \circ base$ returns the g-mintree with the center of r and the base of $base$. The operation ins(g-mintree, $s^g(T)$) connects the g-mintree to the last entry of $s^g(T)$. For simplicity, each g-mintree is hashed into a number. Since each node is visited twice in Euler Traversal, when the center of that g-mintree is visited in the oppose direction, we use another hash function to hash that g-mintree into another number.

Algorithm 1. Generate-g-String

```
Input:T, g; Output:s^g(T)
s^g(T)=Euler-traversal(T, root(T), g, s^g(T))
return s^g(T)
```

Algorithm 2. Euler-Traversal

```
Input:T, r, g, s^g(T); Output:s^g(T)
s^g(T)=Substring-Addition(T, r, g, s^g(T), h)
if r is a non-leaf node then
  for all children c (from left to right) of r do
    s^g(T)=Euler-traversal(T, r, g, s^g(T))
s^g(T)=Substring-Addition(T, r, g, s^g(T), h')
return s^g(T)
```

Algorithm 3. Substring-Addition

```
Input:T, r, g, s^g(T),h; Output:s^g(T)
base=initialize base register full filled with *
if r is a leaf node then
  g-mintree=h(r ∘ base); ins(g-mintree, s^g(T))
else
  for all children c (from left to right) of r do
    base=shift(base, c); g-mintree=h(r ∘ base); ins(g-mintree, s^g(T))
  for j = 1 to g-1 do
    base=shift(base, *); g-mintree=h(r ∘ base); ins(g-mintree, s^g(T))
return s^g(T)
```

4.3 Some Properties of g-String Distance

Sensitivity to Structural Changes In tree-structured data, edits on high degree nodes often have relatively more impact on the tree structure. Our method is sensitive to structural changes: edits on nodes with more children are more likely to cause bigger g-string distance. We demonstrate this point with an example.

Example 4. In Figure 4(a), T is a tree with 10 nodes at height 3. T' is generated by deleting a leaf node and relabeling a leaf node while T'' is generated by deleting a non-leaf node and relabeling a non-leaf node. $TD(T,T')$=$TD(T,T'')$=2 even though T and T' seem more similar. Using 2-string, $\Delta^2(T,T') = 0.2778 < \Delta^2(T,T'') = 0.6111$, edits on high degree nodes cause bigger g-string distance.

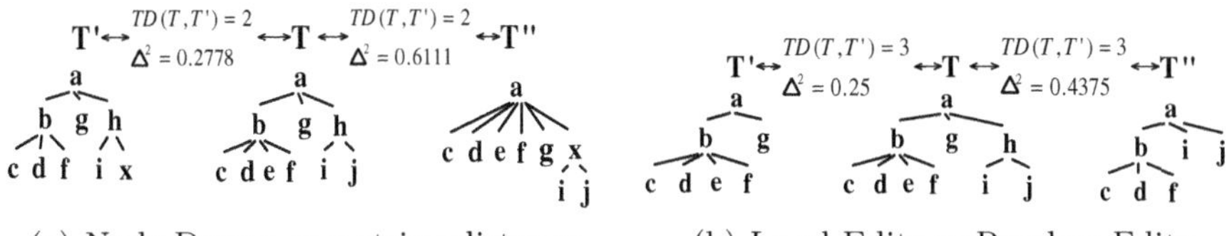

(a) Node Degree vs g-string distance (b) Local Edits vs Random Edits

Fig. 4. g-String Distance is Sensitive to Structure

g-string distance can better detect the local similarity (e.g. two trees share a large subtree). Consider three trees T, T' and T'' and $TD(T,T') = TD(T,T'')$. Suppose that T and T' share a large subtree while T and T'' share large numbers of nodes distributed all over the tree. In many cases like RNA molecules [11], T and T' are more likely to describe similar RNA molecules while T and T'' are more likely to share some nodes just in coincidence. In this situation, T and T' are evaluated more similar with g-string distance. Another case would involve that only a small subtree of T is lost or replaced. The result tree T' should be evaluated with high similarity with T. In our g-string distance, local edits (e.g. delete a subtree from T) are more likely to have less effect than uniformly distributed edits (e.g. random delete a number of nodes from T).

Example 5. In Figure 4(b), T' is generated by deleting a subtree consisting of h, i and j. T'' is generated by deleting a 2-degree node h and two leaf nodes e and g. $TD(T,T')$=$TD(T,T'')$=3 even though T and T' seem more similar. Using 2-string distance, $\Delta^2(T,T') = 0.25 < \Delta^2(T,T'') = 0.4375$. Local edits often have less effect than uniformly distributed edits on g-string distance.

Information Representation in g-String. Two kinds of information is stored in trees: label information and structure information. Our g-string can better represent the two kinds of information than existing transform-based methods. In this subsection, we compare our g-string distance with other methods.

Most transformation-based methods transform trees into sets [8,16,2,13]. However, a set itself has no internal structure, the structure information of trees is contained in the elements of the set. For example, in method pq-gram, each element of the set is a subtree and the structure information is contained in these subtrees. However, a problem rises when choosing the size of these subtrees. If subtrees are small, the global changes can hardly be detected. If the subtrees are large, some label information is over emphasized for these labels exist in too many subtrees. Here we illustrate this point in two examples.

Example 6. In Figure 5(a), T_1 and T_2 are different trees, but in method *pq*-gram, their differences cannot be detected. This is because all the local label and local structure of the two trees are the same and the method *pq*-gram can not detect global structure changes. In our method, this problem is solved for the order of these g-mintrees in *g*-strings represents the global structure information in trees. *g*-string distance is 0 only when two trees are exactly the same.

Example 7. In Figure 5(b), T_1 is a tree with 7 nodes at height 3. T_2 is generated by relabeling a and b in T_1. Using 2,3-grams as the author recommended, the *pq*-distance between T_1 and T_2 are 1 since they share no *pq*-gram. This problem is resulted from that the labels of a and b are over emphasized. Both of the two labels appear in more than half of the *pq*-grams. As a comparison, with *g*-string, this problem will not rise since all the entries in *g*-string are tiny 2-level subtrees. These subtrees are so small that the labels are less likely to be over emphasized.

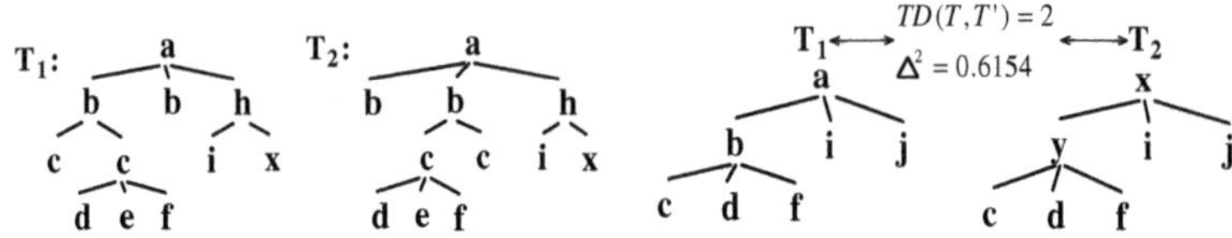

(a) Some set-based methods fail to detect the global changes

(b) Some set-based methods emphasize too much on some node labels

Fig. 5. *g*-string vs set-based method

In our method, the label information and structure information are represented properly:

1. Our *g*-string consists of *g*-mintrees at height 2. These *g*-mintrees are so small that the label information is not likely to be overemphasized too much.
2. *g*-mintrees themselves describe the local structure information of trees.
3. The order of *g*-mintrees represents the global structure information of trees.

Therefore, the *g*-string can represent the label and structure information of the trees more properly than some widely accepted set-based methods.

5 Efficient Approximate XML Join Based on *g*-String

In this section, we present an efficient join algorithm for XML document sets based on *g*-string.

5.1 Approximate Join Algorithm Using *g*-string

From the description in Section 4, the length of *g*-strings is linear in the tree size. Therefore, the computation of the *g*-string distance potentially needs $O(n^2)$

time for two trees both with n nodes. When the trees in two XML databases need to join, each tree pairs between them must be compared. This process may be costly. Set (bag) is a kind of data structure whose similarity can be evaluated more efficiently than string. To make the join process more efficient, we further transform g-strings into g-bags and give a lower bound of g-string distance to accelerate the join process.

Definition 7 (g-Bag). *Let T be a tree and $s^g(T)$ be the g-string of T. In an Euler Traversal, each node is visited twice. The entries generated in the first visit are stored in a bag called* g-bag. *We use the symbol $B^g(T)$ to denote that g-bag.*

Definition 8 (g-Bag distance). *Let T_1 and T_2 be two trees, $B^g(T_1)$ and $B^g(T_2)$ be the their corresponding g-Bags. $1 - 2\frac{B^g(T_1) \bigcap B^g(T_2)}{B^g(T_1) \biguplus B^{pq}(T_2)}$ is the g-Bag distance between $B^g(T_1)$ and $B^g(T_2)$.*

Theorem 3. *g-Bag distance serves as a lower bound to the g-string distance.*

Suppose that F_1 and F_2 are two XML document sets and the goal is to find all the tree pairs in $F_1 \times F_2$ with g-string distance lower than a predefined threshold τ. Algorithm 4 describes our approximate join method. All the trees are first transformed into g-strings (line 1-2) and g-bags. Then we sort-merge all the g-bags in F_i into $List_i$ (line 3-4). The size of each g-bag in F_i is stored in $Size_i$ (line 5). Note that the two $List$s are sorted by the *entry-value*. We check for each g-mintree in which pairs of trees it appears and count the number of g-mintrees that each tree pair shares (line 6-7). Then the g-bag distance between all the tree pairs in $F_1 \times F_2$ is computed without nested-loop. The tree pairs with g-bag distance lower than τ are chosen as candidates (line 8). Next, we only compute the g-string distance of these candidates and output tree pairs whose g-string distance lower than τ as our join results (line 9-12). Since the g-bag distance often serves as a close lower bound of g-string distance, in most cases, our algorithm only compute a very small share of g-string distance directly. Thus the overall efficiency can be nearly as high as those set-based methods.

5.2 An Example for Approximate Join

We take the join on two sets of XML documents F_1 and F_2 in Figure 1(a) as an example. The goal is to find all the tree pairs in $F_1 \times F_2$ with g-string distance lower than 0.25. First, we transform all the trees to g-bags (Shown in Figure 6). T_1 and T_2 are merged into $List_1$ while T_3 and T_4 are merged into $List_2$ (Figure 6). Then it is checked for each g-mintree in $List_1$ and $List_2$ to find in which pairs of trees it appears. Then the number of g-mintrees each pair of g-bags sharing is counted (Figure 6). For example, the g-mintree (a,*,*) appears in T_2, T_3 and T_4 once respectively. The counts in (T_2, T_3), (T_2, T_4) increase by one respectively. After the counting, the g-bag distance between each tree pairs is easy to compute. Since only the g-distance of (T_1, T_3) and (T_2, T_4) is lower than 0.25, we only compute the g-string distance for (T_1, T_3) and (T_2, T_4). Since $\Delta(T_1, T_3)$=0.1667<0.25, $\Delta(T_2, T_4)$=0.2<0.25, (T_1, T_3) and (T_2, T_4) are

Algorithm 4. Approximate XML Join

Input: F_1, F_2, g, τ; **Output:** *Join-result*

for all Trees in F_i **do**
  $s^g(T)_j$=Generate-g-String(T_j,g)
  for Half entries in $s^g(T_j)$ **do**
    $List_i = List_i \uplus (treeID_i, entry\text{-}value, count_i)$
  $Size_i = \Gamma_{treeID_i, SUM(count_i) \rightarrow size_i}(List_i)$
$List' = List_1 \bowtie List_2$
$List'' = \Gamma_{treeId_1, treeId_2, SUM(min(count_1, count_2)) \rightarrow count}(List')$
$candidate \leftarrow \pi_{treeId_1, treeId_2}(\sigma_{1 - \frac{2count}{size_1 + size_2} \leq \tau}(List'' \bowtie Size_1 \bowtie Size_2))$
for all Trees pairs in *candidate* **do**
  compute the g-string distance $\Delta^g(treeId_1, treeId_2)$
  if $\Delta^g(treeId_1, treeId_2) \leq \tau$ **then**
    $Join\text{-}result = Join\text{-}result \uplus (treeId_1, treeId_2)$
return *Join-result*

outputted as the join result. In this example, the g-string distance of (T_1, T_3) and (T_2, T_4) equal to their g-bag distance respectively by coincidence. In fact, except in some extreme situations, the g-bag-distance serves as a very close lower bound for g-string distance.

5.3 Time Complexity Analysis

To be brief, we suppose each of the two XML document set has N trees and all the trees have n nodes. To analyze the time complexity, we summary the approximate join process to three steps:

1. All the trees are transformed to their corresponding g-strings and g-bags.
2. Sort merge and hash join all the g-bags and choose the tree pairs whose g-bag distance lower than τ as candidates.
3. The g-string distance of all the candidate tree pairs is computed and the candidates whose g-string lower than τ are output as the join results.

In the first step, since each tree can be transformed to its corresponding g-string and g-bag in time $O(n)$, the running time in the first step is $O(Nn)$. In the second step, the diversity of the trees would affect the running time. In the best case, when no tree pair in $F_1 \times F_2$ shares g-mintree, the runtime in this step is the time of merging all the g-bags into $List_1$ and $List_2$. That is $O(Nnlog(Nn))$. In the worst case, when all the trees in the two sets are exactly the same. Each g-mintree in one List would match N tuples in the other List. Thus the runtime is $O(Nnlog(Nn) + N^2n)$. From our experiments on various real world databases, the running time in this step is usually close to the best case. In the third step, the g-string distance between a pair of trees is computed in $O(n^2)$ time. It is supposed that M pairs of trees are chosen as candidates. The running time in this step is $O(Mn^2)$. Our experiments demonstrate that M is often $O(N)$. Therefore, the average overall time complexity of our join algorithm is about $O(Nnlog(Nn) + Nn^2)$.

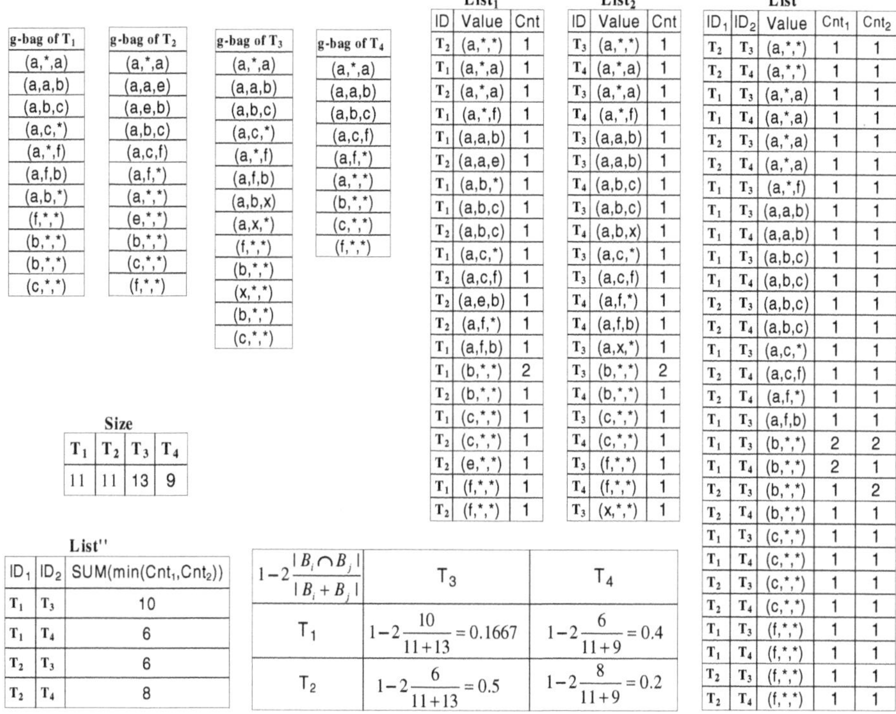

g-bag of T1	g-bag of T2	g-bag of T3	g-bag of T4
(a,*,a)	(a,*,a)	(a,*,a)	(a,*,a)
(a,a,b)	(a,a,e)	(a,a,b)	(a,a,b)
(a,b,c)	(a,e,b)	(a,b,c)	(a,b,c)
(a,c,*)	(a,b,c)	(a,c,*)	(a,c,f)
(a,*,f)	(a,c,f)	(a,*,f)	(a,f,*)
(a,f,b)	(a,f,*)	(a,f,b)	(a,*,*)
(a,b,*)	(a,*,*)	(a,b,x)	(b,*,*)
(f,*,*)	(e,*,*)	(a,x,*)	(c,*,*)
(b,*,*)	(b,*,*)	(f,*,*)	(f,*,*)
(b,*,*)	(c,*,*)	(b,*,*)	
(c,*,*)	(f,*,*)	(x,*,*)	
		(b,*,*)	
		(c,*,*)	

Size

T1	T2	T3	T4
11	11	13	9

List1

ID	Value	Cnt
T2	(a,*,*)	1
T1	(a,*,a)	1
T2	(a,*,a)	1
T1	(a,*,f)	1
T1	(a,a,b)	1
T2	(a,a,e)	1
T1	(a,b,*)	1
T1	(a,b,c)	1
T2	(a,b,c)	1
T1	(a,c,*)	1
T2	(a,c,f)	1
T2	(a,e,b)	1
T2	(a,f,*)	1
T1	(a,f,b)	1
T1	(b,*,*)	2
T2	(b,*,*)	1
T1	(c,*,*)	1
T2	(c,*,*)	1
T2	(e,*,*)	1
T1	(f,*,*)	1
T2	(f,*,*)	1

List2

ID	Value	Cnt
T3	(a,*,*)	1
T4	(a,*,a)	1
T3	(a,*,a)	1
T4	(a,*,f)	1
T3	(a,a,b)	1
T3	(a,a,b)	1
T4	(a,b,c)	1
T3	(a,b,c)	1
T4	(a,b,x)	1
T3	(a,c,*)	1
T3	(a,c,f)	1
T4	(a,f,*)	1
T4	(a,f,b)	1
T3	(a,x,*)	1
T3	(b,*,*)	2
T4	(b,*,*)	1
T3	(c,*,*)	1
T4	(c,*,*)	1
T3	(f,*,*)	1
T4	(f,*,*)	1
T3	(x,*,*)	1

List'

ID1	ID2	Value	Cnt1	Cnt2
T2	T3	(a,*,*)	1	1
T2	T4	(a,*,*)	1	1
T1	T3	(a,*,a)	1	1
T1	T4	(a,*,a)	1	1
T2	T3	(a,*,a)	1	1
T2	T4	(a,*,a)	1	1
T1	T3	(a,*,f)	1	1
T1	T3	(a,a,b)	1	1
T1	T4	(a,a,b)	1	1
T1	T3	(a,b,c)	1	1
T1	T4	(a,b,c)	1	1
T2	T3	(a,b,c)	1	1
T2	T4	(a,b,c)	1	1
T1	T3	(a,c,*)	1	1
T2	T4	(a,c,f)	1	1
T2	T4	(a,f,*)	1	1
T1	T3	(a,f,b)	1	1
T1	T3	(b,*,*)	2	2
T1	T4	(b,*,*)	2	1
T2	T3	(b,*,*)	1	2
T2	T4	(b,*,*)	1	1
T1	T3	(c,*,*)	1	1
T1	T4	(c,*,*)	1	1
T2	T3	(c,*,*)	1	1
T2	T4	(c,*,*)	1	1
T1	T3	(f,*,*)	1	1
T1	T4	(f,*,*)	1	1
T2	T3	(f,*,*)	1	1
T2	T4	(f,*,*)	1	1

List''

ID1	ID2	SUM(min(Cnt1,Cnt2))
T1	T3	10
T1	T4	6
T2	T3	6
T2	T4	8

$1-2\frac{\vert B_i \cap B_j \vert}{\vert B_i + B_j \vert}$	T3	T4
T1	$1-2\frac{10}{11+13}=0.1667$	$1-2\frac{6}{11+9}=0.4$
T2	$1-2\frac{6}{11+13}=0.5$	$1-2\frac{8}{11+9}=0.2$

Fig. 6. An example for our join algorithm

6 Experiments

In this section, we test the efficiency and effectiveness of the g-string distance. All of our experiments were performed on a PC with Intel Core Duo 2GHz, 1G main memory and 250G hard disk. The OS is Windows XP Professional. We implemented our experiments using CodeBlocks.

6.1 Scalability

We evaluate the scalability of our algorithm by comparing it with the tree edit distance [17]. We also test the influence of the parameter g on the runtime in our method. In the case of approximate join between two large tree sets, we compare our method with the pq-gram [2] (one of the most efficient set-based methods).

When comparing our algorithm with the tree edit distance, we produce pairs of trees (T_1, T_2) of size n from 20 up to 15000 nodes. The height of the trees is logarithmic and all the labels are randomly chosen from a label set sized n.

Figure 7(a) shows the running time. For large trees, the runtime of the tree edit distance grows much more dramatically than our method. Figure 7(b) shows the impact of g on the efficiency. In our method, the runtime increases with g.

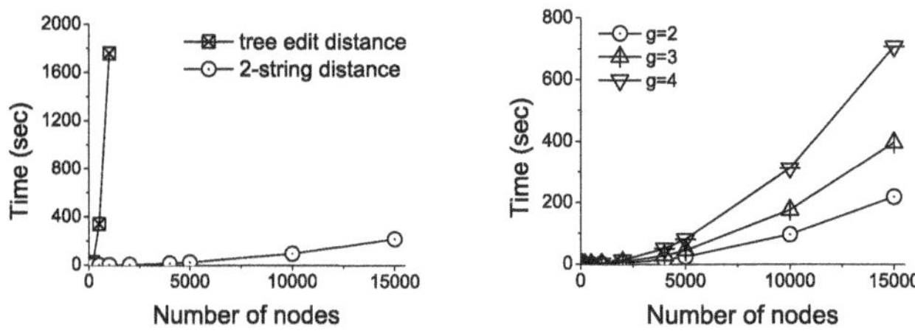

(a) Compare with edit distance (b) Impact of g on efficiency

Fig. 7. Efficiency Test

In the similarity join experiment, we use various XML databases including the Swissprot[1] (bioinformatics), Treebank[2] (linguistics) and DBLP[3] (bibliography). In each database, the top-level XML tags are removed to generate a set of (sub)documents. The three (sub)document sets are very different: Swissprot documents contain big and flat trees. Treebank documents have deep recursive structure. DBLP contains small and flat documents. Each time we randomly choose N documents as the $Source$ and match the $Source$ with itself. The output is all the tree pairs in $Source \times Source$ whose g-string distance lower than a threshold (here we choose 0.3). We compare our efficiency with pq-gram [2] (we apply the "optimized join" [1] to pq-gram [2]). We choose g=2 in our g-string and p=2, q=3 in method pq-gram as the authors recommended. The result is shown in Figure 8(a)-8(c). Our method is nearly as efficient as pq-gram. (We use g-bag distance to give candidates and use g-string distance to refine the candidates).

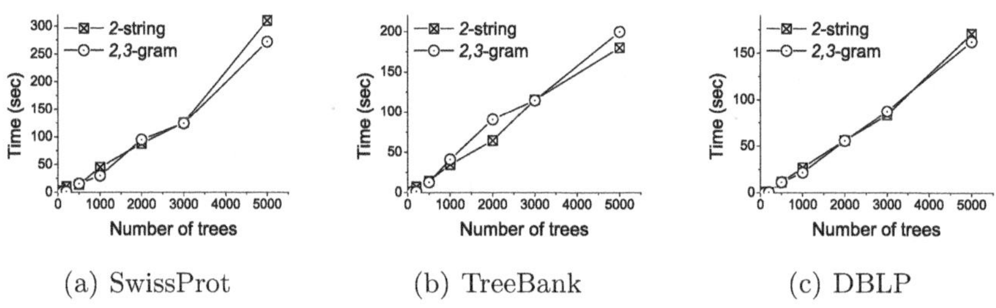

(a) SwissProt (b) TreeBank (c) DBLP

Fig. 8. g-String vs pq-Gram on Efficiency

6.2 Sensitivity to Structural Changes

As analyzed in Section 4.3, the edit operations on high degree nodes would cause bigger g-string distance than the edit operations on low degree nodes. Another

[1] Swissprot: `http://www.expasy.ch/sprot/`

[2] Treebank:`http://www.cis.upenn.edu/~treebank/`

[3] DBLP: `http://dblp.uni-trier.de/xml/`

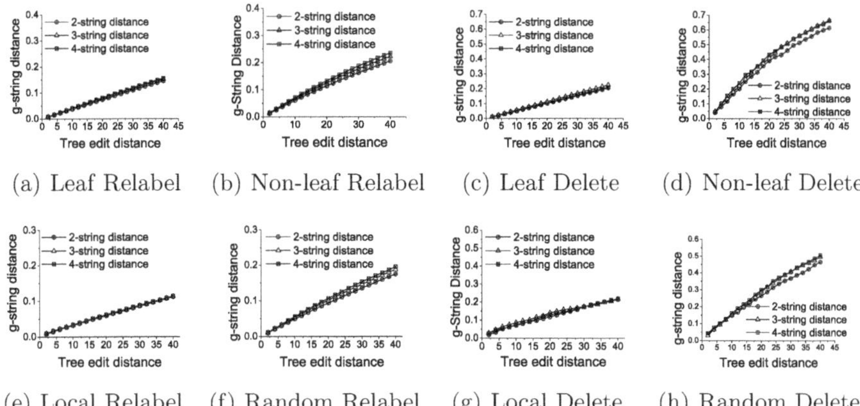

(a) Leaf Relabel (b) Non-leaf Relabel (c) Leaf Delete (d) Non-leaf Delete

(e) Local Relabel (f) Random Relabel (g) Local Delete (h) Random Delete

Fig. 9. Sensitivity to Structural Changes

property is that local edit operations have less effect than uniformly distributed edit operations. In this subsection, we test these properties with experiments.

We create an artificial tree with 200 nodes, 132 leaves at height 8. Since the insert operation is dual to the delete operation, we only test these properties with delete and relabel operation. All experiments in this subsection are repeated independently for 100 times and each g-string distance is the average value.

In Figure 9(a) and 9(b), we relabel a number of leaf nodes and non-leaf nodes respectively. In Figure 9(c) and 9(d), a number of leaf nodes and non-leaf nodes are deleted respectively. The result shows that edit operations on leaf nodes have less impact on the g-string distance than edit operations on non-leaf nodes.

We relabel or delete a subtree of a certain number of nodes. The impact of this kind of local edit is shown in Figure 9(e) and 9(g). Also the impact of random node relabel or deletion on g-string distance is shown in Figure 9(f) and 9(h). Obviously, local edit operations have less impact than random edit operations on g-string distance. We also increase g from 2 to 4. The results show that the structural sensitivity of g-string grows slightly with the parameter g.

6.3 Approximate Join with Real World Data

To test the join quality with real world data, we use the application data from the Municipality of Bozen[4]. The scene is that the Office wants to integrate the apartment data stored in two databases and display that information on a map. We denote the two sources as R and L. For each document T_i^R in R, we find its nearest neighbor T_j^L in L and join them. This join result is denoted as $M_{r \to l}$. For each document T_j^L in L, we also find its nearest neighbor T_i^R in R and join them. We denote this join result as $M_{l \to r}$. The final result is $M_x = M_{r \to l} \cap M_{l \to r}$.

[4] We get the data and source code from the authors in [3], some of our results are cited from [3].

We use the symbol M_c to denote all the correct join. We measure the join quality using precision ($p = \frac{|M_x \cap M_c|}{|M_x|}$), recall ratio ($r = \frac{|M_x \cap M_c|}{|M_c|}$) and F-measure ($F = \frac{2pr}{p+r}$) [15] which considers both recall and precision.

We compare our method with other methods such as tree edit distance [12], *pq*-grams [2], Hashing Tree method [13] ($k = 400$), tree embedding distance [6], the binary branch distance [16] and the bottom-up distance [14]. The result is shown in Figure 10. It is observed that the performance of g-string slightly outperforms tree edit distance and significantly outperforms other methods.

	Correct	False	Recall	Precision	F-Measure
g-string (*g*=2)	251	4	83.9%	98.4%	0.901
g-string (*g*=3)	252	5	84.3%	98.1%	0.898
g-string (*g*=4)	247	5	82.6%	98.0%	0.896
edit distance	247	9	82.6%	96.5%	0.890
pq-gram (*p*=2,*q*=3)	231	4	77.3%	98.3%	0.865
tree-embedding	206	8	68.9%	96.3%	0.803
binary branch	193	14	64.5%	93.2%	0.763
hashing tree	162	14	54.2%	92.0%	0.682
bottom-up	148	12	49.5%	92.5%	0.645

Fig. 10. Street Matching Result Using Different Methods

7 Conclusion

XML documents are often modeled as ordered, labeled trees. To join XML documents efficiently and effectively, in this paper, we propose a new distance measure, the g-string distance, for ordered, labeled trees. In our method, we first Euler traverse a tree and each time we visit a node, a series of very small subtrees are putted into a line to form the g-string. Then we use the g-string distance between these g-strings to evaluate the distance between trees. We also provide the g-bag distance as the lower bound of g-string distance to accelerate the join process. We analyze the scalability and other properties of our method theoretically. Extensive experiments confirm that the join quality based on our method is higher than that based on unit tree edit distance and our join efficiency is nearly as high as the most efficient set-based method.

In this paper, we hash each label into a number and disregard the similarity between different labels. In the future, we will try to consider the similarity between different labels when we evaluate the similarity between XML documents.

Acknowledgements

Many thanks to Michael H. Böhlen [1,2,3] for his source code and test data; and the Municipality of Bolzano for the street matching data. They have been a great help in this research.

References

1. Augsten, N., Böhlen, M.H., Dyreson, C.E., Gamper, J.: Approximate joins for data-centric xml. In: ICDE, pp. 814–823 (2008)
2. Augsten, N., Böhlen, M.H., Gamper, J.: Approximate matching of hierarchical data using pq-grams. In: VLDB, pp. 301–312 (2005)
3. Augsten, N., Böhlen, M.H., Gamper, J.: The pq-gram distance between ordered labeled trees. ACM Trans. Database Syst. 35(1) (2010)
4. Bille, P.: A survey on tree edit distance and related problems. Theor. Comput. Sci. 337(1-3), 217–239 (2005)
5. Demaine, E.D., Mozes, S., Rossman, B., Weimann, O.: An optimal decomposition algorithm for tree edit distance. In: Arge, L., Cachin, C., Jurdziński, T., Tarlecki, A. (eds.) ICALP 2007. LNCS, vol. 4596, pp. 146–157. Springer, Heidelberg (2007)
6. Garofalakis, M.N., Kumar, A.: Xml stream processing using tree-edit distance embeddings. ACM Trans. Database Syst. 30(1), 279–332 (2005)
7. Guha, S., Jagadish, H.V., Koudas, N., Srivastava, D., Yu, T.: Approximate xml joins. In: SIGMOD Conference, pp. 287–298 (2002)
8. Kailing, K., Kriegel, H.-P., Schönauer, S., Seidl, T.: Efficient similarity search for hierarchical data in large databases. In: Bertino, E., Christodoulakis, S., Plexousakis, D., Christophides, V., Koubarakis, M., Böhm, K., Ferrari, E. (eds.) EDBT 2004. LNCS, vol. 2992, pp. 676–693. Springer, Heidelberg (2004)
9. Klein, P.N.: Computing the edit-distance between unrooted ordered trees. In: Bilardi, G., Pietracaprina, A., Italiano, G.F., Pucci, G. (eds.) ESA 1998. LNCS, vol. 1461, pp. 91–102. Springer, Heidelberg (1998)
10. Kuboyama, T.: Matching and Learning in Trees (2007)
11. Shapiro, B.A., Zhang, K.: Comparing multiple rna secondary structures using tree comparisons. Computer Applications in the Biosciences 6(4), 309–318 (1990)
12. Tai, K.-C.: The tree-to-tree correction problem. J. ACM 26(3), 422–433 (1979)
13. Tatikonda, S., Parthasarathy, S.: Hashing Tree-Structured Data: Methods and Applications. In: ICDE (to appear, 2010)
14. Valiente, G.: An efficient bottom-up distance between trees. In: SPIRE, pp. 212–219 (2001)
15. van Rijsbergen, C.J.: Information Retrieval. Butterworth, London (1979)
16. Yang, R., Kalnis, P., Tung, A.K.H.: Similarity evaluation on tree-structured data. In: SIGMOD Conference, pp. 754–765 (2005)
17. Zhang, K., Shasha, D.: Simple fast algorithms for the editing distance between trees and related problems. SIAM J. Comput. 18(6), 1245–1262 (1989)

Linear Computation of the Maximum Simultaneous Forward and Backward Bisimulation for Node-Labeled Trees

Nils Grimsmo, Truls Amundsen Bjørklund, and Magnus Lie Hetland

Norwegian University of Science and Technology
{nilsgri,trulsamu,mlh}@idi.ntnu.no

Abstract. The F&B-index is used to speed up pattern matching in tree and graph data, and is based on the maximum F&B-bisimulation, which can be computed in loglinear time for graphs. It has been shown that the maximum F-bisimulation can be computed in linear time for DAGs. We build on this result, and introduce a linear algorithm for computing the maximum F&B-bisimulation for tree data. It first computes the maximum F-bisimulation, and then refines this to a maximal B-bisimulation. We prove that the result equals the maximum F&B-bisimulation.

1 Introduction

Structure indexes are used to reduce the cost of pattern matching in labeled trees and graphs [5,14,9], by capturing structure properties of the data in a *structure summary*, where some or all of the matching can be performed. Efficient construction of such indexes is important for their practical usefulness [14], and in this paper we reduce the construction cost of the *F&B-index* [9] for tree data.

In a structure index, data nodes are typically *partitioned* into *blocks* based on properties of the surrounding nodes. A structure summary typically has one node per block in the partition, and edges between summary nodes where there are edges between data nodes in the related blocks. Matching in structure summaries is usually more efficient than partitioning the data nodes on label and using structural joins to find full query matches [14,9].

In a *path index*, data nodes are classified by the labels on the paths by which they are reachable [5,14]. For tree data this equals partitioning nodes on their label and the block of the parent node. Figures 1c and 1b show path partitioning and the related summary for the example data in Figure 1a. With path indexes, non-branching queries can be evaluated without processing joins [14,18].

A natural extension of a path index is the F&B-index, where nodes are partitioned on both their label, the partitions of the parents, *and* the partitions of the children, as shown in Figure 1d. This gives an index where more of the pattern matching can be performed on the summary, and also branching queries can be evaluated without processing joins [9].

The focus of this paper is efficient computation of the maximum *simultaneous forward and backward bisimulation* (F&B-bisimulation), which is the underlying

M.L. Lee et al. (Eds.): XSym 2010, LNCS 6309, pp. 18–32, 2010.

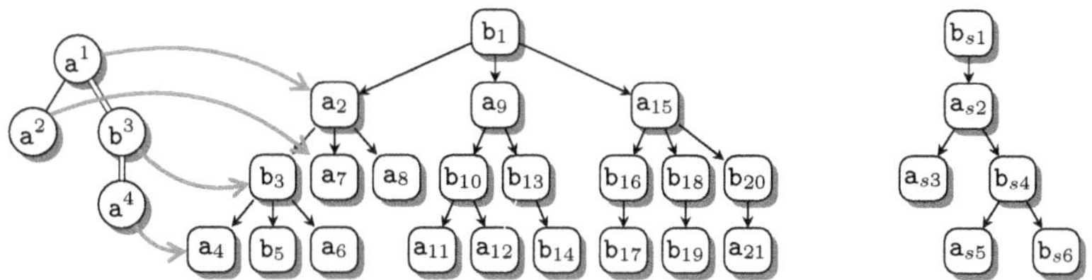

(a) Example query and data. Single/double query edges specify parent–child/ancestor–descendant relationships.

(b) Path summary.

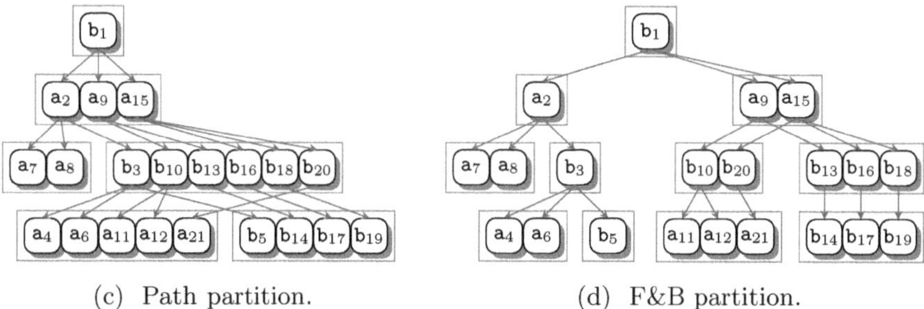

(c) Path partition.

(d) F&B partition.

Fig. 1. Partitioning strategies. Superscripts and subscripts give node identifiers.

concept used to partition nodes in the F&B-index. It can be computed in time loglinear in the number of edges in the graph [9]. A linear construction algorithm for directed acyclic graphs (DAGs) has been presented recently [12], but we show that it is incorrect. On the other hand, there exists a correct algorithm which can compute *either* the maximum *forward bisimulation* (F-bisimulation) *or* the maximum *backward bisimulation* (B-bisimulation) in linear time for DAGs [3]. We extend this algorithm to compute the maximum F&B-bisimulation in linear time for tree data. This has relevance for applications where the underlying data is known to be tree shaped, such as in many uses of XML [6].

2 Background

In this section we present different types of bisimulations, and show how they can be computed by first partitioning on label, and then *stabilizing* the graph.

We use the following notation: A directed graph $G = \langle V, E\rangle$ has node set V and edge set $E \subseteq V \times V$. Let $n = |V|$ and $m = |E|$. For $X \subseteq V$, $E(X) = \{w \mid \exists v \in X : vEw\}$ and $E^{-1}(X) = \{u \mid \exists v \in X : uEv\}$. Each node $v \in V$ has label $L(v)$. A *partition* P of V is a set of *blocks*, such that each node $v \in V$ is contained in exactly one block. For an equivalence relation $\sim \subseteq V \times V$, the equivalence class containing $v \in V$ is denoted by $[v]_\sim$. The equivalence relation arising from the partition P is denoted $=_P$. A relation R_2 is a *refinement* of R_1 iff $R_2 \subseteq R_1$. A partition P_2 is a refinement of the *coarser* P_1 iff $=_{P_2} \subseteq =_{P_1}$. Let the *contraction graph* of a partition P be a graph with one node for each equivalence class of $=_P$, and an edge $\langle [u]_{=_P}, [v]_{=_P}\rangle$ whenever $\langle u, v\rangle \in E$.

The structure summary built for a structure index is typically isomorphic with the contraction graph for the data partition. For a partitioning to be useful, it must yield a summary that somehow simulates the data, such that pattern matching in the summary gives the same results as pattern matching in the data, or at least no false negatives. If nodes are partitioned into blocks where nodes in some way simulate each other, then the contraction graph also simulates the data in the same way.

2.1 Bisimulation and Bisimilarity

Broadly speaking, bisimulations relate nodes that have the same label and related neighbors. We use the following properties of a binary relation $R \subseteq V \times V$ to formally define the different types of bisimulation:

$$vRv' \Rightarrow L(v) = L(v') \tag{1}$$

$$\begin{aligned} vRv' \Rightarrow\ & (uEv \Rightarrow \exists u' : u'Ev' \wedge uRu') \wedge \\ & (u'Ev' \Rightarrow \exists u : uEv \wedge uRu') \end{aligned} \tag{2}$$

$$\begin{aligned} vRv' \Rightarrow\ & (vEw \Rightarrow \exists w' : v'Ew' \wedge wRw') \wedge \\ & (v'Ew' \Rightarrow \exists w : vEw \wedge wRw') \end{aligned} \tag{3}$$

Definition 1 (Bisimulations [13,9]). A relation R is a B-bisimulation iff it satisfies (1) and (2) above, an F-bisimulation iff it satisfies (1) and (3), and an F&B-bisimulation iff it satisfies (1), (2) and (3).

For each type, there exists a unique maximum bisimulation, of which all other bisimulations are refinements [13,9]. We say that two nodes are *bisimilar* if there exists a bisimulation that relates them, i.e., they are related by the maximum bisimulation. Since bisimilarity is an equivalence relation, it can be used to partition the nodes [13,9]. When nodes u and v are backward, forward, and forward and backward bisimilar, we write $u \sim_B v$, $u \sim_F v$ and $u \sim_{F\&B} v$, respectively. Figure 2 illustrates the different types of bisimilarity.

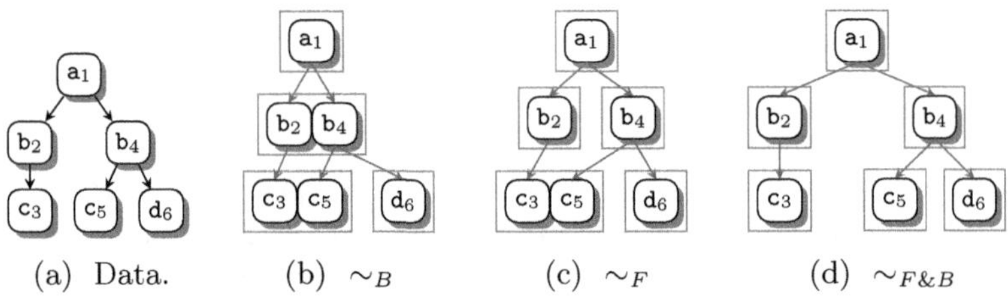

(a) Data. (b) $\sim_B$ (c) $\sim_F$ (d) $\sim_{F\&B}$

Fig. 2. Partitioning on different types of bisimilarity

Two *graphs* are said to be bisimilar if there exists a total surjective bisimulation from the nodes in one graph to the nodes in the other. For a given graph, the smallest bisimilar graph is unique, and is exactly the contraction for bisimilarity [3]. The F&B-bisimilarity contraction is the basis for the F&B-index [9].

2.2 Stability

The different types of bisimilarity listed in the previous section can be computed by first partitioning the data nodes on label, and then finding the coarsest *stable* refinements of the initial partition [15,4,9]. A partition is *successor stable* iff all nodes in a block have incoming edges from nodes in the same set of blocks, and is *predecessor stable* iff all nodes in a block have outgoing edges to the same set of blocks [9]. The coarsest successor, predecessor, and successor and predecessor stable refinement of a label partition, equal a partition on B-bisimilarity, F-bisimilarity and F&B-bisimilarity, respectively [4,9].

Definition 2 (Partition stability [15,9]). Given a directed graph $G = \langle V, E \rangle$, then $D \subseteq V$ is *successor stable* with respect to $B \subseteq V$ if either all or none of the nodes in D are pointed to from nodes in B (meaning $D \subseteq E(B)$ or $D \cap E(B) = \emptyset$), and D is *predecessor stable* with respect to B if either none or all of the nodes in D point to nodes in B (meaning $D \subseteq E^{-1}(B)$ or $D \cap E^{-1}(B) = \emptyset$).

For any combination of successor and predecessor stability, a partition P of V is said to be stable with respect to a block B if all blocks in P are stable with respect to B. A partition P is stable with respect to another partition Q if it is stable with respect to all blocks in Q. P is said to be stable if it is stable with respect to itself.

Figure 3 shows cases where a block can be split to achieve different types of stability. The block D is not stable with respect to B, but we can split it into blocks that are: Assume that D is stable with respect to a union of blocks S such that $B \subset S$. We can split D into blocks that are stable with respect to both B and $S \setminus B$, shown as D_B, D_{BS} and D_S in the figure. Stabilizing also with respect to $S \setminus B$ is crucial for obtaining a $\mathcal{O}(m \log n)$ running time in the partition stabilization algorithm explained in the next section.

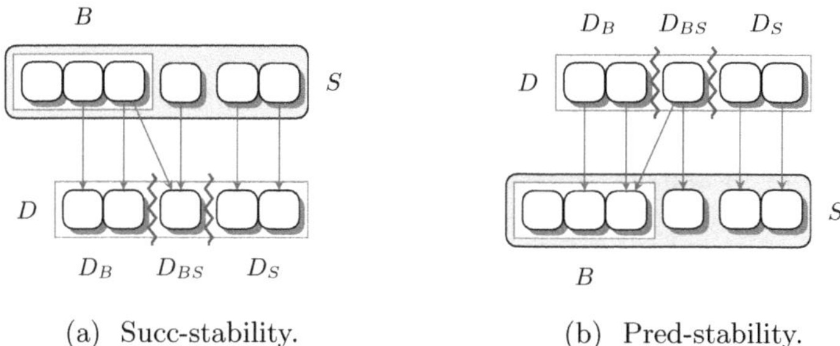

(a) Succ-stability. (b) Pred-stability.

Fig. 3. Refining D into blocks that are stable with respect to B and $S \setminus B$

2.3 Stabilizing Graph Partitions

We now go through Paige and Tarjan's algorithm for refinement to the coarsest predecessor stable partition [15], extended to simultaneous successor and predecessor stability by Kaushik et al. [9], as shown in Algorithm 1. The input to the algorithm is a partition P and the set of flags *Directions* $\subseteq \{\textsc{Succ}, \textsc{Pred}\}$, which specifies whether P is to be successor and/or predecessor stabilized.

Algorithm 1. Graph partition stabilization

```
▷ P is the initial partition.
function StabilizeGraph(P, Directions):
    for dir ∈ Directions:
        InitialRefinement(P, dir)
    X ← {⋃_{B∈P} B}
    while P ≠ X:
        Extract B ∈ P such that B ⊂ S ∈ X and |B| ≤ |S|/2.
        Replace S by B and S \ B in X.
        for dir ∈ Directions:
            StabilizeWRT(copy of B, P, dir)
```

Figure 4 illustrates an example run of the algorithm with *Directions* $= \{\textsc{Succ}, \textsc{Pred}\}$. In addition to the current partition P, the algorithm maintains a partition X, where the blocks are unions of blocks in P. Initially X contains a single block that is the union of all blocks in P, and the algorithm maintains the loop invariant that P is stable with respect to X by Definition 2. The algorithm terminates when the partitions P and X are equal, which means P must be stable with respect to itself. But the loop invariant may not be true for the given input partition initially: Blocks containing both roots and non-roots are not successor stable with respect to X, because non-roots have incoming edges from the single block $S \in X$, while roots do not. Similarly, blocks containing both leaves and non-leaves are not predecessor stable with respect to X. In Algorithm 1 initial stability is achieved by calls to InitialRefinement(), which splits blocks in a simple linear pass. Initial splitting is illustrated by the step from line (a) to line (b) in Figure 4.

The algorithm repeatedly selects a block $S \in X$ that is a *compound* union of blocks from P, and selects a *splitter block* $B \subset S$ with size at most half of S. Then S is replaced by B and $S \setminus B$ in X, as shown when extracting $B = \{\mathtt{a}_2, \mathtt{a}_9, \mathtt{a}_{15}\}$ between lines (b) and (c) in Figure 4. The call to StabilizeWRT() uses the strategies depicted in Figure 3 to stabilize P with respect to both B and $S \setminus B$, to make sure P is stable with respect to the new X. It is important to use a *copy* of B as splitter, as the stabilization may cause B itself to be split. The step from line (b) to (c) in the figure shows that a block of nodes labeled $\mathtt{a}$ is split when successor stabilizing with respect to $B = \{\mathtt{a}_2, \mathtt{a}_9, \mathtt{a}_{15}\}$.

Efficient implementation of the above requires some attention to detail [15]: The partition X can be realized through a set $\mathcal{X}$ containing sets of pointers to

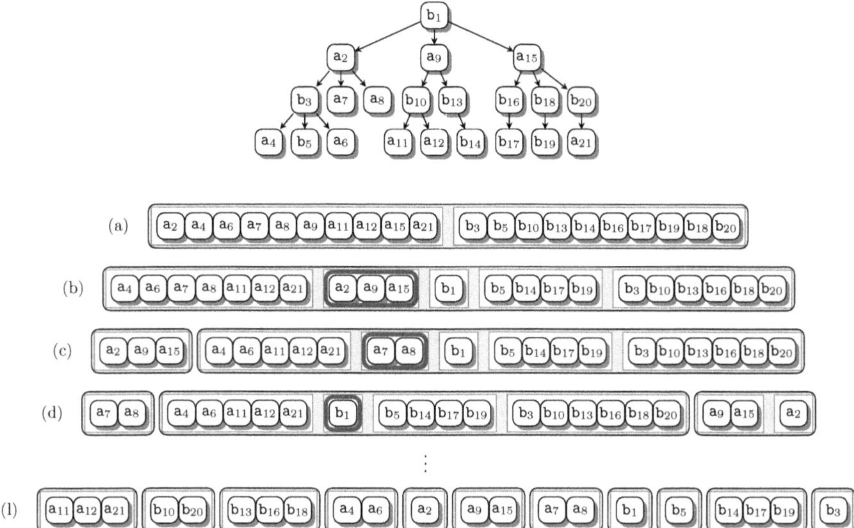

Fig. 4. Algorithm 1 doing successor and predecessor stabilization on a label partition of the data from Figure 1a. The white boxes are the current blocks in P, while the gray boxes are the current blocks in X. Line (a) shows initial label partition. Step (a)–(b) shows refinement separating roots from non-roots and leaves from non-leaves, and steps (b)–(l) show simultaneous predecessor and successor stabilization.

blocks in P, such that for each $S \in X$ we have $S = \bigcup_{B \in \mathcal{S}} B$ for the related $\mathcal{S} \in \mathcal{X}$. To extract a $B \subset S \in X$ in constant time, we also maintain the set of compound unions $\mathcal{C} = \{\mathcal{S} \in \mathcal{X} \mid 1 < |\mathcal{S}|\}$. A block $B \subset S$ such that $|B| \leq |S|/2$ can be found by choosing the smalllest of the two first blocks in any $\mathcal{S} \in \mathcal{C}$. Note that we can check if $P = X$ by checking whether $\mathcal{C}$ is empty, and neither P, X nor $\mathcal{X}$ need to be materialized, as they are never used directly. You only need to maintain $\mathcal{C}$, and a $\mathcal{P} \subseteq P$ containing the blocks in P not in some $\mathcal{S} \in \mathcal{C}$. For inserting and removing elements in constant time, the sets are implemented as doubly linked list. In addition, each $v \in B$ has a pointer to B, and each $B \in \mathcal{S}$ has a pointer to $\mathcal{S}$. This allows keeping the data structures updated throughout the evaluation.

As all operations in the while-loop excluding the calls to StabilizeWRT() are constant time operations on linked lists, the complexity of the loop is bounded by the number of splitter blocks selected, which again is bounded by the number of times a node may be part of such a splitter. Splitter blocks at most half the size of a compound union are always selected, and no node in this block is part of a splitter again before the block itself has become a compound union. This means that the number of times a given node is part of a splitter block is $\mathcal{O}(\log n)$, and that the total number of splitter blocks used is $\mathcal{O}(n \log n)$ [15].

Algorithm 2 shows how all blocks in a partition P can be successor (or predecessor) stabilized with respect to a block $B \in P$ and $S \setminus B$, where $B \subset S \in X$, in time linear in the number of edges going out from (or into) B [15]. For successor stability, only blocks D pointed to from B are affected, and they are stabilized with respect to both B and $S \setminus B$ without involving $S \setminus B$ directly. This is done by maintaining for each node $v \in V$, the number of times it is pointed to from each set $S \in X$, and storing references to these records from the related edges. We can then differentiate between nodes pointed to from B, pointed to from both B and $S \setminus B$, and pointed to only from $S \setminus B$. Nodes from the first two categories are moved into new blocks, while the rest are untouched.

Algorithm 2. Stabilizing with respect to a block

```
function StabilizeWRT(B, P, d):
    Assume dir = Succ.                                        (or Pred)
    for D ∈ P pointed to from B:                 (or pointing into B)
        Initialize D_B and D_BS and associate with D.
    for v ∈ D ∈ P pointed to from B:             (or pointing into B)
        if v is pointed to only from B:     (or pointing only into B)
            D' ← D_B
        else:
            D' ← D_BS
        if D' ∉ P: Insert D' after D in P
        Move v from D to D'.
        if D = ∅: Remove D from P.
```

As the cost of a single call to StabilizeWRT() is bounded by the number of nodes in the splitter block and the number of outgoing (or incoming) edges, the total cost for the calls is $\mathcal{O}((m + n) \log n)$, as a given node or edge is used for splitting $\mathcal{O}(\log n)$ times. Assuming $n \in \mathcal{O}(m)$, the cost of Algorithm 1 is $\mathcal{O}(n)$ for the initial refinement, $\mathcal{O}(n \log n)$ for the while-loop excluding StabilizeWRT(), and $\mathcal{O}(m \log n)$ for the StabilizeWRT() calls, giving a total of $\mathcal{O}(m \log n)$ [15,9].

3 Linear Time Stabilization

Linear time computation of F&B-bisimilarity for DAG data has been attempted earlier. The SAM algorithm [12] partitions the data separately on B-bisimilarity and F-bisimilarity, and then combines the partitions by putting two nodes in the same final block iff they are in the same blocks in both partitions. It builds on the following theorem, which is stated without proof or reference: "*Node n_1 and node n_2 satisfy F&B-bisimulation if and only if they satisfy F-bisimulation and B-bisimulation.*" The *only if* part is of course true, but the *if* part is not, as can be seen from the partitioning of a tree with six nodes in Figure 2. Here $c_3 \sim_B c_5$ and $c_3 \sim_F c_5$, but $c_3 \not\sim_{F\&B} c_5$, because for the parent nodes $b_2 \not\sim_{F\&B} b_4$. Also note that it is assumed for the running time of the SAM algorithm that the number of edges to and from each node can be viewed as a constant.

3.1 Stabilizing DAG Partitions

We now present an algorithm for refining a partition of the nodes in a DAG *either* to successor stability *or* to predecessor stability. It is based on two different previous algorithms: Paige and Tarjan's loglinear algorithm for stabilizing general graphs [15], and Dovier, Piazza and Policriti's algorithm for computing F-bisimilarity on unlabeled graphs [3], which has linear complexity for DAG data. A difference between these two algorithms is that the former is given an initial partition as input, which is then *refined*, while the latter starts with the set of singleton blocks, from which the final partition is *constructed*. These are called *negative* and *positive* strategies, respectively [3]. Dovier et al. describe how their algorithm can be extended to compute F-bisimilarity for *labeled* data, but when developing an algorithm for refining to simultaneous successor and predecessor stability in the next section, we use the result of a predecessor stabilization as input to a successor stabilization, and hence cannot use a positive strategy.

Dovier et al.'s algorithm initially computes the *rank* of each node in the DAG, which is the length of the longest path from the node to a leaf. We extend the notion of rank to both directions in the DAG:

Definition 3 (Rank). In a DAG G, the successor and predecessor rank of $v \in V(G)$ is defined as:

$$rank_{\text{SUCC}}(v) = \begin{cases} 0 & \text{if } v \text{ is a root in } G \\ 1 + \max_{\langle u,v\rangle \in E(G)} rank_{\text{SUCC}}(u) & \text{otherwise} \end{cases}$$

$$rank_{\text{PRED}}(v) = \begin{cases} 0 & \text{if } v \text{ is a leaf in } G \\ 1 + \max_{\langle v,w\rangle \in E(G)} rank_{\text{PRED}}(w) & \text{otherwise} \end{cases}$$

Algorithm 3 shows our modification of Paige and Tarjan's algorithm [15] based on Dovier et al.'s principles [3]. It refines a partition of a DAG *either* to predecessor *or* to successor stability, and runs in linear time, due to the order in which splitter blocks are chosen.

Algorithm 3. DAG partition stabilization

▷ Assume sets are ordered.
function StabilizeDAG(P, dir):
  RefineAndSortOnRank(P, dir)
  $X \leftarrow \{\bigcup_{B \in P} B\}$
  while $P \neq X$:
    Extract first $B \in P$ such that $B \subset S \in X$.
    Replace S by B and $S \setminus B$ in X.
    StabilizeWRT(B copy, P, dir)

A run of the algorithm with dir = PRED is illustrated in Figure 5. Instead of only separating between leaves and non-leaves (or roots and non-roots) as in

Algorithm 1, blocks are initially split such that predecessor (or successor) rank is uniform within each block, and sorted, such that the rank is monotonically increasing in the partition. This is done in the function RefineAndSortOnRank(), which is described later in this section. An initial refinement and sorting on predecessor rank is shown when going from line (a) to line (b) in Figure 5.

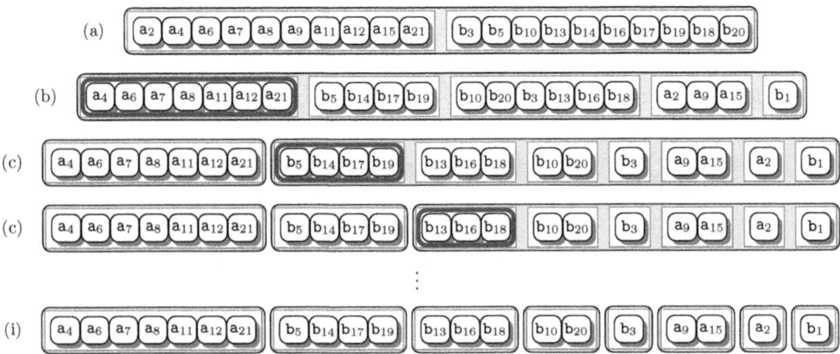

Fig. 5. Using Algorithm 3 to predecessor stabilize a label partition of the data from Figure 1a. The first step shows refinement on predecessor rank.

In a partition that respects a given type of rank, let the rank of a block be equal to the rank of the contained nodes. The following lemma implies that the initial refinement on rank does not split blocks unnecessarily:

Lemma 1. Given nodes $u, v \in V(G)$ and a partition P of G, if P is successor stable then $[u]_{=P} = [v]_{=P} \Rightarrow rank_{\text{SUCC}}(u) = rank_{\text{SUCC}}(v)$, and if P is predecessor stable then $[u]_{=P} = [v]_{=P} \Rightarrow rank_{\text{PRED}}(u) = rank_{\text{PRED}}(v)$.

Proof. For F-bisimilarity $[u]_{\sim F} = [v]_{\sim F} \Rightarrow rank_{\text{PRED}}(u) = rank_{\text{PRED}}(v)$ [3]. If P is predecessor stable, then $=_P$ is an F-bisimulation [4], and therefore a refinement of partitioning on $\sim_F$, such that $[u]_{=P} = [v]_{=P} \Rightarrow [u]_{\sim F} = [v]_{\sim F}$. The case for successor stability is symmetric. □

The next lemma implies that if blocks are chosen as splitters in order of their rank, a node will be part of a block that is used as a splitter at most once. This property is used to achieve a linear complexity in our algorithm.

Lemma 2 ([3]). Given a DAG G, a partition P of G that respects predecessor rank and a block $B \in P$, predecessor stabilization of P with respect to B only splits blocks D where $rank_{\text{PRED}}(D) > rank_{\text{PRED}}(B)$.

This is symmetric for successor stabilization and successor rank, as a reversed DAG is also a DAG.

In Algorithm 3 the blocks in the current partition P are maintained ordered on rank. This is implemented through a detail in our method for stabilization with respect to a block in Algorithm 2, which is different from the original description [15]: The new blocks D_B and D_{BS} are inserted into P on the position after the old block D, and not at the end of P. The sets of blocks which make up the unions in X are also ordered such that their concatenation yields an ordered list of blocks. This is maintained by inserting B followed by $S \setminus B$ on the original position of S in X. Notice how blocks never change positions during the stabilization shown in lines (b)–(i) in Figure 5.

In Dovier et al.'s algorithm, rank is computed by performing a topological traversal of the DAG depth first [3]. Because we need to *refine* a given partition on rank, as opposed to *constructing* a partition on rank from scratch, the problem is slightly more involved. Algorithm 4 shows how a partitioning can be refined and sorted on successor or predecessor rank in a single pass. The algorithm traverses the DAG with a hybrid between a topological sort and a breadth first search, implemented using edge counters and a queue. Blocks are refined and sorted on the fly.

Algorithm 4. Refining and sorting on rank

```
function RefineAndSortOnRank(P, dir):
    Assume dir = SUCC                                  (or dir = PRED)
    Q is a queue.
    for v ∈ V:
        v.count ← |{x | ⟨x, v⟩ ∈ E}|                   (or |{x | ⟨v, x⟩ ∈ E}|)
        if v.count = 0:
            v.rank_dir ← 0
            PushBack(Q, v)
    for B ∈ P:
        B.currRank ← −1
    while Q:
        v ← PopFront(Q)
        Let B ∋ v.
        if v.rank_dir ≠ B.currRank:
            B.rankedB ← {}
            Append B.rankedB at the end of P.
            B.currRank ← v.rank_dir
        Move v from B to B.rankedB
        Remove B from P if empty.
        for x where ⟨v, x⟩ ∈ E:                        (or ⟨x, v⟩ ∈ E)
            x.count ← x.count − 1
            if x.count = 0:
                x.rank_dir ← v.rank_dir + 1
                PushBack(Q, x)
```

Lemma 3. Algorithm 4 refines and orders P on successor (or predecessor) rank in $\mathcal{O}(m + n)$ time.

Proof (Sketch). Because the queue is initialized with the roots, and a node is added to the queue when the last parent is popped from the queue, the nodes are queued and popped in order of successor rank, and this distance is calculated from the parent node with the greatest successor rank. As the successor rank of the nodes that are moved to a new block grows monotonically, only one associated block $B.rankedB$ is created per successor rank found in block B, and all such blocks are appended to P in sorted order. As a node is only queued once, and the cost of processing a node is proportional to the number of outgoing edges, the total running time of the algorithm is $\mathcal{O}(m + n)$. The case for predecessor rank is symmetric. □

Theorem 1. Algorithm 3 yields the coarsest refinement of a partition of a DAG that is successor (or predecessor) stable.

Proof (Sketch). For predecessor stability, the only differences from Paige and Tarjan's algorithm are the initial refinement and the order in which splitter blocks are chosen. By Lemma 1 blocks are not refined unnecessarily when refininig on rank, and the order of split operations is not used in the correctness proof for the original algorithm [15]. Successor stability is symmetric. □

To implement Algorithm 3 we use the same underlying data structures as for Algorithm 1: doubly linked lists $\mathcal{C}$ and $\mathcal{P}$ realizing X and P. In Algorithm 3, the extract operation is implemented by removing the first $B \in \mathcal{S}$ from the first $\mathcal{S} \in \mathcal{C}$. The replace operation is implemented by moving B from $\mathcal{S}$ to the end of $\mathcal{P}$, and if only one block B' is left in $\mathcal{S}$, this B' is also moved from $\mathcal{S}$ to $\mathcal{P}$, and $\mathcal{S}$ is removed from $\mathcal{C}$.

Theorem 2. The running time of Algorithm 3 is $\mathcal{O}(m + n)$.

Proof (Sketch). We analyze the cost of StabilizeWRT() separately. Outside the while loop, the call to RefineAndSortOnRank() has cost $\mathcal{O}(m+n)$ by Lemma 3, and the construction of $\mathcal{C}$ and $\mathcal{P}$ has cost $\mathcal{O}(|P|) \subseteq \mathcal{O}(n)$. As splitters are chosen in order of their rank, by Lemma 2 a splitter block is not later split itself. This means that each node is only part of a splitter once, and that the while-loop is run $\mathcal{O}(n)$ times. The loop condition is implemented by checking if $\mathcal{C} \neq \emptyset$. As all the operations on linked lists inside the loop have complexity $\mathcal{O}(1)$, the total cost of the while-loop is $\mathcal{O}(n)$. The StabilizeWRT() function is called $\mathcal{O}(n)$ times, and the cost of one call is linear in the number of nodes and edges used [15]. As nodes are only part of a splitter block once, edges are also only used for splitting once, and the total cost is $\mathcal{O}(m + n)$. □

3.2 Stabilizing Trees

We now present an algorithm for finding the coarsest successor *and* predecessor stable refinement of the nodes in a tree. It uses the solution for DAGs from the previous section to refine a partition *first* to the coarsest predecessor stable refinement, and *then* to the coarsest successor stable refinement, as shown in

Algorithm 5. Stabilization for trees

```
function StabilizeTree(P, Directions):
    if PRED ∈ Directions:
        StabilizeDAG(P, PRED)
    if SUCC ∈ Directions:
        StabilizeDAG(P, SUCC)
```

Algorithm 5. For trees this yields a partition that is still predecessor stable, as we prove in the following.

Figure 6 shows with a continuation of Figure 5 how Algorithm 5 is used to find a successor and predecessor stable refinement. The starting point in the figure is a predecessor stable refinement found after calling StabilizeDAG(P, PRED). This partition is then successor stabilized by calling StabilizeDAG(P, SUCC), which first refines and sorts on successor rank, shown between lines (i) and (j) in the figure, and then uses the blocks in the current P as splitters in order, shown in lines (j)–(t). Compare this partition with the F&B-bisimilarity partition in Figure 1d.

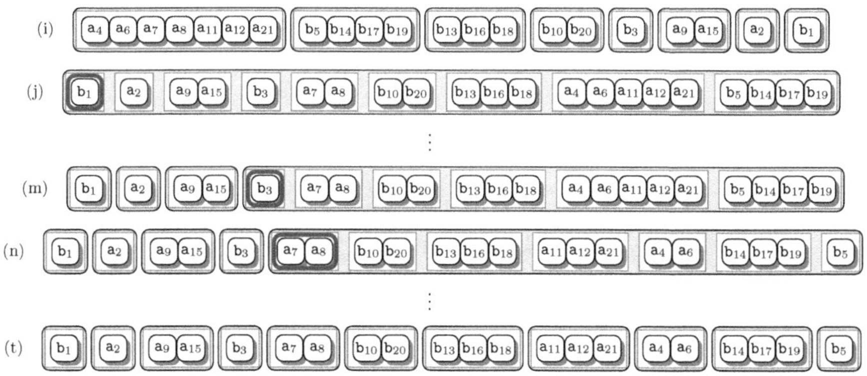

Fig. 6. Continuing Fig. 5: Line (i) shows predecessor stable partition, step (i)–(j) shows successor rank refinement, and steps (j)–(t) show successor stabilization

Theorem 3. If a predecessor stable partition of the nodes in a tree is refined to successor stability, the resulting partition is still predecessor stable.

Proof (Sketch). Blocks are split in three ways: To refine on rank, with respect to a block $B \in P$, or as a side effect with respect to $S \setminus B$ in Algorithm 2. By Lemma 1, the first type of split does not cause any split that would not eventually be caused by an algorithm that iteratively refines P with respect to a random block $B \in P$, and from the correctness proof of Paige and Tarjan's algorithm [15], neither does splitting with respect to $S \setminus B$.

We now use induction on the refinement steps, and show that the partition P remains predecessor stable. It is true initially by assumption. The induction step is to split a block $D \in P$ on successor stability with respect to a block $B \in P$.

B will split D into two parts D_B and D_S, containing the nodes pointed to and not pointed to from B, respectively. The splitting of D may only affect the predecessor stability of the new blocks D_B and D_S with respect to their descendants, and of the set of blocks $\mathcal{B}$ pointing into D with respect to D_B and D_S. After the split, $B \subseteq E^{-1}(D_B)$ and $B \cap E^{-1}(D_S) = \emptyset$, and for all other $B' \in \mathcal{B}$ we have that $B' \cap E^{-1}(D_B) = \emptyset$ and $B' \subseteq E^{-1}(D_S)$, because these B' by assumption have pointers into D, but by the fact that the data is a tree, do not have pointers into D_B.

For any block G pointed to from some node in D, $D \subseteq E^{-1}(G)$ by the initial assumption of predecessor stability, meaning all nodes in D point into G. This means that all nodes in D_B and D_S also point into G, and thus D_B and D_S are predecessor stable with respect to G. □

Figure 7a illustrates this theorem. By contrast, assuming the data was not a tree, the blocks $B' \in \mathcal{B}$ would not necessarily be predecessor stable after splitting D, as shown in Figure 7b.

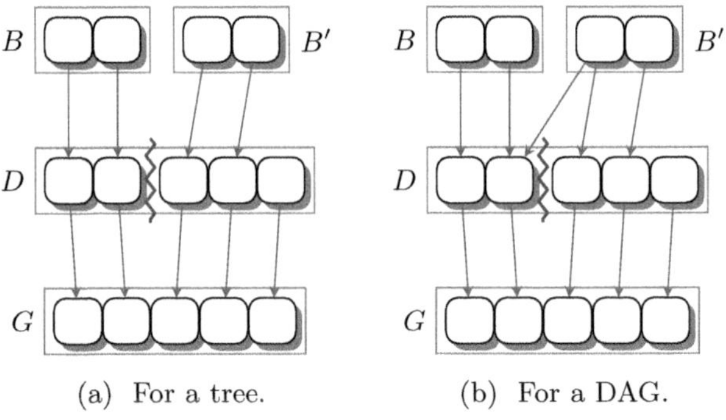

Fig. 7. Splitting D for successor stability w.r.t. B in a partition P. This does not impact predecessor stability for any block given tree data, but may break predecessor stability in a DAG.

Theorem 4. Algorithm 5 finds the coarsest refinement of a partition of the nodes in tree that is successor and predecessor stable in $\mathcal{O}(n)$ time.

Proof. From Theorems 1, 2 and 3, and the fact that $m \in \mathcal{O}(n)$ for tree data. □

Corollary 1. The F&B-index can be built in $\mathcal{O}(n)$ time for tree data using Algorithm 5.

Proof (Sketch). The coarsest successor and predecessor stable refinement of a partitioning on label gives the maximum F&B-bisimulation [9], and the summary structure can be constructed from the contraction graph [9].

4 Related Work

There are many variations of structure summaries for graph data, such as partitionings on similarity [8,14], the F+B-index [9], the A(k) index [11], and the D(k)-index [2]. Note that an implication of Theorem 3 is that the F+B-index and the F&B-index are identical for tree data. The cost of matching in the summary can be reduced by label-partitioning it and using specialized joins [1], or using multi-level structure indexing [17]. For queries using ancestor–descendant edges on graph data, different graph encodings offer trade-offs between space usage and query time [20]. For a general overview of indexing and search in XML see the survey by Gou and Chirkova [6]. There is previous research on updates of bisimilarity partitions [10,19,16]. Some of these methods trade update time for coarseness, as refinements of bisimilarity may be cheaper to compute after a data update. Single directional bisimulations are used in many fields, such as modal logic, concurrency theory, set theory, formal verification, etc. [3], but to our knowledge, F&B-bisimulation is not frequently used outside XML search.

5 Conclusions and Future Work

In this paper we have improved the running time for refining a partition to the coarsest simultaneous successor and predecessor stability for tree data from $\mathcal{O}(n \log n)$ to $\mathcal{O}(n)$, and with that the computation of F&B-bisimilarity, and construction of the F&B-index.[1] An incorrect linear algorithm for DAGs has been presented recently [12], and it would be interesting to know whether the problem is actually solvable in linear time for DAGs.

A natural extension of our work would be to reduce the cost of updates in F&B-bisimilarity partitions for trees. A particularly interesting direction would be to improve indexing performance for typical XML document collections, where there is a large number of small independent documents. It may be possible to iteratively add documents to the index with (expected) cost dependent only on the size of the documents.

Acknowledgments. This material is based upon work supported by the iAd Project funded by the Research Council of Norway and the Norwegian University of Science and Technology. Any opinions, findings and conclusions or recommendations expressed in this material are those of the authors, and do not necessarily reflect the views of the funding agencies.

References

1. Bača, R., Krátký, M., Snášel, V.: On the efficient search of an XML twig query in large DataGuide trees. In: Proc. IDEAS (2008)
2. Chen, Q., Lim, A., Ong, K.W.: D(k)-index: an adaptive structural summary for graph-structured data. In: Proc. SIGMOD (2003)

[1] See the extended version of this paper for some performance experiments [7].

3. Dovier, A., Piazza, C., Policriti, A.: A fast bisimulation algorithm. In: Berry, G., Comon, H., Finkel, A. (eds.) CAV 2001. LNCS, vol. 2102, p. 79. Springer, Heidelberg (2001)
4. Fernandez, J.-C.: An implementation of an efficient algorithm for bisimulation equivalence. Sci. Comput. Program. 13(2-3) (1990)
5. Goldman, R., Widom, J.: DataGuides: Enabling query formulation and optimization in semistructured databases. In: Proc. VLDB (1997)
6. Gou, G., Chirkova, R.: Efficiently querying large XML data repositories: A survey. Knowl. and Data Eng. (2007)
7. Grimsmo, N., Bjørklund, T.A., Hetland, M.L.: Linear computation of the maximum simultaneous forward and backward bisimulation for node-labeled trees (extended version). Technical Report IDI-TR-2010-10, NTNU, Trondheim, Norway (2010)
8. Henzinger, M.R., Henzinger, T.A., Kopke, P.W.: Computing simulations on finite and infinite graphs. In: Proc. FOCS (1995)
9. Kaushik, R., Bohannon, P., Naughton, J.F., Korth, H.F.: Covering indexes for branching path queries. In: Proc. SIGMOD (2002)
10. Kaushik, R., Bohannon, P., Naughton, J.F., Shenoy, P.: Updates for structure indexes. In: Proc. VLDB (2002)
11. Kaushik, R., Shenoy, P., Bohannon, P., Gudes, E.: Exploiting local similarity for indexing paths in graph-structured data. In: Proc. ICDE (2002)
12. Liu, X., Li, J., Wang, H.: SAM: An efficient algorithm for F&B-index construction. In: Proc. APWeb/WAIM (2007)
13. Milner, R.: Communication and concurrency. Prentice-Hall, Inc., Englewood Cliffs (1989)
14. Milo, T., Suciu, D.: Index structures for path expressions. In: Beeri, C., Bruneman, P. (eds.) ICDT 1999. LNCS, vol. 1540, pp. 277–295. Springer, Heidelberg (1998)
15. Paige, R., Tarjan, R.E.: Three partition refinement algorithms. SIAM J. Comput. (1987)
16. Saha, D.: An incremental bisimulation algorithm. In: Proc. FSTTCS (2007)
17. Wu, X., Liu, G.: XML twig pattern matching using version tree. Data & Knowl. Eng. (2008)
18. Yang, B., Fontoura, M., Shekita, E., Rajagopalan, S., Beyer, K.: Virtual cursors for XML joins. In: Proc. CIKM (2004)
19. Yi, K., He, H., Stanoi, I., Yang, J.: Incremental maintenance of XML structural indexes. In: Proc. SIGMOD (2004)
20. Yu, J.X., Cheng, J.: Graph reachability queries: A survey. In: Managing and Mining Graph Data (2010)

Extending the Tractability Results on XPath Satisfiability with Sibling Axes

Yasunori Ishihara[1], Shogo Shimizu[2], and Toru Fujiwara[1]

[1] Osaka University, Japan
{ishihara,fujiwara}@ist.osaka-u.ac.jp
[2] Advanced Institute of Industrial Technology, Japan
shimizu-syogo@aiit.ac.jp

Abstract. This paper extends the tractability results on XPath satisfiability with sibling axes under DC-DTDs, which were presented by the authors at DBPL 2009, in the following two directions. First, we provide a condition to extend a class of DTDs without spoiling the tractability of XPath satisfiability, provided that only child, descendant-or-self, parent, ancestor-or-self, following-sibling, and preceding-sibling axes, path union, and qualifier are taken into account. By applying the condition to DC-DTDs, we obtain a strictly broader but still tractable class of DTDs, where operators ? (zero or one occurrence) and + (one or more occurrences) are allowed in regular expressions in a restricted manner. Second, we extend the existing method of analyzing the satisfiability under DC-DTDs to a broader class of XPath expressions. Then, we show that the extended satisfiability analysis can be performed efficiently for a new subclass of XPath expressions.

1 Introduction

XPath satisfiability is one of the major theoretical topics in the field of XML databases. XPath is a query language for XML documents, where an XML document is often regarded as an unranked labeled ordered tree. An XPath expression specifies a pattern of (possibly branching) paths from the root of a given XML document. The answer to an XPath expression for an XML document T is a set of nodes v of T such that the specified path pattern matches the path from the root to v. A given XPath expression p is satisfiable under a given DTD (Document Type Definition) D if there is an XML document T conforming to D such that the answer to p for T is a nonempty set.

Research on XPath satisfiability is strongly motivated by query optimization. When (a part of) an XPath expression is found unsatisfiable, we can always replace the expression with the empty set without evaluating it. However, it is known that satisfiability under unrestricted DTDs is in P only for a very small subclass of XPath expressions [1,2]. Genevès and Layaïda tackled the intractability of XPath satisfiability itself. Their approach is to translate XPath expressions to formulas in monadic second-order (MSO) logic [3] and in a variant of μ-calculus [4,5]. Regular tree grammars [6], which are a general model

M.L. Lee et al. (Eds.): XSym 2010, LNCS 6309, pp. 33–47, 2010.

of XML schemas and a proper superclass of DTDs, are also translated to such formulas. Then, satisfiability is verified by fast decision procedures for MSO and μ-calculus formulas. On the other hand, several research works focused on investigating the relationship among XPath classes, DTD classes, and the complexity of the satisfiability. In [1,2], Benedikt et al. investigated how the combinations of XPath components such as downward/upward axes, qualifiers, attribute-value equalities, and negations affect the complexity of the satisfiability problem. Then, in [2,7], they took sibling axes into account. Data equality operator was explored in several research works, e.g., [1,2,8]. In [8], Figueira showed that the combination of the equality operator and downward axes brings EXPTIME-hardness to the satisfiability problem even in the absence of DTDs.

Of course, the purpose of the investigation of such relationship is to find a tractable combination of XPath classes and DTD classes. In [1,2,7], non-recursive and disjunction-free DTDs were considered. However, non-recursiveness does not broaden the tractable class of XPath. Disjunction-freeness definitely broadens the tractable class of XPath, but disjunction-free DTDs are too restricted from a practical point of view. Montazerian et al. presented two tractable subclasses of DTDs, called duplicate-free DTDs and covering DTDs [9]. Intuitively, a DTD is *duplicate-free* if every tag name appears at most once in each content model. A DTD is *covering* if each content model allows a sequence consisting of all the tag names which appear in the content model. They also claimed that most of the real-world DTDs are duplicate-free or covering. However, the examined class of XPath was rather small. Especially, neither upward axes nor sibling axes were handled. Suzuki and Fukushima [10] found that satisfiability of an XPath expression with child, parent, and sibling axes under duplicate-free DTDs is tractable. On the other hand, in [11], the tractability of covering DTDs was shown to be fragile against upward and sibling axes.

In our previous work [11], we proposed *disjunction-capsuled DTDs*, or *DC-DTDs* for short, which are a proper superclass of disjunction-free DTDs but a proper subclass of covering DTDs. A DTD is disjunction-capsuled if in each content model, every disjunction operator appears within a scope of a Kleene star operator. For example, $a(b|c)^*$ is DC but $(a|b)c^*$ is not. In [11], XPath expressions were supposed to consist of $\downarrow$ (child axis), $\downarrow^*$ (descendant-or-self axis), $\uparrow$ (parent axis), $\uparrow^*$ (ancestor-or-self axis), $\rightarrow^+$ (following-sibling axis), $\leftarrow^+$ (preceding-sibling axis), $\cup$ (path union), and $[\ ]$ (qualifier). Then, it was shown that the satisfiability under DC-DTDs for XPath expressions without upward axes or qualifiers is tractable.

The purpose of this paper is to extend the tractability results in [11] to a broader class of DTDs and to a broader class of XPath expressions. First, we propose a condition to extend a class of DTDs without spoiling the tractability of XPath satisfiability, provided that the class of XPath expressions consists of the above components. As the first contribution, we obtain *$DC^{?+}$-DTDs* by applying the condition to DC-DTDs. A DTD allowing operators ? (zero or one occurrence) and + (one or more occurrences) in its content models is said to be $\text{DC}^{?+}$ if all the content models obtained by replacing every + with $*$ and by deleting every ?

Table 1. Results of this paper

<table>
<tr><th>↓</th><th>↓*</th><th>↑</th><th>↑*</th><th>→+</th><th>←+</th><th>∪</th><th>[ ]</th><th>covering DTDs</th><th>DC?+-DTDs</th><th>DC-DTDs</th><th>disjunction-free DTDs</th></tr>
<tr><td>+</td><td>+</td><td></td><td></td><td></td><td></td><td>+</td><td>+</td><td>P[9]</td><td>P</td><td>P</td><td>P[2]</td></tr>
<tr><td colspan="2">+</td><td></td><td></td><td colspan="2">+</td><td></td><td>+</td><td>NPC[11]</td><td>P(§3)</td><td>P[11]</td><td>P</td></tr>
<tr><td colspan="2">+</td><td colspan="2">+</td><td colspan="2">+</td><td>+</td><td></td><td>NPC[11]</td><td>P(§3)</td><td>P[11]</td><td>P</td></tr>
<tr><td>+</td><td>+</td><td></td><td></td><td>+</td><td>+</td><td>+</td><td>+</td><td>NPC[11]</td><td>P(§3)</td><td>P[11]</td><td>P</td></tr>
<tr><td>+</td><td>+</td><td>+</td><td>+</td><td>+</td><td>+</td><td>+</td><td></td><td>NPC[11]</td><td>P(§3)</td><td>P[11]</td><td>P</td></tr>
<tr><td>+</td><td></td><td colspan="2">+</td><td colspan="2">+</td><td></td><td>+</td><td>NPC[11]</td><td>P(§3, §4)</td><td>P(§4)</td><td>P</td></tr>
<tr><td>+</td><td></td><td>+</td><td>+</td><td></td><td></td><td></td><td>+</td><td>NPC</td><td>NPC</td><td>NPC</td><td>NPC(§4)</td></tr>
<tr><td>+</td><td></td><td>+</td><td></td><td></td><td></td><td>+</td><td>+</td><td>NPC</td><td>NPC</td><td>NPC</td><td>NPC[2]</td></tr>
<tr><td></td><td>+</td><td></td><td>+</td><td></td><td></td><td></td><td>+</td><td>NPC</td><td>NPC</td><td>NPC</td><td>NPC[11]</td></tr>
<tr><td colspan="2">+</td><td colspan="2">+</td><td>+</td><td>+</td><td></td><td>+</td><td>NPC</td><td>NPC</td><td>NPC</td><td>NPC[11]</td></tr>
</table>

- A "+" in a multicolumn means "one of them." For example, the second row of the table represents the class with one of ↓ and ↓*, one of $\rightarrow^+$ and $\leftarrow^+$, and [ ].
- NPC stands for NP-complete.
- Bold letters indicate the contributions of this paper.

are disjunction-capsuled. For example, $a^?(b|c)^+$ is $\mathrm{DC}^{?+}$ because $a(b|c)^*$, which is obtained by replacing + with * and by deleting ?, is DC. Note that any regular expression equivalent to $a^?(b|c)^+$ (e.g., $(a|\epsilon)(b|c)(b|c)^*$) is not DC. On the other hand, $(a|b)^?c^+$ is not $\mathrm{DC}^{?+}$ because $(a|b)c^*$ is not DC. Obviously $\mathrm{DC}^{?+}$-DTDs are a proper superclass of DC-DTDs but a proper subclass of covering DTDs. The extension of DC to $\mathrm{DC}^{?+}$ has a great impact from a practical point of view, because ? and + are used very often in real-world DTDs. To show the impact, we examined 22 real-world DTDs, 950 rules. The numbers of $\mathrm{DC}^{?+}$-DTDs and $\mathrm{DC}^{?+}$-rules were 13 and 928, respectively. Moreover, all the covering DTDs were $\mathrm{DC}^{?+}$-DTDs and there was only one rule that was covering but not $\mathrm{DC}^{?+}$. On the other hand, there were only 7 DC-DTDs and 853 DC-rules. Thus, $\mathrm{DC}^{?+}$-DTDs are much broader than DC-DTDs and almost covering in the real world.

Second, we extend the method of analyzing the satisfiability under DC-DTDs in [11] to a broader class of XPath expressions. Then, as the second contribution, we obtain that the satisfiability under DC-DTDs is tractable for XPath expressions consisting of child axis, one of the upward axes, one of the sibling axes, and qualifier. Since the known tractable classes of XPath expressions must not contain upward axes and qualifier simultaneously, this result is definitely new. Moreover, we obtain that the satisfiability under DC-DTDs becomes intractable for XPath expressions consisting of child axis, *both* of the upward axes, and qualifier. Thus, a slight difference of the combination drastically affects the tractability of the satisfiability problem. Table 1 summarizes the results of this paper.

The rest of the paper is organized as follows. Preliminary definitions are given in Section 2. Then, the first and the second contributions are presented in Sections 3 and 4, respectively. Section 5 summarizes the paper.

2 Definitions

2.1 XML Documents

An XML document is represented by an unranked labeled ordered tree. The label of a node v, denoted $\lambda(v)$, corresponds to a tag name. We extend λ to a function on sequences, i.e., for a sequence $v_1 \cdots v_n$ of nodes, let $\lambda(v_1 \cdots v_n) = \lambda(v_1) \cdots \lambda(v_n)$. Attributes are not handled in this paper.

2.2 DTDs

A regular expression over an alphabet Σ consists of constants ϵ (empty sequence) and the symbols in Σ, and operators $\cdot$ (concatenation), $*$ (zero or more occurrences), and $|$ (disjunction). We exclude $\emptyset$ (empty set) because we are interested in only nonempty regular languages. The concatenation operator is often omitted as usual. The string language represented by a regular expression e is denoted by $L(e)$.

A regular expression is *disjunction-capsuled*, or *DC* for short, if it is in the form of $e_1 e_2 \cdots e_n$ $(n \geq 1)$, where each e_i $(1 \leq i \leq n)$ is either a symbol in Σ or in the form of $(e'_i)^*$ for any regular expression e'_i. For example, $(a|bc)^* d(ab^*)^*$ is disjunction-capsuled, but $a^*|(bc)^*$ is not. Note that ϵ is disjunction-capsuled because $\epsilon = \epsilon^*$. The *length* of a disjunction-capsuled regular expression $e = e_1 e_2 \cdots e_n$, where each e_i $(1 \leq i \leq n)$ is either a symbol in Σ or in the form of $(e'_i)^*$, is defined as n and denoted by $len(e)$. Moreover, i $(1 \leq i \leq len(e))$ is called a *position* and each e_i is called the i-th subexpression of e.

A regular expression e is *disjunction-free* if e contains no disjunction operators. A regular expression e over an alphabet Σ is *covering* if $L(e)$ contains a string consisting of all the symbols in Γ_e, where $\Gamma_e \subseteq \Sigma$ is the set of symbols appearing in e. A disjunction-free regular expression is vacuously disjunction-capsuled. Moreover, a disjunction-capsuled regular expression is always covering. To see this, regard a regular expression as a string generator. Since disjunctions are only inside the scope of Kleene stars, we can generate a string by repeating the Kleene-starred subexpressions so that all the operands of disjunctions simultaneously appear in the string.

Definition 1. *A* DTD *is a 3-tuple* $D = (\Sigma, r, P)$*, where:*

- Σ *is a finite set of* labels,
- $r \in \Sigma$ *is the* root label, *and*
- P *is a mapping from* Σ *to the set of regular expressions over* Σ*.* $P(a)$ *is called the* content model *of label* a*.*

A disjunction-free DTD *is a DTD such that* $P(a)$ *is disjunction-free for every* $a \in \Sigma$*. A* disjunction-capsuled DTD*, a* DC-DTD *for short, is a DTD such that* $P(a)$ *is disjunction-capsuled for every* $a \in \Sigma$*. A* covering DTD *is a DTD such that* $P(a)$ *is covering (i.e.,* $L(P(a))$ *contains a string consisting of all the symbols in* $\Gamma_{P(a)}$*) for every* $a \in \Sigma$*.*

Definition 2. *A tree T* conforms *to a DTD $D = (\Sigma, r, P)$ if*

- *the label of the root of T is r, and*
- *for each node v of T and its children sequence $v_1 \cdots v_n$, $L(P(\lambda(v)))$ contains $\lambda(v_1 \cdots v_n)$.*

Let $TL(D)$ denote the set of all the trees conforming to D.

In this paper, we assume that every DTD $D = (\Sigma, r, P)$ contains no useless symbols. That is, for each $a \in \Sigma$, there is a tree T conforming to D such that the label of some node of T is a.

The size of a regular expression is the number of constants and operators appearing in the regular expression. The size of a DTD is the sum of the size of all content models.

2.3 XPath Expressions

The syntax of an XPath expression p is defined as follows:

$$p ::= \chi :: l \mid p/p \mid p \cup p \mid p[q],$$
$$\chi ::= \downarrow \mid \uparrow \mid \downarrow^* \mid \uparrow^* \mid \rightarrow^+ \mid \leftarrow^+,$$
$$q ::= p \mid q \wedge q \mid q \vee q,$$

where $l \in \Sigma$. Each $\chi \in \{\downarrow, \uparrow, \downarrow^*, \uparrow^*, \rightarrow^+, \leftarrow^+\}$ is called an *axis*. Also, a subexpression in the form of $[q]$ is called a *qualifier*. The *size* of an XPath expression p is defined as the number of subexpressions in the form of $\chi :: l$ in p.

Definition 3. *The semantics of an XPath expression over a tree T is defined as follows, where p and q are regarded as binary and unary predicates on paths from the root node of T, respectively. In what follows, v_0 denotes the root of T, and v and v' denote nodes of T. Also, w, w', and w'' are nonempty sequences of nodes of T starting by v_0, unless otherwise stated.*

- $T \models (\downarrow :: l)(w, wv')$ *if path wv' exists in T and $\lambda(v') = l$.*
- $T \models (\uparrow :: l)(wv, w)$ *if path wv exists in T and the label of the last node of w is l.*
- $T \models (\downarrow^* :: l)(w, ww')$ *if path ww' exists in T and the label of the last node of ww' is l, where w' is a possibly empty sequence of nodes of T.*
- $T \models (\uparrow^* :: l)(ww', w)$ *if path ww' exists in T and the label of the last node of w is l, where w' is a possibly empty sequence of nodes of T.*
- $T \models (\rightarrow^+ :: l)(wv, wv')$ *if paths wv and wv' exist in T, v' is a following sibling of v, and $\lambda(v') = l$.*
- $T \models (\leftarrow^+ :: l)(wv, wv')$ *if paths wv and wv' exist in T, v' is a preceding sibling of v, and $\lambda(v') = l$.*
- $T \models (p/p')(w, w')$ *if there is w'' such that $T \models p(w, w'')$ and $T \models p'(w'', w')$.*
- $T \models (p \cup p')(w, w')$ *if $T \models p(w, w')$ or $T \models p'(w, w')$.*
- $T \models (p[q])(w, w')$ *if $T \models p(w, w')$ and $T \models q(w')$.*

- $T \models p(w)$ *if there is* w' *such that* $T \models p(w, w')$.
- $T \models (q \wedge q')(w)$ *if* $T \models q(w)$ *and* $T \models q'(w)$.
- $T \models (q \vee q')(w)$ *if* $T \models q(w)$ *or* $T \models q'(w)$.

It would be reasonable to define p and q as predicates on the last nodes of the paths, rather than the entire paths, because T is a tree and therefore the last nodes are enough to determine the entire paths uniquely. However, this redundant definition will be useful when discussing the correctness of the proposed satisfiability analysis method.

Let v_0 be the root node of T. A tree T *satisfies* an XPath expression p if there is a path w from v_0 such that $T \models p(v_0, w)$. An XPath expression p is *satisfiable* under a DTD D if some $T \in TL(D)$ satisfies p.

Following the notation of [1,2,7], a subclass of XPath is indicated by $\mathcal{X}(\cdot)$. For example, the subclass with child axes and qualifiers is denoted by $\mathcal{X}(\downarrow, [\,])$.

3 Extending the Tractable Class of DTDs

In this section, we first show a condition to extend a class of DTDs *without spoiling* the tractability of XPath satisfiability, provided that the class of XPath expressions is (a subclass of) $\mathcal{X}(\downarrow, \downarrow^*, \uparrow, \uparrow^*, \rightarrow^+, \leftarrow^+, \cup, [\,])$. Then, we apply the condition to DC-DTDs and obtain a broader class of DTDs, called *$DC^{?+}$-DTDs*, which inherits the tractability of DC-DTDs.

3.1 Extending the Class of DTDs without Spoiling Tractability

Let e and e' be regular expressions. We write $e \sim e'$ if they satisfy the following two conditions:

- every $w \in L(e)$ is a subsequence (i.e., can be obtained by deleting zero or more symbols) of some $w' \in L(e')$; and
- every $w' \in L(e')$ is a subsequence of some $w \in L(e)$.

For example, it is not difficult to see that $(aa)^* \sim a(aa)^*$. To see another example, let $e = (a|\epsilon)(b|c)(b|c)^*$ and $e' = a(b|c)^*$. Then, $e \sim e'$ because

- for every $w \in L(e) - L(e') = L((b|c)(b|c)^*)$, there is $w' = aw \in L(e')$, where w is a subsequence of w', and
- $L(e') - L(e) = \{a\}$, and a is a subsequence of, say, $w = ab \in L(e)$.

Let $D = (\Sigma, r, P)$ and $D' = (\Sigma, r, P')$. We write $D \sim D'$ if $P(a) \sim P'(a)$ for each $a \in \Sigma$. Since DTDs are assumed to have no useless symbols, $D \sim D'$ implies that

- every $T \in TL(D)$ can be obtained by deleting zero or more subtrees of some $T' \in TL(D')$; and
- every $T' \in TL(D')$ can be obtained by deleting zero or more subtrees of some $T \in TL(D)$.

The following lemma says that the satisfiability of any XPath expression in $\mathcal{X}(\downarrow, \downarrow^*, \uparrow, \uparrow^*, \rightarrow^+, \leftarrow^+, \cup, [\,])$ under DTDs D and D' coincides if $D \sim D'$.

Lemma 1. *Let $p \in \mathcal{X}(\downarrow, \downarrow^*, \uparrow, \uparrow^*, \rightarrow^+, \leftarrow^+, \cup, [\,])$. Suppose that $D \sim D'$. Then, p is satisfiable under D if and only if p is satisfiable under D'.*

Proof. By the symmetry of D and D', it suffices to show the "only if" part. Let $T \in TL(D)$ be a tree such that $T \models p(w, w')$ at some paths w and w' from the root of T. Since $D \sim D'$, there is a tree $T' \in TL(D')$ that contains T as a subgraph. By induction on the structure of p, we show that $T' \models p(w, w')$ at the "same" paths w and w'. The rest of the proof is straightforward and therefore omitted because T' contains T as a subgraph. Note that neither $\rightarrow^+$ nor $\leftarrow^+$ is sensible of the immediate siblings. Therefore, if $T \models (\chi_{\leftrightarrow} :: l)(w, w')$, where $\chi_{\leftrightarrow} \in \{\rightarrow^+, \leftarrow^+\}$, then $\chi_{\leftrightarrow} :: l$ is also satisfied at w and w' of any tree obtained by inserting zero or more nodes between the last nodes of w and w' in T. □

The next theorem states a condition where the tractability of the satisfiability problem under a class C of DTDs is preserved under another (possibly broader) class C'.

Theorem 1. *Suppose that classes C and C' of DTDs satisfy the following property: for each DTD $D' \in C'$, there exists $D \in C$ such that $D \sim D'$ and D can be computed efficiently from D'. Then, for any subclass X of $\mathcal{X}(\downarrow, \downarrow^*, \uparrow, \uparrow^*, \rightarrow^+, \leftarrow^+, \cup, [\,])$, if the satisfiability problem for X under C is tractable, the same problem is also tractable under C'.*

Proof. Assume that the satisfiability problem for X under C is tractable. Let (p, D') be an arbitrary instance of the satisfiability problem for X under C'. By the assumption on C and C', we can efficiently compute a DTD $D \in C$ such that $D \sim D'$. The satisfiability of p under D' is preserved under D by Lemma 1, and is decidable efficiently by the assumption. □

3.2 A Broader Tractable Class of DTDs

Now, we introduce DC$^{?+}$-DTDs, a proper superclass of DC-DTDs, and show that they satisfy the condition stated in Theorem 1. Thus, DC$^{?+}$-DTDs are broader than DC-DTDs but still inherit the tractability of DC-DTDs. In what follows, we consider regular expressions that may involve two more operators ? (zero or one occurrence) and + (one or more occurrences) as well as the standard three operators introduced in Section 2.

Definition 4. *A regular expression e is* DC$^{?+}$ *if e is in the form of $e_1 e_2 \cdots e_n$ ($n \geq 1$), where each e_i ($1 \leq i \leq n$) is either*

- *a symbol in Σ,*
- *in the form of $(e'_i)^*$ for a regular expression e'_i,*
- *in the form of $(e'_i)^?$ for a DC$^{?+}$ regular expression e'_i, or*
- *in the form of $(e'_i)^+$ for a regular expression e'_i.*

A DTD $D = (\Sigma, r, P)$ is DC$^{?+}$ *if $P(a)$ is DC$^{?+}$ for every $a \in \Sigma$.*

For example, both $a^?b$ and $(a|b)^+$ are DC$^{?+}$. By using only the standard three operators of regular expressions, $a^?b$ is equivalent to $(a|\epsilon)b$, $ab|b$, etc., but none of them is DC. Similarly, $(a|b)^+$ is equivalent to $(a|b)(a|b)^*$, $(a(a|b)^*)|(b(a|b)^*)$, etc., but none of them is DC. Thus, DC$^{?+}$-DTDs are a proper superclass of DC-DTDs from the perspective of not only the syntax but the expressive power.

To apply Theorem 1 to DC- and DC$^{?+}$-DTDs, we introduce the following mapping δ:

- $\delta(\epsilon) = \epsilon$,
- $\delta(a) = a$ for each $a \in \Sigma$,
- $\delta(e_1 \cdot e_2) = \delta(e_1) \cdot \delta(e_2)$,
- $\delta(e^*) = \delta(e)^*$,
- $\delta(e_1|e_2) = \delta(e_1)|\delta(e_2)$,
- $\delta(e^?) = \delta(e)$, and
- $\delta(e^+) = \delta(e)^*$.

Intuitively, δ removes all the ? operators and replaces all the + operators with $*$ operators. Note that δ maps a DC$^{?+}$ regular expression into a DC one.

The next lemma states that δ preserves the satisfiability of XPath expressions in $\mathcal{X}(\downarrow, \downarrow^*, \uparrow, \uparrow^*, \rightarrow^+, \leftarrow^+, \cup, [\,])$.

Lemma 2. *Let e be a regular expression possibly involving operators ? and +. Then, $e \sim \delta(e)$.*

Proof. The lemma is shown by induction on the structure of e. For the base step, suppose that $e = \epsilon$ or $e = a$ for some $a \in \Sigma$. In either case, $\delta(e) = e$, and therefore, the lemma holds.

For the inductive step, first, suppose that $e = e_1 \cdot e_2$. By the inductive hypothesis, $e_1 \sim \delta(e_1)$ and $e_2 \sim \delta(e_2)$. Therefore, any $w = w_1 \cdot w_2 \in L(e_1 \cdot e_2)$ is a subsequence of some $w' = w'_1 \cdot w'_2 \in \delta(e_1) \cdot \delta(e_2)$, and vice versa. The cases when $e = (e_1)^*$ and $e = e_1|e_2$ can be shown similarly. Next, suppose that $e = (e_1)^?$. We have $L((e_1)^?) = L(e_1) \cup \{\epsilon\}$ and $L(\delta((e_1)^?)) = L(\delta(e_1))$. Since ϵ is a subsequence of any sequence and $e_1 \sim \delta(e_1)$ by the inductive hypothesis, it holds that $(e_1)^? \sim \delta((e_1)^?)$. Lastly, suppose that $e = (e_1)^+$. We have $L(\delta((e_1)^+)) = L(\delta(e_1)^*) = L(\delta(e_1)^+) \cup \{\epsilon\}$. Thus, in a similar way to the case when $e = (e_1)^?$, it can be concluded that $(e_1)^+ \sim \delta((e_1)^+)$. □

For a DTD $D = (\Sigma, r, P)$, let $\delta(D)$ denote the DTD $(\Sigma, r, \delta(P))$, where $\delta(P)(a) = \delta(P(a))$ for each $a \in \Sigma$. By Lemma 2 we have $D \sim \delta(D)$, and obviously $\delta(D)$ can be computed efficiently from D. Moreover, as stated above, $\delta(D)$ is DC if D is DC$^{?+}$. Hence, from Theorem 1, we can conclude the fact that DC$^{?+}$-DTDs inherit the tractability of DC-DTDs:

Corollary 1. *For any subclass X of $\mathcal{X}(\downarrow, \downarrow^*, \uparrow, \uparrow^*, \rightarrow^+, \leftarrow^+, \cup, [\,])$, if the satisfiability problem for X under DC-DTDs is tractable, the same problem is also tractable under DC$^{?+}$-DTDs.*

We discuss the practical impact of extending DC-DTDs to DC$^{?+}$-DTDs. Table 2 shows the numbers of rules in the forms of covering, DC$^{?+}$, and DC regular

Table 2. The numbers of covering, $DC^{?+}$, and DC rules in real-world DTDs

DTD Names	Numbers of Rules			
	Total	Covering	$DC^{?+}$	DC
LevelOne	31	29	29	21
Ecoknowmics	224	222	222	221
XML Schema	26	20	20	5
OSD	15	14	14	14
Opml	15	15	15	14
Rss	31	30	30	29
TV-Schedule	10	10	10	8
Xbel-1.0	9	9	9	6
XHTML1-strict	77	75	74	72
Newspaper	7	7	7	7
DBLP	37	37	37	37
Music ML	12	12	12	9
XMark DTD	77	76	76	70
Yahoo	32	32	32	32
Reed	16	16	16	16
SigmodRecord	11	11	11	10
Ubid	32	32	32	32
Ebay	32	32	32	32
News ML	118	114	114	100
PSD	66	64	64	55
Mondial	40	40	40	30
321gone	32	32	32	32
Total	950	929	928	852

expressions in 22 real-world DTDs [9]. By extending DC to $DC^{?+}$, the number of covered rules increases by 76 rules in 14 DTDs. Moreover, 13 out of 22 DTDs are $DC^{?+}$-DTDs, that is, all the rules in DTDs are $DC^{?+}$ regular expressions. On the other hand, among 929 covering rules, there is only one rule that is covering but not $DC^{?+}$. Thus, $DC^{?+}$-DTDs are much broader than DC-DTDs and almost covering in the real world. The only rule that is covering but not $DC^{?+}$ is in the form of $(ab|ba)$. Such a form causes intractability for even small XPath classes, e.g., $\mathcal{X}(\downarrow, \rightarrow^+, [\,])$. Actually, the 3SAT problem can be reduced to the satisfiability under $\mathcal{X}(\downarrow, \rightarrow^+, [\,])$ in a similar manner to Theorem 1 in [11]. In the reduction, the DTD has rules in the form of $P(a_{k-1}) = (a_k b_k | b_k a_k)$, where the value of a variable x_k is encoded by the order of the two sibling nodes a_k and b_k. The order of a_k and b_k can be checked by the following XPath expressions: $\cdots/\downarrow :: a_k/\rightarrow^+ :: b_k$ and $\cdots/\downarrow :: b_k/\rightarrow^+ :: a_k$.

There are 21 rules which are not even covering. All of them are in the form of $(a|b)$ or $(a|b)^?$. Again, it is not difficult to see that allowing rules of these forms causes intractability.

4 Extending the Tractable Class of XPath Expressions under DC-DTDs

In our previous work [11], we showed that the satisfiability of XPath expressions without upward axes or qualifiers is tractable under DC-DTDs. To show the fact, we introduced a notion of a schema graph G of a DC-DTD D, which is a structural summary of D. After that, we defined two kinds of satisfaction relation between G and an XPath expression p. Then, we showed that the satisfaction relation between G and p coincides with the satisfiability of p under D. Finally, we showed that the satisfaction relation can be determined efficiently.

In this section, we first extend one of the satisfaction relation to the full class of XPath expressions. Then, we show that the extended satisfaction relation still coincides with the satisfiability. Finally, we show the extended satisfaction relation can be determined efficiently for a subclass of XPath expressions. The subclass contains both upward axes and qualifiers, and therefore, the subclass is a new tractability result on the satisfiability under DC-DTDs.

4.1 Schema Graphs and SG Mappings

Definition 5. *The* schema graph *[11] $G = (U, E)$ of a DC-DTD $D = (\Sigma, r, P)$ is a directed graph defined as follows:*

- *A node $u \in U$ is either*
  - *$(\perp, 1, -, r)$, where $\perp$ is a new symbol not in Σ, or*
  - *(a, i, ω, b), where a, $b \in \Sigma$, $1 \leq i \leq len(P(a))$ such that b appears in the i-th subexpression e_i of $P(a)$, and $\omega =$ "$-$" if e_i is a single symbol in Σ and $\omega =$ "$*$" otherwise.*

  The first, second, third and fourth components of u are denoted by $\lambda_{par}(u)$, $pos(u)$, $\omega(u)$, and $\lambda(u)$, respectively. Especially, $\lambda(u)$ is called the label *of u. λ_{par}, pos, and λ are extended to functions on sequences.*
- *An edge from u to u' exists in E if and only if $\lambda(u) = \lambda_{par}(u')$.*

If $T \in TL(D)$, then each node of T can be associated with a node of the schema graph of D. More precisely, there exists a mapping θ, called an *SG mapping* [11] of T, from the set of nodes of T to the set of nodes of the schema graph of D with the following properties:

- θ maps the root node of T to $(\perp, 1, -, r)$.
- Let v be a node of T and $v_1 \cdots v_n$ be the children sequence of v. Then, $\theta(v_j) = (\lambda(v), i_j, \omega_{i_j}, \lambda(v_j))$, where $1 \leq i_j \leq len(P(\lambda(v)))$, $\omega_{i_j} =$ "$-$" if the i_j-th subexpression of $P(\lambda(v))$ is a single symbol in Σ and $\omega_{i_j} =$ "$*$" otherwise, and $i_j \leq i_{j'}$ if $j \leq j'$. Moreover, for every maximum subsequence $v_j \cdots v_{j'}$ such that $i_j = \cdots = i_{j'}$, $\lambda(v_j \cdots v_{j'})$ matches the i_j-th subexpression of $P(\lambda(v))$.

4.2 Extending the Satisfaction Relation by Schema Graphs

In our previous work [11], we introduced a satisfaction relation $\models_{\mathbb{G}}$ between schema graphs and XPath expressions without qualifiers. In the next definition, we extend $\models_{\mathbb{G}}$ to the full class of XPath expressions in our formulation, i.e., $\mathcal{X}(\downarrow,\downarrow^*,\uparrow,\uparrow^*,\rightarrow^+,\leftarrow^+,\cup,[\,])$. Here, an XPath expression will be regarded as a binary predicate on paths from $(\perp,1,-,r)$ on G.

Definition 6. *A satisfaction relation* $\models_{\mathrm{G}}$ *between a schema graph* G *and an XPath expression* $p \in \mathcal{X}(\downarrow,\downarrow^*,\uparrow,\uparrow^*,\rightarrow^+,\leftarrow^+,\cup,[\,])$ *is defined as follows. Let* u *and* u' *be nodes of* G*. Also, let* s*,* s'*, and* s'' *be nonempty sequences of nodes of* G *starting by* $(\perp,1,-,r)$*, unless otherwise stated.*

- $G \models_{\mathrm{G}} (\downarrow\!::l)(s, su')$ *if path* su' *exists in* G *and* $\lambda(u') = l$.
- $G \models_{\mathrm{G}} (\uparrow\!::l)(su, s)$ *if path* su *exists in* G *and the label of the last node of* s *is* l.
- $G \models_{\mathrm{G}} (\downarrow^*\!::l)(s, ss')$ *if path* ss' *exists in* G *and the label of the last node of* ss' *is* l*, where* s' *is a possibly empty sequence of nodes of* G.
- $G \models_{\mathrm{G}} (\uparrow^*\!::l)(ss', s)$ *if path* ss' *exists in* G *and the label of the last node of* s *is* l*, where* s' *is a possibly empty sequence of nodes of* G.
- $G \models_{\mathrm{G}} (\rightarrow^+\!::l)(su, su')$ *if paths* su *and* su' *exist in* G*,* $\lambda(u') = l$*, and* $pos(u) < pos(u')$ *if* $\omega(u) =$ "$-$" *and* $pos(u) \le pos(u')$ *if* $\omega(u) =$ "$*$".
- $G \models_{\mathrm{G}} (\leftarrow^+\!::l)(su, su')$ *if paths* su *and* su' *exist in* G*,* $\lambda(u') = l$*, and* $pos(u) > pos(u')$ *if* $\omega(u) =$ "$-$" *and* $pos(u) \ge pos(u')$ *if* $\omega(u) =$ "$*$".
- $G \models_{\mathrm{G}} (p/p')(s, s')$ *if there is* s'' *such that* $G \models_{\mathrm{G}} p(s, s'')$ *and* $G \models_{\mathrm{G}} p'(s'', s')$.
- $G \models_{\mathrm{G}} (p \cup p')(s, s')$ *if* $G \models_{\mathrm{G}} p(s, s')$ *or* $G \models_{\mathrm{G}} p'(s, s')$.
- $G \models_{\mathrm{G}} (p[q])(s, s')$ *if* $G \models_{\mathrm{G}} p(s, s')$ *and* $G \models_{\mathrm{G}} q(s')$.
- $G \models_{\mathrm{G}} p(s)$ *if there is* s' *such that* $G \models_{\mathrm{G}} p(s, s')$.
- $G \models_{\mathrm{G}} (q \wedge q')(s)$ *if* $G \models_{\mathrm{G}} q(s)$ *and* $G \models_{\mathrm{G}} q'(s)$.
- $G \models_{\mathrm{G}} (q \vee q')(s)$ *if* $G \models_{\mathrm{G}} q(s)$ *or* $G \models_{\mathrm{G}} q'(s)$.

Let G be the schema graph of a DC-DTD D. In the rest of this section, we show that the extended satisfaction relation $\models_{\mathrm{G}}$ of G and p still coincides with the satisfiability of p under D. The outline of the proof of the coincidence is almost the same as [11]. The following theorem is almost obvious because G captures all the possible topologies of the trees conforming to D. Formally, it can be proved by induction on the structure of p.

Theorem 2. *Let* $p \in \mathcal{X}(\downarrow,\downarrow^*,\uparrow,\uparrow^*,\rightarrow^+,\leftarrow^+,\cup,[\,])$*. Let* D *be a DC-DTD. Suppose that* $T \models p(w, w')$ *for some* $T \in TL(D)$ *with an SG mapping* θ*. Then,* $G \models_{\mathrm{G}} p(\theta(w), \theta(w'))$.

The converse of Theorem 2 is also shown by induction on the structure of p. As a part of the inductive step, we show the following lemma:

Lemma 3. *Let* D *be a DC-DTD. Let* T_1 *and* T_2 *be in* $TL(D)$ *with SG mappings* θ_1 *and* θ_2*, respectively. Suppose that* $T_1 \models p_1(w_1, w_1')$*,* $T_2 \models p_2(w_2, w_2')$*, and* $\theta_1(w_1') = \theta_2(w_2)$*. Then, there are* $T \in TL(D)$*, its SG mapping* θ*, and paths* w *and* w' *from the root of* T *such that* $\theta(w) = \theta_1(w_1)$*,* $\theta(w') = \theta_2(w_2')$*, and* $T \models (p_1/p_2)(w, w')$.

Proof. T can be constructed from T_1 and T_2 in the same way as Lemma 4 of [11]. In what follows, the construction method is briefly explained. Let v_1 and v_2 be nodes of T_1 and T_2, respectively. Also, let w_1'' and w_2'' be the paths from the roots to v_1 and v_2, respectively. Suppose that $\theta_1(w_1'') = \theta_2(w_2'')$ (and therefore, $\theta_1(v_1) = \theta_2(v_2)$). If $\omega(\theta_1(v_1)) =$ "$-$", then v_1 and v_2 are merged into one node in T. If $\omega(\theta_1(v_1)) =$ "$*$", T has both copies of v_1 and v_2. Moreover, if v_1 is a node on w_1', then T has two copies of v_2 on both sides of a copy of v_1, so that sibling axes work correctly. For more explanation, refer to the proofs of Lemmas 2 and 4 of [11]. □

The case when expressions are in other forms such as $p[q]$ and $q_1 \wedge q_2$ can be proved by the same construction method. Hence, we have the following theorem:

Theorem 3. *Let $p \in \mathcal{X}(\downarrow, \downarrow^*, \uparrow, \uparrow^*, \rightarrow^+, \leftarrow^+, \cup, [\,])$. Let D be a DC-DTD. If $G \models_G p(u, u')$, then there are $T \in TL(D)$, its SG mapping θ, and its nodes v and v' such that $\theta(v) = u$, $\theta(v') = u'$, and $T \models p(v, v')$.*

Thus, satisfiability of $p \in \mathcal{X}(\downarrow, \downarrow^*, \uparrow, \uparrow^*, \rightarrow^+, \leftarrow^+, \cup, [\,])$ under a DC-DTD D is equivalent to whether $G \models_G p((\bot, 1, -, r), u')$ for some u'.

4.3 A New Tractable Class of XPath Expressions under DC-DTDs

Now, our purpose is to find a class of XPath expressions such that we can decide efficiently whether $G \models_G p((\bot, 1, -, r), u')$ for some u'. To do this, we introduce an abstract machine M_p that, for a given s, computes s' such that $G \models_G p(s, s')$.

To be precise, let Ω be a special value denoting that "the execution of M_p is unsuccessful." Nondeterministic abstract machines M_p and N_q are defined below. It is not difficult to see that $M_p(s)$ returns s' such that $G \models_G p(s, s')$ if such s' exists, and Ω otherwise. It is also not difficult to see that $N_q(s)$ returns s if $G \models_G q(s)$, and Ω otherwise. Thus, p is satisfiable if and only if some execution of $M_p((\bot, 1, -, r))$ returns a value other than Ω.

Definition 7. *The behavior of $M_p(s)$ is defined as follows:*

- *For any p, return Ω if $s = \Omega$.*
- *Suppose that $p = \downarrow :: l$. If there is a node u' such that there is an edge from the last node of s to u' and $\lambda(u') = l$, then return su'. Otherwise, return Ω.*
- *Suppose that $p = \downarrow^* :: l$. Let u be the last node of s. If there is a node u' such that there is a path us' from u to u' and $\lambda(u') = l$, then return ss'. Otherwise, return Ω.*
- *Suppose that $p = \uparrow :: l$. If s is in the form of $s'u'u$ such that $\lambda(u') = l$, then return $s'u'$. Otherwise, return Ω.*
- *Suppose that $p = \uparrow^* :: l$. If s is in the form of $s'u's''$ such that $\lambda(u') = l$, then return $s'u'$. Otherwise, return Ω.*
- *Suppose that $p = \rightarrow^+ :: l$. Let $s = s'u$. Suppose that there is a node u' such that $pos(u) < pos(u')$ if $\omega(u) =$ "$-$", $pos(u) \leq pos(u')$ if $\omega(u) =$ "$*$", and $\lambda(u') = l$. Then, return su'. If such u' does not exist, return Ω.*

- *Suppose that* $p = \leftarrow^+ :: l$. *Let* $s = s'u$. *Suppose that there is a node* u' *such that* $pos(u) > pos(u')$ *if* $\omega(u) =$ "$-$", $pos(u) \geq pos(u')$ *if* $\omega(u) =$ "$*$", *and* $\lambda(u') = l$. *Then, return* su'. *If such* u' *does not exist, return* Ω.
- *Suppose that* $p = p_1/p_2$. *Return* $M_{p_2}(M_{p_1}(s))$.
- *Suppose that* $p = p_1 \cup p_2$. *Return* $M_{p_1}(s)$ *or* $M_{p_2}(s)$ *nondeterministically.*
- *Suppose that* $p = p'[q]$. *Return* $N_q(M_{p'}(s))$.

Also, the behavior of $N_q(s)$ *is defined as follows:*

- *For any* q, *return* Ω *if* $s = \Omega$.
- *Suppose that* $q = p$. *Return* s *if* $M_p(s) \neq \Omega$, *and* Ω *otherwise.*
- *Suppose that* $q = q_1 \wedge q_2$. *Return* s *if both* $N_{q_1}(s) \neq \Omega$ *and* $N_{q_2}(s) \neq \Omega$, *and* Ω *otherwise.*
- *Suppose that* $q = q_1 \vee q_2$. *Return* s *if either* $N_{q_1}(s) \neq \Omega$ *or* $N_{q_2}(s) \neq \Omega$, *and* Ω *otherwise.*

Deciding whether some execution of $M_p((\perp, 1, -, r))$ returns a value other than Ω is intractable. However, there are several restrictions each of which makes the decision tractable. In our previous work [11], we presented two of such restrictions as tractability results of XPath satisfiability. The first restriction was that each parameter of the machines can be represented by only the last node of a path, and was achieved by excluding upward axes. The second restriction was that copying the value of the input parameter never occurs during the execution. Note that during the execution of N_q, the value of the input parameter must be preserved because it is used as the returned value. This restriction was achieved by excluding qualifiers.

This paper presents another, new restriction: the execution of M_p is deterministic and the length of the parameters are bounded by some polynomial in the length of p. It is obvious that the decision is tractable under the new restriction, because just running M_p will do. In what follows, we examine what class of XPath achieves the new restriction.

First, consider $\mathcal{X}(\downarrow, \uparrow, \rightarrow^+, [\,])$. From Definition 7, axes $\downarrow$ and $\rightarrow^+$ seem to bring the nondeterminism. However, since only left-to-right sibling traversal is possible by $\mathcal{X}(\downarrow, \uparrow, \rightarrow^+, [\,])$, M_p can always choose the "leftmost node" among the candidate nodes. More formally, let M'_p be the same machine as M_p except that if $p = \downarrow :: l$ or $p = \rightarrow^+ :: l$, M'_p always chooses the node u with the least value of $pos(u)$ among the candidate nodes. Then, it suffices to show that $M'_p((\perp, 1, -, r)) \neq \Omega$ if and only if some execution of $M_p((\perp, 1, -, r))$ returns a value other than Ω. The "only if" part is obvious. The "if" part can be proved by the induction on the number of nondeterministic choices where non-leftmost nodes are selected. Moreover, the length of the parameters is bounded by the length of p because $\downarrow^*$ is not in the current class of XPath expressions.

Next, consider $\mathcal{X}(\downarrow, \uparrow^*, \rightarrow^+, [\,])$. The nondeterminism by $\uparrow^*$ can be eliminated by always choosing the "bottommost node" among the candidate nodes.

Using the symmetry of $\rightarrow^+$ and $\leftarrow^+$, we have the following, new result on the tractability:

Theorem 4. *Satisfiability of* $\mathcal{X}(\downarrow, \chi_\uparrow, \chi_\leftrightarrow, [\,])$, *where* $\chi_\uparrow \in \{\uparrow, \uparrow^*\}$ *and* $\chi_\leftrightarrow \in \{\rightarrow^+, \leftarrow^+\}$, *under DC-DTDs is tractable.*

4.4 A New Intractable Class of XPath Expressions under Disjunction-Free DTDs

In contrast to our new tractability result, the following theorem says that using *both* of upward axes in a qualifier brings intractability, even under disjunction-free DTDs. This is also a tight bound between tractability and intractability of satisfiability under DC-DTDs.

Theorem 5. *Satisfiability of* $\mathcal{X}(\downarrow, \uparrow, \uparrow^*, [\ ])$ *is NP-complete even under disjunction-free DTDs.*

Proof. We show only the NP-hardness, by providing a reduction from the 3SAT problem. For an instance $\phi = (L_{1,1} \vee L_{1,2} \vee L_{1,3}) \wedge \cdots \wedge (L_{n,1} \vee L_{n,2} \vee L_{n,3})$ of 3SAT, where each $L_{i,j}$ is a member of $\{x_1, \ldots, x_m, \bar{x}_1, \ldots, \bar{x}_m\}$, define a disjunction-free DTD $D = (\Sigma, r, P)$ as follows:

- $\Sigma = \{r, x_0, \ldots, x_{m+1}\}$,
- $P(r) = x_0$,
  $P(x_i) = (x_i x_{i+1})^*$ for each i $(0 \leq i \leq m)$, and
  $P(x_{m+1}) = \epsilon$.

Also, an XPath expression p is defined as

$$\downarrow :: x_0/p_1/\cdots/p_m/\downarrow :: x_{m+1}[(q_{1,1} \vee q_{1,2} \vee q_{1,3}) \wedge \cdots \wedge (q_{n,1} \vee q_{n,2} \vee q_{n,3})],$$

where

$$p_i = \downarrow :: x_i/\downarrow :: x_i/\uparrow^* :: x_i \quad \text{for each } i \ (1 \leq i \leq m),$$
$$q_{i,j} = \begin{cases} \uparrow^* :: x_{k+1}/\uparrow :: x_k/\uparrow :: x_{k-1} & \text{if } L_{i,j} = x_k, \\ \uparrow^* :: x_{k+1}/\uparrow :: x_k/\uparrow :: x_k/\uparrow :: x_{k-1} & \text{if } L_{i,j} = \bar{x}_k. \end{cases}$$

The subexpression p_i nondeterministically specifies one of the two x_i nodes which are in a parent-child relation. Thus, the subexpression $\downarrow :: x_0/p_1/\cdots/p_m/\downarrow :: x_{m+1}$ specifies a node v with label x_{m+1} such that on the path from the root to v, each label x_i appears either only once or consecutively twice. In this reduction, the path from the root to v is regarded as a truth assignment, where variable x_i is true if label x_i appears only once on the path and variable x_i is false if label x_i appears consecutively twice. □

5 Conclusions

This paper has extended the tractability results [11] on XPath satisfiability under DC-DTDs in two directions. First, we have proposed a condition to extend a class of DTDs without spoiling the tractability of XPath satisfiability, provided that the class of XPath expressions is (a subclass of) $\mathcal{X}(\downarrow, \downarrow^*, \uparrow, \uparrow^*, \rightarrow^+, \leftarrow^+, \cup, [\ ])$. By applying the condition to DC-DTDs, we obtain DC$^{?+}$-DTDs, which are much broader than DC-DTDs from the practical point of view, but still tractable. Second, we extend the satisfaction relation between a schema graph and an XPath expression, which is a basis for analyzing the satisfiability, to a broader class of XPath expressions. Then, we show a new tractable class of XPath expressions for which the satisfiability under DC-DTDs is tractable.

The tractability of the satisfiability under DC-DTDs for $(\downarrow^*, \uparrow, [\,])$ and its variations remains open, and we are trying to solve it. Also, we are investigating the complexity when the size of a given DC-DTD is considered to be fixed.

Acknowledgment

The authors gratefully appreciate the helpful and constructive comments by the anonymous reviewers to improve the paper. This research is supported in part by Grant-in-Aid for Scientific Research (C) 20500092 from Japan Society for the Promotion of Science.

References

1. Benedikt, M., Fan, W., Geerts, F.: XPath satisfiability in the presence of DTDs. In: Proceedings of the Twenty-fourth ACM SIGACT-SIGMOD-SIGART Symposium on Principles of Database Systems, pp. 25–36 (2005)
2. Benedikt, M., Fan, W., Geerts, F.: XPath satisfiability in the presence of DTDs. Journal of the ACM 55(2) (2008)
3. Genevès, P., Layaïda, N.: A system for the static analysis of XPath. ACM Transactions on Information Systems 24(4), 475–502 (2006)
4. Genevès, P., Layaïda, N.: Deciding XPath containment with MSO. Data & Knowledge Engineering 63(1), 108–136 (2007)
5. Genevès, P., Layaïda, N., Schmitt, A.: Efficient static analysis of XML paths and types. In: Proceedings of the ACM SIGPLAN 2007 Conference on Programming Language Design and Implementation, pp. 342–351 (2007)
6. Murata, M., Lee, D., Mani, M., Kawaguchi, K.: Taxonomy of XML schema languages using formal language theory. ACM Transactions on Internet Technology 5(4), 660–704 (2005)
7. Geerts, F., Fan, W.: Satisfiability of XPath queries with sibling axes. In: Bierman, G., Koch, C. (eds.) DBPL 2005. LNCS, vol. 3774, pp. 122–137. Springer, Heidelberg (2005)
8. Figueira, D.: Satisfiability of downward XPath with data equality tests. In: Proceedings of the 28th ACM SIGMOD-SIGACT-SIGART Symposium on Principles of Database Systems, pp. 197–206 (2009)
9. Montazerian, M., Wood, P.T., Mousavi, S.R.: XPath query satisfiability is in PTIME for real-world DTDs. In: Barbosa, D., Bonifati, A., Bellahsène, Z., Hunt, E., Unland, R. (eds.) XSym 2007. LNCS, vol. 4704, pp. 17–30. Springer, Heidelberg (2007)
10. Suzuki, N., Fukushima, Y.: Satisfiability of simple XPath fragments in the presence of DTD. In: Proceedings of the 11th International Workshop on Web Information and Data Management, pp. 15–22 (2009)
11. Ishihara, Y., Morimoto, T., Shimizu, S., Hashimoto, K., Fujiwara, T.: A tractable subclass of DTDs for XPath satisfiability with sibling axes. In: Gardner, P., Geerts, F. (eds.) Database Programming Languages. LNCS, vol. 5708, pp. 68–83. Springer, Heidelberg (2009)

Extending XQuery with a Pattern Matching Facility

Peter M. Fischer, Aayush Garg, and Kyumars Sheykh Esmaili

Systems Group
ETH Zurich
8092 Zurich, Switzerland
petfisch@inf.ethz.ch, garga@student.ethz.ch, kyumarss@inf.ethz.ch

Abstract. Considering the growing usage of XML for communication and data representation, the need for more advanced analytical capabilities on top of XQuery is emerging. In this regard, a pattern matching facility can be considered as a natural extension to empower XQuery. In this paper we first provide some use cases for XML pattern matching. After showing that current XQuery falls short in meeting basic requirements, we propose an extension to XQuery which imposes no changes into current model, while covering a wide range of important use cases. We also implemented our proposal into the MXQuery prototype and show through experiments that, compared to the existing pattern matching means, our extension is not only more expressive, but also more efficient.

Keywords: XQuery, Pattern Matching

1 Introduction

There is a growing interest in the area of applications that deal with finding patterns in data items. These applications include:

- Security applications to detect unusual behavior
- Financial applications to detect market trends
- RFID and Sensor data processing
- Complex document analysis and formatting

While expressing tree patterns is fairly natural in XPath (and XSLT for more expressiveness), there is no comprehensive approach for sequence pattern matching on XML that takes into account its properties, its data model(s), and the query languages. As the *FORSEQ* window extension [4] shows, XQuery fits nicely with sequence processing. The existing language features are, however, not sufficient for expressive and effective pattern matching.

As a running example, we define the sequence S:

$$S = (B, A, B, C, A, B, B, B, B, C) \quad (1)$$

A simple pattern which specifies the occurrence of three consecutive $< B/ >$ elements (written as B for brevity) would see possible instances (B, B, B) at the positions (5, 6, 7), (6, 7, 8).

M.L. Lee et al. (Eds.): XSym 2010, LNCS 6309, pp. 48–57, 2010.

1.1 Example Use Case

MASTER [1] is a project which tries to solve the problem of compliance in Service-Oriented Architecture (SOA) systems. An important part of this project is SOA Monitoring. This is realized by observing the message flow between services and then checking particular properties on this message sequence.

For example, upon invocation of operations of a browsing/shopping service, the following events are captured from a service wrapper or message bus:

```
<event operation="Login" uid="511" time="10:00"/>
<event operation="Search" uid="101" time="10:01"/>
<event operation="Logout" uid="511" time="10:03"/>
```

The monitoring system is given a set of expected or not-expected patterns, which it detects in this event sequences, (e.g. the pattern `SearchNoBuy`) and report them. Since the messages are exchanged between services in XML format, relational pattern matching systems cannot be applied.

1.2 Requirements for a Pattern Matching Language

A language to describe patterns needs to cover several aspects:

Pattern Structure: Patterns can be represented in a number of ways. The most common approaches are *regular expressions*, and *temporal logic*; we chose regular expressions since they are more widely used. Regular expressions are composed of a set of variables that uses quantification and grouping. Supposing a regular expression is A^*B^+ applied on S, the following pattern match instances are generated: {B}, {A, B}, {A, B, B, B, B},{B, B, B, B}.

Variable Binding: In contrast to classical regular expressions, in which the variable symbols directly correspond to the symbols in in the sequence, general pattern matching requires more expressiveness: Let's assume that we want to detect a pattern in which there are several increasing values, followed by at least one decreasing value. The pattern structure is A^*B^+, where A is a sequence representing increasing values (e.g. as a predicate comparing consecutive values), and B accordingly, with a correlation to A.

Instance Relationship and Selection: In order to properly identify a pattern instance, a user needs to specify 1) how far a pattern should extend if there are fitting elements, and 2) where the next pattern matching instance should be started in relation to the curent one. For example, the well known '*' quantifier expresses zero or more matches. For a pattern A^* and a sequence (A,A,A), always returning (A,A,A) might not be the desired result. In certain scenarios, (A) and (A,A) would also be valid results.

1.3 Paper Structure

The paper is structured as follows: Section 2 and Section 3 describe pattern matching capabilites in the relational world and existing features of XQuery supporting patterns, respectively. Section 4 describes our XQuery pattern matching extension proposal. Section 5 describes our prototype implementation and a summary of the evaluation. Then we conclude in Section 6.

2 Related Work in Relational and Streaming Databases

A lot of previous work has been done in the field of pattern matching. For this work, the areas of relational database systems and data streams are most relevant. While most of these focus on optimizations, there is a number of language-oriented proposals. The ANSI 2007 proposal defines the MATCH_RECOGNIZE clause for SQL[3]: Patterns are defined as (restricted) regular expressions over sequences of rows, with an extensive discussion on how to bind the variables to columns, and how to relate match instances. SASE+[8] supports Kleene closure over event streams, and provides a formal analysis of the expressibility of this language. A particular emphasis has been given to event selection strategies, in particular non-contiguous matches. Cayuga[5] presents a query language based on Cayuga Algebra for naturally expressing complex event patterns. This query language uses many SQL-like constructs.

Compared to these approaches, our language proposal does not re-invent the wheel: We aim for similar pattern structure and match selection, so that implementation and optimization strategies can be utilized. A significant difference is in the area of variable binding expressions, which are richer in the XML world.

3 Existing Pattern Matching Features In XQuery

3.1 String Matching

XPath and XQuery provide textual pattern matching based on regular expression matching, such `fn:matches(string, pattern)`. The XQuery Fulltext facility also provides textual matching facilities, taking into account text or XML structure. While in particular the pattern structure part of `fn:matches` is quite rich, text functions are not really suitable for general pattern matching.

3.2 Tree Pattern Matching

The notion of pattern matching is often associated with tree pattern matching in an XML environment. There is a tremendous amount of theoretical work (e.g [9]) in this area; from a practical point of view XPath expressions (for rigid tree patterns) and XSLT (for unknown, complex structures) provide the necessary facilities. A recent work [6] applies the new higher-order functions in XQuery 1.1 to achieve XSLT-like recursive matching. XPath or XSLT tree pattern matching is by design limited to a single document; the expressiveness of pattern structure, variable binding, and match selection is quite restricted.

3.3 Window Clause

The window clause of XQuery 1.1 gives the ability of selecting subsequences over a possibly infinite stream. It added a new language construct for XQuery called

FORSEQ that integrates seamlessly into the *FLWOR* expression. A detailed description of the *FORSEQ* clause can be found in [4], here we will describe its basic features. Windows boundaries are determined using predicates, stated as `start` and `end` expressions, which can refer to "previous", "current", or "next" items at the current position as well, as the explicit position. Window instance relationships can be specified as *tumbling*, *sliding*, and *landmark*

Pattern Structure. Simple patterns like A^+ can be expressed directly as windows which open on the occurrence of an A element and close whenever the next item is not an A element. More complex patterns need to be expressed differenly: Pattern structure needs to be expressed as joins over windows for the individual variables, with the window boundary positions as join criteria. Consider the following regular expression: A^+B^+C. A possible XQuery 1.1 query can be given as:

```
forseq $w in $seq/stream/event sliding window
    start curItem $ax, position $ap when $ax/person eq "A"
    end nextItem $ay, position $aq when not($ay/person eq "A")
    return
    forseq $s in $seq/stream/event tumbling window
        start curItem $bx, position $bp when $bx/person eq "B"
        end nextItem $by, position $bq when not($by/person eq B")
        where $bp eq ($aq + 1)
        return
         ...
```

This query uses a FORSEQ to create a sequences of A+ variable bindings, with their end positions expressed in `$aq`. Nested into this expression is another FORSEQ expression to create a B+ sequence, which is joined on its start position `$bp`. This approach can then be repeated for other variables. While it is possible to express complex patterns this way, they are cumbersome to write and, as we will see in the experiment section, difficult to optimize. Additional problems arise when variables use the "*" quantifier, since FORSEQ cannot create bindings to empty sequences, thus necessitating a refactoring of the pattern. For details of this refactoring and more examples, we refer to the technical report[7].

Variable Bindings. While the predicate-based window boundaries of FORSEQ are quite expressive, there is no support in the current XQuery model to close a window based on its contents. For example, assume that a trader has a daily limit of 50 million dollars. Expressing this specification using a tumbling window, the windows close at the close of the day, and then an aggregation of the trades will be performed. Clearly for this case, we will get the results only after the day has closed, so execeeding the limit is easily possible. When using a landmark window, it is opened for the change of the day and closed at every trade; then aggregation is performed. Since landmark windows can almost never be discarded, the cost for memory management and computations will be extremely high. In addition, the underlying tumbling nature of the windows is no longer visible in the query.

4 Extending XQuery with a Pattern Matching Facility

4.1 Overview

Since a simple extension of XQuery is not really feasible, we propose to integrate a *PatternClause* into the FLWORExpr, thus representing pattern instances (and possibly also the parts out of which they were composed) as variables bound to sequences, contributing to the "'tuple stream"' as defined in XQuery 1.1.

```
    FLWORExpr ::= InitialClause IntermediateClause* ReturnClause
InitialClause ::= ForClause|LetClause|WindowClause|PatternClause
PatternClause ::= "pattern" "$" VarName (WindowTypeClause)
                   (SelectionClause) "in" ExprSingle RegExpClause
                   "using" (PatternVarClause)+
```

Covering the requirements stated in Section 1.2, *WindowTypeClause* and *SelectionClause* are introduced to cover Match Selection, *RegExpClause* for the pattern structure, and *PatternVarClause*es to determine the variables used in the RegExpClause. A pattern like $A^{+}B^{+}C$ would be expressed follows:

```
pattern $p tumbling maximal in $seq $a $b $c using
    $a as item()+ pcur $q1 when $q1 eq ''A''
    $b as item()+ pcur $q2 when $q2 eq ''B''
    $c as item() pcur $q3 when $q3 eq ''C''
```

The output on S can be written (in "tuple" notation) as:

```
($p = {A,B,C}, $a = {A}, $b = {B}, $c = {C})
($p = {A,B,B,B,B,C}, $a = {A}, $b = {B,B,B,B}, $c = {C})
```

4.2 Pattern Structure as Regular Expression

Similar to the relational approaches, we represent the structure as regular expressions, where the alphabet is formed by the variables later defined in the *PatternVarClauses*. Repetition of groups (aka nested repetitions, such as $((AB) * C)+$) has not gained much support in the relation world due to the possibly high evaluation cost and the lack of use cases [10,8,5]. We therefore exclude nested groups, which brings an additional benefit, as we can use normal XQuery variables as regular expression variables, simplifying the integration. In Sections 4.3 and 4.5, we show how to express nesting using the composability of XQuery and the `Pattern` clause. The proposed grammar thus looks as follows:

```
RegExpClause ::= RegTerm | "(" RegExpClause ")" "or" "(" RegTerm ")"
     RegTerm ::= RegPrimary | RegTerm RegPrimary
  RegPrimary ::= VarRef | RegExpClause
```

Patterns are contiguous, i.e., there must be no gap in the bindings of the underlying stream to pattern variables. A common case of such gaps are partitions; these are naturally supported (see Section 4.5). For other cases, these gaps can be simulated using dummy variables.

4.3 Pattern Variable Clauses

Since we use regular XQuery variables in the pattern structure, we define a binding expression, in which a predicate is evaluated over a candidate sequence:

```
PatternVarClause ::= "$"VarName SequenceType (PatternVars)? "when"
                     ExprSingle
```

SequenceType contains an XQuery type, which acts as a type selector, while its occurrence indicator becomes the quantifier. As an example, when declaring a variable $\$a$ as part of a^+, containing at least one <a/> element, we can write:

```
$a as element(a)+ when fn:true()
```

We propose five variables to express predicates over the (candidate) sequence:

- `before` Represents the element directly before the sequence
- `after` Represents the element directly after the sequence
- `all` Denotes all of the elements of the sequence so far
- `pprev` Running variable representing the previous item in the sequence
- `pcur` Running variable representing the current item in the sequence

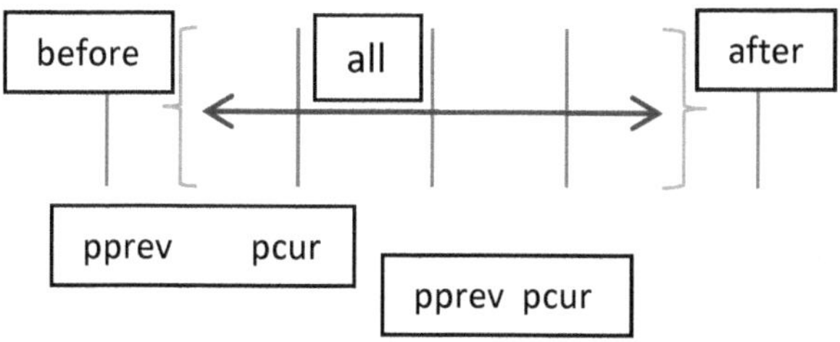

Fig. 1. Pattern Variables

The set of variables form a superset of the variables in the window clause in [4], since `all` now provides access to the contents of the sequence observed after `before`, not just the boundary elements. `pprev` and `pcur` are essentially syntactic sugar that simplify writing monotonic relationships over the sequence. Instead of using these five variables, we also provide the possibility to expose an unrestricted sequence **nested** to a nested *Window* or *Pattern Expression*, on which the first produced sequence is bound to the variable defined by nested.

To summarize the semantics: items become part of the pattern variable as long as the type matches, the occurrence indicator allows adding more elements, and computing the effective booleans value (EBV) of ExprSingle gives *true*.

Table 1 gives an example of the variable bindings for the pattern A^+, where A is an increasing value in the sequence, applied to the sequence $\{10, 15, 20, 25, 30, 5\}$. The pattern variable clause can be written as:

```
$p as xs:integer+  pprev $b, pcur $c when $b lt $c
```

The result includes 15 to 30, since comparing () and $\{10\}$ yields *false*.

Table 1. Evaluation Stages and Variable Bindings for A^+, increasing values

before($a)	pprev($b)	pcur($c)	all($u)	after($d)	ExprSingle
()	()	10	(10)	15	false
10	10	15	(15)	20	true
10	15	20	(15, 20)	25	true
10	20	25	(15, 20, 25)	30	true
10	25	30	(15, 20, 25, 30)	5	true
10	30	5	(15, 20, 25, 30, 5)	()	false

4.4 Match Selection

The relationship of the individual pattern instances and the selection of the variable parts play an important role in the semantics of the pattern clause. Table 2 gives an example of the interaction of the individual modifiers, which we will new explain now step by step.

Selection Policy: The *SelectionClause* provides three options, which determine how much of a sequence should be matched for greedy operators such as * or $^+$. This is similar to MATCH_RECOGNIZE; FORSEQ does not have such issues, since fulfilling a predicate is precise.

```
SelectionClause ::= AllMatch | Maximal| Incremental
```

- `AllMatch` gives the all possible variants of patterns in the sequence
- `Maximal` mode finds only the longest matching pattern
- `Incremental` mode increases the match candidates incrementally by a single item (starting from the empty sequence) and applies the `Maximal` match to every such partition. The union of all such matches then forms the output

Restart Policy. The *WindowTypeClause* specifies where to start a new pattern:

```
WindowTypeClause ::= Tumbling| Sliding
```

- `Tumbling` specifies that the next pattern will be searched after the last element of the previous pattern, ensuring non-overlapping patterns.
- `Sliding` allows overlapping patterns. It matches the next pattern past the first element of the previous pattern which is not part of an existing result.

The semantics of both `Tumbling` and `Sliding` clauses correspond closely to both the clauses of the same name in the Window Extension [4], besides suppressing already contained pattern instances, as well as the SKIP PAST LAST ROW and SKIP TO NEXT ROW clauses in MATCH_RECOGNIZE [3].

Order of Matches. Results are produced by the order of the first element of the pattern, with shorter pattern instances (generated by `INCREMENTAL` or `ALLMATCH`) before longer matches. This is again similar to what MATCH_RECOGNIZE and the Window Clause in XQuery 1.1 do. If ordering by the end of a pattern instance is needed, this can be achieved by using an `order by` clause.

Table 2. Selection for Pattern: (A*B*) or (B*A*); Input: $a_1a_2b_1b_2a_3b_3$

<table>
<tr><th></th><th>Maximal</th><th>Incremental</th><th>AllMatch</th></tr>
<tr><td>Tumbling</td><td>$\{a_1,a_2,b_1,b_2\}$
$\{a_3,b_3\}$</td><td>$\{a_1\}$ $\{a_1,a_2\}$ $\{a_1,a_2,b_1\}$
$\{a_1,a_2,b_1,b_2\}$
$\{a_3\}$ $\{a_3,b_3\}$</td><td rowspan="2">$\{a_1\}$ $\{a_1,a_2\}$ $\{a_1,a_2,b_1\}$
$\{a_1,a_2,b_1,b_2\}$
$\{a_2\}$ $\{a_2,b_1\}$ $\{a_2,b_1,b_2\}$
$\{b_1\}$ $\{b_1,b_2\}$ $\{b_1,b_2,a_3\}$
$\{b_2\}$ $\{b_2,a_3\}$
$\{a_3\}$ $\{a_3,b_3\}$
$\{b_3\}$</td></tr>
<tr><td>Sliding</td><td>$\{a_1,a_2,b_1,b_2\}$
$\{b_1,b_2,a_3\}$
$\{a_3,b_3\}$</td><td>$\{a_1\}$ $\{a_1,a_2\}$ $\{a_1,a_2,b_1\}$
$\{a_1,a_2,b_1,b_2\}$
$\{b_1,b_2,a_3\}$
$\{a_3,b_3\}$</td></tr>
</table>

4.5 Wrapping Up

We have compiled a list of use cases that shows the expressiveness and usefulness of our proposed pattern extension [7]. Given the space constraints, we are only showing a few interesting aspects here:

Partitioning: A typical use case is the detection of patterns on partitions of the original sequence, e.g., the shopping habits of an individual user in the general clickstream of a web store. Given the integration of the pattern clause into the FLWOR expression, this can be expressed very naturally:

```
for $a in $events
     group by $a/user
     pattern $p ... in $a
     ...
     return  <p> $p </p>
```

`Group by` splits the variable binding/tuple stream into n substreams according to the values generated by \$a/user, assigning all relevant variables, in this case \$a. The nested pattern clauses then work on each of these partitions individually. It is also possible to apply the partitioning after detecting a pattern.

Repeating Groups and Nested Variables: As stated above, we do not allow patterns like $(A^+B^*)^*$ to be expressed directly. Given the composable nature of XQuery, we can express this by using a nested pattern clause as input for the full pattern clauses (similar to [5,8]) or by variables using the `nested` keyword:

```
pattern $p  in $events $v using
$v item ()* nested $n when pattern $pn in $n ($a $b) using $a
               element(a)+ when fn:true() $b element (b) when
                                       fn:true() return $pn[1]
     return <p> $p </p>
```

The sequence of the values considered for $\$v$ (named $\$n$) is consumed by the nested pattern expression, yielding matches, which are then bound to to $\$v$.

5 Implementation and Evaluation

We extended the Micro XQuery Engine (MXQuery) [2] and integrated an initial implementation of our proposed pattern matching extension into it. MXQuery lends itself well for the pattern extension, since it pioneered the XQuery Window extension [4] and the extension of XDM to infinite data [4]. Its architecture follows a classic parser/optimizer/runtime approach: It uses an iterator-based runtime, and a token-based representation of XDM. Given the existing MXQuery infrastructure, the initial implementation of the pattern matching extension could be done using roughly 1500 LOC. The bulk of the extension went to the runtime, in which the logic of a pattern structure matching, variable binding, and match selection were encapsulated into an iterator. This iterator follows the same implementation as the FOR, LET, and FORSEQ iterators in terms of variable binding "mechanics". The predicate evaluation for pattern variable clauses is then mapped on existing iterators, using the variables bound by the pattern iterator. Many optimizations are possible in the predicate evaluation, but they are not implemented yet; in particular, incremental evaluation on predicates over `all` would be promising. The *RegExpClause*, and the corresponding *PatternVarClauses* can be translated in a fairly straightforward way into a Non-deterministic Finite State Machine (NFA), similar to the approaches taken in relational pattern matching [5,8]. It should be noted that expressing the pattern clause as a single iterator encapsulating a NFA is just one possibility to implement it. Other approaches might express the pattern as a combination of relational or XML iterators, similar to recent approaches in event processing [10].

In order to validate the quality and usefulness of our implementation, we carried out a number of performance experiments. The main goals were to compare the cost relative to the FORSEQ-based translations of patterns, and to establish an understanding of the impact of particular parameters on the pattern matching implementations. Due to space restrictions, we are only summarizing the results of two experiments here, more results can be found in the technical report [7]. All experiments were run on an Intel Xeon 3050, 2.13 GHz with 8GB RAM, running Windows Vista, 64 bit version and the latest Sun JVM.

We evaluated the pattern A^+B^+C, which can be translated to FORSEQ fairly directly using joins, as shown in Section 3. Table 3 shows the timing result of a (`sliding, maximal`) pattern matching clause and a `sliding` window in the *FORSEQ* clause on a flat sequence of elements A,B and C. The pattern extension is significantly more efficient than the $FORSEQ$ translation, creating only a linear overhead over the parsing and FLWOR execution cost, since multi-sequence joins can be avoided. In contrast, the cost of FORSEQ increases in a $O(n^2)$ fashion because of the two-way join for the B and C elements. We performed similar experiments for different patterns expressed using FORSEQ, and the pattern clause; they showed the same trends and an even greater benefit for more complex patterns. For trivial patterns (like $A+$ for a simple window condition), the costs for FORSEQ and the pattern clause were comparable, as nearly the same work needed to be performed.

Table 3. Processing time (s): Pattern A^+B^+C sliding maximal

Sequence Length (items)	50	100	500	1000	5000	10000
Parse+FLWOR	0.006	0.01	0.02	0.027	0.092	0.172
Pattern	0.035	0.031	0.177	0.312	1.191	2.312
FORSEQ	0.14	0.051	1.429	5.906	113.671	438.73

We also performed a brief sensitivity analysis for the individual pattern structure and match selection parameters. Since these are very similar to the related relational approaches, we saw similar tradeoffs there. For example, the different combinations of *SelectionClause* and *WindowClause* on the same pattern structure/variables behaved as expected: The cost of running each variant had an almost linear relationship to the size of the output sets produced by each of the variants, showing that even our straightforward implementation provided a good scaleup to more complex requirements.

6 Conclusions

In this paper, we proposed our pattern matching extension for XQuery that is seamlessly integrated with existing *FLWOR*. We found that pattern matching is a needed and useful feature in XQuery and, since the current support for it is not sufficient, a separate pattern matching clause is needed. The proposal provides rich match selection and variable binding semantics, while balancing pattern structure expressiveness and cost in a similar way as relational approaches. Implementing this proposal on an open-source XQuery engine, and relevant benchmarking results prove that our extension is practical.

References

1. MASTER: Managing Assurance, Security, and Trust in sERvices, `http://www.master-fp7.eu/`
2. MXQuery, `http://mxquery.org/`
3. Anonymous: Pattern matching in sequences of rows. Technical report (2007)
4. Botan, I., et al.: Extending XQuery with Window Functions. In: VLDB (2007)
5. Brenna, L., et al.: Cayuga: a High-Performance Event Processing Engine. In: SIGMOD (2007)
6. Candillon, W., Brantner, M., Knochenwefel, D.: XQuery Design Patterns. In: Balisage (2010)
7. Garg, A.: Pattern Matchin In XQuey. Master's Thesis, ETH Zurich (2010)
8. Gyllstrom, D., et al.: SASE: Complex Event Processing over Streams. In: CIDR (2007)
9. Lu, J., Ling, T.W., Bao, Z., Wang, C.: Extended XML Tree Pattern Matching: Theories and Algorithms. In: TKDE (2010)
10. Mei, Y., Madden, S.: ZStream: a Cost-Based Query Processor for Adaptively Detecting Composite Events. In: SIGMOD (2009)

A Schema-Based Translation of XQuery Updates

Leonidas Fegaras

University of Texas at Arlington
fegaras@cse.uta.edu

Abstract. We address the problem of translating XQuery updates to plain XQuery expressions. The resulting XQuery code reconstructs the mutable state (the updated XML data), reflecting the updated values in the new state. The translation is done using source-to-source, compositional transformations only. Unlike related approaches that use framework-specific algebras to achieve a similar goal, our work can be incorporated into any existing XQuery engine.

1 Introduction

A major part of web programming nowadays involves querying and updating XML data, since most data available from web services and other data providers come in the form of XML. To handle these data, there was an increasing need by web developers for a well-supported XML query language, powerful enough to let them do most of the XML processing in a single language, without having to embed it into scripts or to use low-level APIs, such DOM or SAX. XQuery [17], a functional query language for XML data, was introduced by W3C to cover this need. XQuery has recently gained widespread adoption in the web programming and database communities mostly because it is supported by most database and web development software vendors. Its resemblance to SQL, a query language already familiar to all web programmers, and its conformance to W3C standards have also contributed to make XQuery a recent favorite for web programming. Web programmers though, comfortable with the imperative style of scripting languages, such as JavaScript for client-side and PHP for server-side programming, found it hard to do some programming tasks using a purely functional programming language. More specifically, there was a need for imperative language extensions to XQuery that would allow one to transform XML data before they are fed into some other web service or application. Furthermore, there is a recent interest to use XQuery on the Web browser for client-side programming [12] to dynamically modify the Web page content displayed on a Web browser. Finally, people working with XML databases wanted to use XQuery to actually update the underlying databases. As a result, there is a recent proposal by W3C for extending XQuery with updates, called the XQuery Update Facility (XUF) [18], that addresses these needs.

Although XQuery expressions can be composed in arbitrary ways, XUF imposes many syntactic and semantic restrictions on updates. The most important static restriction is that updates are permitted to appear in certain places only,

M.L. Lee et al. (Eds.): XSym 2010, LNCS 6309, pp. 58–72, 2010.

such as in the return part of a FLWOR (For-Let-Where-Order-Return) expression only. In addition, the target of insert, replace, and rename updates should be a singleton sequence, which can only be checked at run-time. XUF uses snapshot semantics, indicating that the results of the updates are not visible during query evaluation (that is, updates cannot commit during querying). In other words, updates are accumulated during the query evaluation and are executed at the end of the query. The XUF operational semantics [18] uses a pending update list to accumulate updates during the query execution. This update list is a collection of update primitives, which represent node state changes that have not yet been applied [18].

Although the XUF proposal fulfills an important need for web programmers, it also introduces some problems. The most important problem is the optimization of XQuery updates. While there are many optimization techniques and evaluation strategies based on various storage mappings for plain XQuery, there is still much work to be done on XUF query optimization. Current work uses framework-specific algebras for optimization [11,4], which makes it hard to apply to other frameworks that use different algebras. In addition, one of the intended use of XQuery updates is to use them in various schema mappings and integration scenarios, where XML is used as an integration medium (as a virtual or materialized view) while a relational database is used for storage. Then, view updates expressed in XUF must be reflected to the underlying database [7], while SQL updates must result to the incremental modification of the XML view, if the view is materialized [8]. Both tasks can be greatly facilitated if XQuery updates and view mappings (which are typically expressed in XQuery) are fused and optimized in the same framework.

Currently, many people wrongly believe that there is no straightforward and efficient translation from XUF to XQuery, despite that both XQuery and XUF are computationally complete. One of the reasons for this belief is that XUF updates destructively update XML data while preserving their node identity, which cannot be simulated directly in plain XQuery. Another reason is that it may be very hard to develop a translator from XUF to XQuery that preserves the complex XUF semantics, as is currently described in terms of pending lists of updates. Naive XUF translators that use recursive XQuery functions to apply the updates to the qualified XML nodes may satisfy the XUF semantics but the resulting recursive programs are difficult to optimize.

In this paper, we address the problem of translating XUF queries to plain (side-effect-free) XQuery expressions. The resulting XQuery reconstructs the mutable XML state, reflecting the updated values in the new state. The mutable state s of an XUF query is an XML tree that consists of all XML data whose nodes are updated by the XUF query. Central to our approach is the concept of the *S-complement*: Let v be a sequence of XML nodes $(v_1, \ldots, v_n)$, s be the mutable state, and u be a function, called a *context mapping function*, that can be applied to each of these v nodes. The S-complement of v is a function f so that the application of f to s and u, that is, the function call $(f\, s\, u)$, returns a copy of the state s in which, for all i, the nodes that have the same node identity as v_i have been replaced with $(u\,v_i)$. Our approach is to compile any XUF expression e to pure XQuery code that calculates the S-complement of the value of e. That is, this code creates a copy of the state that is equal to the original state in all places except those reachable by the expression e. The latter places are transformed by the context mapping function, which allows us to change their values at will. When e is used as an update destination, then updates targeting e can be translated to state transformations by just providing the appropriate context mapping. For example, if we want to insert a new node x before the node retrieved by the XQuery e (specified as **insert node** x **before** e in XUF), then we synthesize the S-complement of e and use the context function $u\,v = (x, v)$. This S-complement returns a copy of the state in all places except at the node v of the result of e, which is replaced by concatenating x with v.

The key contribution of our work is in the development of a novel framework for translating XQuery updates to plain XQuery that has the following characteristics:

- It uses source-to-source, compositional transformations only. Unlike related approaches that use framework-specific algebras to achieve a similar goal [11,4], our work can be incorporated into any existing XQuery engine.
- It can be used for XQuery update optimization since it maps XUF updates to plain XQuery, which is amenable to optimization. XQuery optimization has already been addressed by related work [16,10,7].
- It can be used for XUF type-checking and validation by simply type-checking the resulting XQuery code, a task that has already been described by XQuery semantics [17].
- It enables other transformations that are important to databases, such as the incremental maintenance of materialized XML views to make them consistent with the source data, without recreating the entire view from the database after each source update. Updates to the source data must be propagated through the view to become view updates, which can be done effectively if we translate updates to state transformations [8].

The most important limitation of our approach is that it is schema-based. There is a good reason for requiring a schema: without a schema, one has to use recursive XQuery functions to apply each update to the qualified nodes. Then, the resulting code would be recursive, which is very hard to optimize. Another limitation is that the framework presented in this paper is not quite based on the XUF semantics [18], as our pending updates are not reordered according to the official semantics (which requires that insertions be done before updates and deletes). Finally, we have not covered some parts the XUF syntax, such as backward steps, but we believe that there is no fundamental reason why our framework cannot be extended to cover the full syntax.

2 Overview

Consider the following XQuery variable declaration:

declare variable $v **as** tp := doc('bib.xml');

where the type tp is equivalent to the XQuery type:

```
element bib { element article { element title string, element year string,
                                element author string* }* }
```

and the XUF query, QUERY1

```
for $i in $v/article[author="Smith"]
where contains($i/title, "XQuery")
return replace value of node $i/year with 2009
```

which finds all articles published by Smith whose title contains the word XQuery, and replaces their year with 2009. Because of the snapshot semantics, the query result is:

```
for $i in $v/article[author="Smith"]
where contains($i/title, "XQuery")
return if count($i/year) = 1 then () else error()
```

that is, the replace update is translated to a simple test that imposes the XUF semantic restriction that the update destination must always return a singleton sequence. However, as a side-effect, QUERY1 changes the value of $v and these changes are visible to the follow-up queries. The new value of $v after this update is equivalent to the result of the following XQuery expression:

```
<bib>{ for $z in $v/article
        return if $z/author="Smith"
               then if contains($z/title, "XQuery")
                    then <article>{ $z/title, <year>2009</year>,
                                    $z/author }</article>
                    else $z else $z }</bib>
```

That is, the new value of $v is the same as the old value, except of the years of the qualified articles, which have been replaced by 2009. There is an important discrepancy though. The XUF semantic requires that all nodes that are not updated should preserve their identity and document order, which is not true for the previous bib, article, and year element constructions. In a purely functional setting though, these properties can be brought into effect using an explicit node ID for each XML node, which is not directly accessible to programs, but is used indirectly for node comparisons. To preserve the node identity though, we expect that some system-generated programs, such as those that translate XUF to plain XQuery, to be the only ones permitted to explicitly modify the node identity during querying. The document order can be taken to be the node identity as long as each newly constructed element is assigned a succeeding ID, such as when an XML parser parses a document and stores it into memory. For instance, our implementation (HXQ [9]) uses the system attribute _id to assign a unique id to an element construction. (Although atomic values need node identity for node comparisons too, their identities do not need to be changed by our translations.) Then, the opening tag of each element construction must bind this attribute to the appropriate value to propagate the article identity:

```
<bib _id="{$v/@_id}">{
   for $z in $v/article
   return if $z/author="Smith"
            then if contains($z/title, "XQuery")
                 then <article _id="{$z/@_id}">{
                               $z/title,
                               <year _id="{$z/year/@_id}">2009</year>,
                               $z/author }</article>
                 else $z else $z }</bib>
```

To simplify our presentation, although essential, this node identity propagation is not shown in our rules and examples.

From the previous example, it is clear that, to translate an XUF query to a plain XQuery, one has to know the detailed type of the mutable state. It is actually easy to derive the mutable state of a given XUF query: it consists of all global variables (variables defined by a declare variable statement) that are used, directly or indirectly, in the destination of some XUF update in the query. These are the only variables accessible to the follow-up XUF queries; all other side effects are simply ignored since they cannot affect the results of the other queries. If, for example, an XUF query updates doc("bib.xml") directly, these changes would not be visible to the other queries, as long as they do not become persistent in a database and they do not rewrite the document, because if another query reads doc("bib.xml"), it will get the document nodes under different IDs. We call these variables, *mutable variables*. For example, the variable $v in the previous example is mutable, since the replace expression uses the variable $i, which depends on $v. Our framework imposes a very important restriction, called *non-interference*: There should be no two nodes in the XML data returned by the mutable variables with the same identity. Node interference is caused by aliasing. For example, the mutable variable $v := let $x := e return ($x,$x) violates non-interference since it duplicates the nodes of e. Essentially, the reason this restriction is imposed is that updates to a node must propagate to all its replicas, which is hard (but not impossible) to do in a purely functional setting. This restriction is not needed for hypothetical queries (transform queries), described in Section 3.5. The extended version of this paper [6] presents a method that removes this restriction.

Suppose that the mutable state of a given XUF query consists of the mutable variables $\$v_1, \ldots, \$v_n$ defined by:

$$\textbf{declare variable } \$v_i \textbf{ as } t_i \;:=\; e_i;$$

where the type t_i can be omitted since it can be inferred from e_i. Combining all these mutable variables, we derive the state type S, expressed as follows in the XQuery type system:

$$\text{element state } \{ \text{ element } v_1\ t_1,\ \ldots,\ \text{element } v_n\ t_n \ \}$$

For the previous XUF query, the only mutable variable is $v, which indicates that the mutable state has the type:

```
element state { element v { element bib { element article {
                                          element title string,
                                          element year string,
                                          element author string* }* } } }
```

For each XUF query, our framework generates a **declare variable** statement that defines the variable $state to be the new mutable state, while each mutable variable $\$v_i$ is redefined to be $state/$v_i$.

In our framework, given a state s of type S, an XUF expression e that returns a sequence of nodes of type t is translated to a pure XQuery expression of type S that reconstructs the state s, reflecting the updates in e. This is done in a compositional way, using source-to-source transformations. Our translation function $\mathcal{C}[\![e]\!]\,\sigma\,s\,u$ is parameterized by the *context mapping* u of type $t\!\rightarrow t'$ that maps the current context of e (the XQuery 'dot' value) to a new value. An identity mapping leaves the context as is; if e needs to be changed, then u must return a new value that replaces the current context of e with the new value. Basically, if e does not contain side-effects, $\mathcal{C}[\![e]\!]\,\sigma\,s\,u$ creates an exact copy of the state s but with the values associated with the results of e wrapped inside u. That way, if e is used as an update destination, then one simply needs to provide the proper mapping u to update e.

For example, as we will show in the next section, the XPath expression $v/article[author="Smith"]/year is translated to

```
<state><v><bib>{
        for $w in $state/v/bib/article
        return if $w/author="Smith"
                then <article>{ $w/title, u($w/year), $w/author }</article>
                else $w
}</bib></v></state>
```

which allows us to 'update' the values returned by the XPath expression by providing an appropriate mapping u. This is exactly the S-complement of the XPath result. Note that, even though the XPath expression may return multiple years (the years of articles published by Smith), the context mapping u is applied to each individual year.

The environment σ in $\mathcal{C}[\![e]\!]\,\sigma\,s\,u$ is a binding list that maps XQuery variables to functions that, given a state s and a context mapping u, calculate a new state, thus encapsulating the context mappings associated with the variable. That is, an XQuery variable in our mappings is bound to the S-complement of the variable value. For example, since $i in QUERY1 iterates over $v/article[author="Smith"], it is bound to the translation of this expression, which is

```
λs.λu. <state><v><bib>{
                for $w in s/v/bib/article
                return if $w/author="Smith" then u($w) else $w
        }</bib></v></state>
```

where an anonymous function, such as $\lambda x.\lambda y.\,x+y$, is equivalent to the function f with $f\,x\,y\ =\ x+y$. (Note that, although we use higher-order mappings for convenience, the resulting XQuery code is first-order. In fact, the mapping algorithm can be implemented in a language that does not support anonymous functions, such as C, provided that we implement function substitution explicitly.)

When $i is used in the path step $i/year, we replace u in the $i binding with

λx. <article>{ x/title, u(x/year), x/author }</article>

which is derived from the type of $i. Then, updating $i/year in 'replace value of node $i/year with 2009', is simply using $u =$ λx. <year>2009</year> to replace the current context with a new value.

3 Translating XQuery Updates to Plain XQuery

In this section, we provide the detailed rules for the source-to-source translation of XUF to plain XQuery. Since many of our translation rules are guided by data types, we impose certain limitations on XML types: we can currently handle non-recursive XML types of the following form (for the types t, t_1, and t_2):

$$
\begin{aligned}
t ::= &\ \text{element } A\ t \ \mid\ \text{attribute } A\ t \ \mid\ (t_1, t_2) \\
&\mid\ () \ \mid\ t* \ \mid\ t+ \ \mid\ t? \ \mid\ \text{`an XQuery base type'}
\end{aligned}
$$

The types and type checking rules for the XQuery data model (XDM) are described in detail by the XQuery Formal Semantics recommendation [17]. Furthermore, we do not handle ambiguous types, such as element A { element B t*, element B t* }. Other types, such as unions, are treated in the extended version of this paper [6].

Our goal in this section is to translate an XUF expression Q to a plain XQuery. We assume that the mutable state of Q, which consists of the mutable variables $\$v_1, \ldots, \$v_n$, satisfies the non-interference constraint. Given an XUF expression e and a state s of type S, the $\mathcal{C}[\![e]\!]\,\sigma\,s\,u$ derives a pure XQuery expression that reconstructs the state s, reflecting the updates in e. Essentially, the function $\mathcal{C}[\![e]\!]\,\sigma$ synthesizes an XQuery that calculates the S-complement of e. It is of type $S \rightarrow (t \rightarrow t') \rightarrow S$, where t is the type of the FLWOR variable $\$v$ in **for** $\$v$ **in** e **return** ..., that is, $u : t \rightarrow t'$ is applied to each node in the sequence returned by e. Basically, $\mathcal{C}[\![e]\!]\,\sigma\,s\,u$ reconstructs the entire state s by ignoring all side-effect-free expressions and by incorporating side-effects into the context mapping function u. The environment σ is a binding list that maps XQuery variables to functions that, given a state s and a context mapping function u, calculate a new state, thus mapping the variable to the S-complement of its value. The notation $\sigma[\$v]$ extracts the binding of the variable $\$v$, while $\sigma[\$v/f]$ extends the environment with a new binding from $\$v$ to f. Initially, e is the XUF query Q, u is the identity function **id** that leaves the current context unchanged, s is the state before the XUF query:

<state><v_1>{\$$v_1$}</$v_1$> $\cdots$ <v_n>{\$$v_n$}</$v_n$></state>

and σ contains the bindings from each mutable variable $\$v_i$ to

$\lambda s.\lambda u.$ <state>{ $s/v_1, \ldots,$ <v_i>{$u(s/v_i/\text{node}())$}</v_i>$, \ldots, s/v_n$ }</state>

based on the previously defined type S. For the XUF query Q, our framework generates the new state, $\$ns$:

declare variable $\$ns := \mathcal{C}[\![Q]\!]\,\sigma\, s\,$ **id**;

which is used to redefine each mutable variable:

declare variable $\$v_i := \$ns/v_i/$node();

The actual value of the XUF query Q is $\mathcal{E}[\![Q]\!]\,(\text{error}())$, where the mapping function $\mathcal{E}[\![e]\!]\,x$ returns the expression e, where all XUF update expressions (except the transform updates) have been removed and the current context (dot) has been replaced with x. The following are some of the rules for $\mathcal{E}[\![e]\!]$:

$$\mathcal{E}[\![.]\!]\,x = x \qquad\qquad \mathcal{E}[\![\$v]\!]\,x = \$v$$
$$\mathcal{E}[\![(e_1,e_2)]\!]\,x = (\mathcal{E}[\![e_1]\!]\,x, \mathcal{E}[\![e_2]\!]\,x) \qquad\qquad \mathcal{E}[\![\textbf{delete node}\, e]\!]\,x = ()$$
$$\mathcal{E}[\![\textbf{replace node}\, e_1\, \textbf{with}\, e_2]\!]\,x = \textbf{if}\, \text{count}(\mathcal{E}[\![e_1]\!]\,x) = 1\, \textbf{then}\, ()\, \textbf{else}\, \text{error}()$$

For example, $\mathcal{E}[\![A/B]\!]\,x$ is equal to $x/A/B$ since the path expression A/B is equivalent to $./A/B$. Note that a mutable variable $\$v$ is bound to its original value before the XUF query. The translation of transform updates (hypothetical queries) is given in Section 3.5.

In addition to type correctness: $e : t^* \;\;\Rightarrow\;\; \mathcal{C}[\![e]\!]\,\sigma : S \rightarrow (t \rightarrow t') \rightarrow S$, we have provided a correctness proof sketch for our XUF translation algorithm. More specifically, we have proved that the XQuery expressions composed by our translation algorithm modify the XML data in the way described by the XUF update semantics. In the standard XUF semantics [18], an XUF update results to a pending list of update primitives, which is reordered before is evaluated, so that insertions are done before updates and deletes. Our translation algorithm generates programs that are precisely equivalent to the results of these pending lists but without the reordering.

Lemma 1. *The $\mathcal{C}[\![e]\!]\,\sigma$ algorithm synthesizes a pure XQuery expression that calculates the S-complement of e.*

Theorem 1. *The resulting state calculated by $\mathcal{C}[\![e]\!]\,\sigma\, s$ **id** is equivalent to the result of applying (without reordering) the pending update list of e to the state s.*

Both proofs are given in the extended version of this paper [6], which also addresses the reordering of the pending updates (using multiple state transformers).

3.1 Update Translation

We first describe the rules for $\mathcal{C}[\![e]\!]\,\sigma\, s\, u$ in which e is an XUF update expression.

Replacing Nodes and Values. Replace updates may take two forms: The first form replaces a single node (the result of the update destination e_1) with a new sequence of zero or more nodes (from e_2):

$$\mathcal{C}[\![\textbf{replace node}\, e_1\, \textbf{with}\, e_2]\!]\,\sigma\, s\, u \;=\; \mathcal{C}[\![e_1]\!]\,\sigma\, s\,(\lambda x.\, u(\mathcal{E}[\![e_2]\!]\,x)) \qquad \text{(repl)}$$

The XUF semantics requires that neither e_1 nor e_2 may contain an update expression (that is, they must be plain XQueries). This is also true for the other update expressions. The resulting code reconstructs the state by copying all its nodes except those nodes x returned by e_1, which are replaced by the value of e_2, which is $\mathcal{E}[\![e_2]\!]\,x$. The second form of the replace expression modifies the value of a node e_1 while preserving its node identity:

$$\begin{aligned}&\mathcal{C}[\![\textbf{replace value of node}\,e_1\,\textbf{with}\,e_2]\!]\,\sigma\,s\,u \qquad \text{(repl-val)}\\ &\quad = \mathcal{C}[\![e_1]\!]\,\sigma\,s\,(\lambda x.\,u(<A>\{\mathcal{E}[\![e_2]\!]\,x\}</A>))\end{aligned}$$

given that e_1 is of type, element $A\,t$. There is a similar rule for attribute values. Recall that the node identity can be propagated to newly constructed elements as a special attribute value derived from the original nodes.

Deleting Nodes. A delete expression deletes zero or more nodes from e:

$$\mathcal{C}[\![\textbf{delete node}\,e]\!]\,\sigma\,s\,u \;=\; \mathcal{C}[\![e]\!]\,\sigma\,s\,(\lambda x.\,u(())) \qquad \text{(del)}$$

Unlike the other updates, the update destination e does not have to return a singleton sequence. The generated code replaces the current context with (), which, when embedded in a sequence, will result to the removal of the element.

Inserting Nodes. There are five variations of the insert expression. Using the insert-last expression, the inserted nodes e_1 become the last children of the target node e_2:

$$\begin{aligned}&\mathcal{C}[\![\textbf{insert node}\,e_1\,\textbf{as last into}\,e_2]\!]\,\sigma\,s\,u \qquad \text{(insl)}\\ &\quad = \mathcal{C}[\![e_2]\!]\,\sigma\,s\,(\lambda x.\,u(<A>\{x/\text{node}(),\,\mathcal{E}[\![e_1]\!]\,x\}</A>))\end{aligned}$$

given that e_2 is of type, element $A\,t$. The resulting code reconstructs each node from e_1 by appending the node sequence e_2 to the children nodes. Using the insert-first expression, the inserted nodes e_1 become the first children of the target node e_2:

$$\begin{aligned}&\mathcal{C}[\![\textbf{insert node}\,e_1\,\textbf{as first into}\,e_2]\!]\,\sigma\,s\,u \qquad \text{(insf)}\\ &\quad = \mathcal{C}[\![e_2]\!]\,\sigma\,s\,(\lambda x.\,u(<A>\{\mathcal{E}[\![e_1]\!]\,x,\,x/\text{node}()\}</A>))\end{aligned}$$

given that e_2 is of type, element $A\,t$. The **insert node** e_1 **into** e_2 expression simply makes the nodes e_1 children of the target node e_2. The positions of the inserted nodes among the children of the target node are implementation-dependent, so we may implement this operation as an insert-last expression. Using the insert-before expression, the inserted nodes e_1 become the preceding siblings of the target node e_2:

$$\mathcal{C}[\![\textbf{insert node}\,e_1\,\textbf{before}\,e_2]\!]\,\sigma\,s\,u \;=\; \mathcal{C}[\![e_2]\!]\,\sigma\,s\,(\lambda x.\,u((\mathcal{E}[\![e_1]\!]\,x,\,x))) \qquad \text{(insb)}$$

Finally, using the insert-after expression, the inserted nodes e_1 become the following siblings of the target node e_2:

$$\mathcal{C}[\![\textbf{insert node}\,e_1\,\textbf{after}\,e_2]\!]\,\sigma\,s\,u \;=\; \mathcal{C}[\![e_2]\!]\,\sigma\,s\,(\lambda x.\,u((x,\,\mathcal{E}[\![e_1]\!]\,x))) \qquad \text{(insa)}$$

Renaming Nodes. A rename expression replaces the name property of a data node e with a new name q:

$$\begin{aligned}&\mathcal{C}[\![\textbf{rename node}\, e\, \textbf{with}\, q]\!]\, \sigma\, s\, u \\ &\quad = \mathcal{C}[\![e]\!]\, \sigma\, s\, (\lambda x.\, u(\textbf{element}\, \{\mathcal{E}[\![q]\!]\, x\}\, \{x/\text{node}()\})) \end{aligned} \qquad \text{(renm)}$$

This rule applies when e is of an element type. There is a similar rule when e is of an attribute type.

3.2 The Translation of Plain XQuery Expressions

We now present the rules for reconstructing the mutable state for the XUF expressions that are plain XQuery expressions. If none of the rules applies, then $\mathcal{C}[\![e]\!]\, \sigma\, s\, u = s$. Variables are introduced by FLWOR expressions (for-loops and let-bindings). Based on the XUF semantics, a FLWOR expression can only have updates in its return body. A for-loop is translated as follows:

$$\mathcal{C}[\![\textbf{for}\, \$v\, \textbf{in}\, e_1\, \textbf{where}\, p\, \textbf{return}\, e_2]\!]\, \sigma\, s\, u \;=\; \mathcal{C}[\![e_2]\!]\, \sigma'\, s\, u \qquad \text{(for)}$$

where σ' extends σ with a new binding: $\sigma' = \sigma[\$v/f]$ so that

$$f = \lambda s.\lambda u.\, \mathcal{C}[\![e_1]\!]\, \sigma\, s\, (\lambda x.\, \text{subst}\, \$v\, x\, (\textbf{if}\, \mathcal{E}[\![p]\!]\, x\, \textbf{then}\, u(x)\, \textbf{else}\, x))$$

where $(\text{subst}\, \$v\, x\, e)$ substitutes all occurrences of the variable $\$v$ in the term e with the term x. This rule indicates that the resulting state is equal to the state of the for-loop return expression, e_2, under the binding of the for-loop variable $\$v$ to the S-complement of e_1. The predicate p is moved inside the mapping function so that if the predicate is true, the context is mapped through u; otherwise the context is returned unchanged. Let-bindings are translated in a similar way:

$$\mathcal{C}[\![\textbf{let}\, \$v\, := \, e_1\, \textbf{return}\, e_2]\!]\, \sigma\, s\, u \;=\; \mathcal{C}[\![e_2]\!]\, \sigma'\, s\, u \qquad \text{(let)}$$

where $\sigma' = \sigma[\$v/(\lambda s.\lambda u.\, \text{subst}\, \$v\, x\, (\mathcal{C}[\![e_1]\!]\, \sigma\, s\, u))]$. The variable bindings are used in variable translations:

$$\mathcal{C}[\![\$v]\!]\, \sigma\, s\, u = \sigma[\$v]\, s\, u \qquad \text{(subst)}$$

XPath predicates are translated in a way similar to FLWOR predicates:

$$\mathcal{C}[\![e[p]]\!]\, \sigma\, s\, u \;=\; \mathcal{C}[\![e]\!]\, \sigma\, s\, (\lambda x.\, \textbf{if}\, \mathcal{E}[\![p]\!]\, x\, \textbf{then}\, u(x)\, \textbf{else}\, x) \qquad \text{(cond)}$$

The $e/\text{node}()$ expression extracts the child nodes of e:

$$\mathcal{C}[\![e/\text{node}()]\!]\, \sigma\, s\, u \;=\; \mathcal{C}[\![e]\!]\, \sigma\, s\, (\lambda x.\, \text{<}A\text{>}\{u\, (x/\text{node}())\}\text{</}A\text{>}) \qquad \text{(node)}$$

given that e is of type, element $A\, t$. For element constructions, we have:

$$\mathcal{C}[\![\text{<}A\text{>}\{e\}\text{</}A\text{>}]\!]\, \sigma\, s\, u \;=\; \mathcal{C}[\![e]\!]\, \sigma\, s\, (\lambda x.\, (u\, (\text{<}A\text{>}\{x\}\text{</}A\text{>}))/\text{node}()) \quad \text{(constr)}$$

A sequence concatenation is handled by using the resulting state of the first sequence component as the initial state of the second component:

$$\mathcal{C}[\![(e_1,e_2)]\!]\,\sigma\,s\,u = \mathcal{C}[\![e_2]\!]\,\sigma\,(\mathcal{C}[\![e_1]\!]\,\sigma\,s\,u)\,u \tag{seq}$$

Given a non-recursive updating function $f(\$v_1,\ldots,\$v_n) = \textit{body}$, a call to f is translated to:

$$\mathcal{C}[\![f(e_1,\ldots,e_n)]\!]\,\sigma\,s\,u \;=\; \mathcal{C}[\![\textit{body}]\!]\,[\$v_1/(\mathcal{C}[\![e_1]\!]\,\sigma),\ldots,\$v_n/(\mathcal{C}[\![e_n]\!]\,\sigma)]\,s\,u \tag{appl}$$

It binds the function parameters to the mappings derived from the call arguments and uses these bindings to derive the mapping of the function body.

3.3 Translation of XPath Steps

The rules for translating XPath steps are the most complex ones. Let e be a sequence of nodes of type t, then:

$$\mathcal{C}[\![e/\text{axis::test}]\!]\,\sigma\,s\,u \;=\; \mathcal{C}[\![e]\!]\,\sigma\,s\,(\lambda x.\,\mathcal{P}[\![t]\!]\,x\,(\text{axis::test})\,0\,u) \tag{step}$$

This rule uses the function $\mathcal{P}[\![t]\!]\,x\,(\text{axis::test})\,n\,u$ to handle forward XPath steps, where the XML nesting level n is initially zero (must be 1 to apply the child step) and x is the current context. It generates an expression of type t that creates a copy of the value of x (which is of type t), except of the nodes that can be reached by the path, which are wrapped by the function u. Currently, the rules for $\mathcal{P}[\![t]\!]$, which are guided by the type t of e, can handle child, descendant, self, and attribute steps only. First, if the type t is an element type and the step is not applicable to the type t (that is, if it always returns ()), then:

$$\mathcal{P}[\![\text{element}\,A\,t]\!]\,x\;\text{step}\;n\,u \;=\; \mathcal{P}[\![\text{element}\,A\,t*\,]\!]\,x\;\text{step}\;n\,u \;=\; x/\text{self::}A \tag{p-expr}$$

For the self step, we have to be at the nesting level 0 to check whether the step tag matches the element tag:

$$\mathcal{P}[\![\text{element}\,A\,t]\!]\,x\,(\text{self::}B)\,0\,u \;=\; \begin{cases} u(x/\text{self::}A) & \text{if } A = B \vee B = * \\ x/\text{self::}A & \text{otherwise} \end{cases} \tag{p-self}$$

For a child step though, we have to be at the nesting level 1:

$$\mathcal{P}[\![\text{element}\,A\,t]\!]\,x\,(\text{child::}B)\,1\,u \;=\; \begin{cases} u(x/\text{self::}A) & \text{if } A = B \vee B = * \\ x/\text{self::}A & \text{otherwise} \end{cases} \tag{p-child}$$

For a descendant step, we have to apply u recursively to all applicable nodes at any level, generating code to reconstruct the elements as we proceed:

$$\mathcal{P}[\![\text{element}\,A\,t]\!]\,x\,(\text{descendant::}B)\,n\,u \;=\; \begin{cases} u(z) & \text{if } n > 0 \wedge (A = B \vee B = *) \\ z & \text{otherwise} \end{cases}$$

where $z = <A>\{\mathcal{P}[\![t]\!]\,(x/\text{self::}A/\text{node}())\,(\text{descendant::}B)\,(n+1)\,u\}</A>$. Attribute steps can only apply at level 0:

$$\mathcal{P}[\![\text{attribute}\,A\,t]\!]\,x\,(\text{attribute::}B)\,0\,u \;=\; \begin{cases} u(x/@A) & \text{if } A = B \vee B = * \\ x/@A & \text{otherwise} \end{cases} \qquad \text{(p-attr)}$$

Otherwise (for child step at level 0 or descendant step at any level), we generate code that reconstructs the node and we apply our method recursively:

$$\begin{aligned} &\mathcal{P}[\![\text{element}\,A\,t]\!]\,x\ \text{step}\ n\,u && \text{(p-step)} \\ &\quad = <A>\{\mathcal{P}[\![t]\!]\,(x/\text{self::}A/\text{node}())\ \text{step}\ (n+1)\,u\}</A> \end{aligned}$$

Sequence types are simple to handle:

$$\mathcal{P}[\![(t_1, t_2)]\!]\,x\ \text{step}\ n\,u \;=\; (\mathcal{P}[\![t_1]\!]\,x\ \text{step}\ n\,u,\ \mathcal{P}[\![t_2]\!]\,x\ \text{step}\ n\,u) \qquad \text{(p-seq)}$$

Finally, for a star type, we generate a for-loop:

$$\begin{aligned} &\mathcal{P}[\![\ \text{element}\,A\,t*\ ]\!]\,x\ \text{step}\ n\,u && \text{(p-star)} \\ &= \textbf{for}\ \$z\ \textbf{in}\ x/\text{self::}A\ \textbf{return}\ <A>\{\mathcal{P}[\![t]\!]\,(\$z/\text{node}())\ \text{step}\ (n+1)\,u\}</A> \end{aligned}$$

3.4 Example

As an example, we translate QUERY1. For clarity, the environment σ is omitted. Initially, the mutable variable $v has type: element bib {...}, given in Section 2, and is bound to λs.λu.<state><v>{u (s/v/node())}</v></state> in σ. From Rules (step), (subst), (p-step), (p-star), and (p-child), we can deduce that:

```
C⟦$v/article⟧ s u
= C⟦$v⟧ s (λx. P⟦element bib {...}⟧ x (child::article) 0 u)
= <state><v>{
      P⟦element bib {...}⟧ (s/v/node()) (child::article) 0 u }</v></state>
= <state><v>{
      P⟦element article {...}*⟧ (s/v/node()/self::bib/node()) (child::article) 1 u
  }</v></state>
= <state><v>{
      for $z in P⟦element article {...}⟧ (s/v/bib/node()/self::article) (child::article) 1
      return u($z) }</v></state>
= <state><v>{ for $z in s/v/bib/article return u($z) }</v></state>
```

Using this result and Rule (cond), we get:

```
C⟦ $v/article[author="Smith"] ⟧ s u
= C⟦$v/article⟧ s (λx. if E⟦author="Smith"⟧ x then u(x) else x)
= <state><v>{ for $z in s/v/bib/article
                 return if E⟦author="Smith"⟧ $z then u($z) else $z }</v></state>
= <state><v>{ for $z in s/v/bib/article
                 return if $z/author="Smith" then u($z) else $z }</v></state>
```

Using Rule (for), QUERY1 is translated to 𝒞⟦ replace value of node $i/year with 2009⟧ s u, where variable $i is bound to

```
λs.λu. 𝒞⟦$v/article[author="Smith"]⟧ s
        (λz. if ℰ⟦contains(z/title,"XQuery")⟧ z then u(z) else z)
 = λs.λu. 𝒞⟦$v/article[author="Smith"]⟧ s
            (λz.if contains(z/title,"XQuery") then u(z) else z)
 = λs.λu. <state><v>{
                for $z in s/v/bib/article
                return if $z/author="Smith"
                        then if contains($z/title,"XQuery") then u($z) else $z
                        else $z }</v></state>
```

Letting u' x = u(<year>2009</year>) and using Rule (repl-val), we have:

```
𝒞⟦ replace value of node $i/year with 2009 ⟧ s u
 = 𝒞⟦$i/year⟧ s (λx. u(<year>2009</year>))
 = 𝒞⟦$i/year⟧ s u'
 = 𝒞⟦$i⟧ s (λx.𝒫⟦element article {...}⟧ x (child::year) 0 u')
```

As before:

```
𝒫⟦element article {...}⟧ x (child::year) 0 u'
 = <article>{ 𝒫⟦(element title string, ...)⟧
                 (x/self::article/node()) 1 u' }</article>
 = <article>{ x/self::article/node()/self::title,
              u'(x/self::article/node()/self::year),
              x/self::article/node()/self::author }</article>
 = <article>{ x/self::article/title, u'(x/self::article/year),
              x/self::article/author }</article>
```

Therefore, using Rule (subst), we get:

```
𝒞⟦replace value of node $i/year with 2009⟧ s u
 = 𝒞⟦$i⟧ s (λx. <article>{ x/self::article/title,
                            u(<year>2009</year>),
                            x/self::article/author }</article>)
 = <state><v>{
      for $z in s/v/bib/article
      return if $z/author="Smith"
              then if contains($z/title,"XQuery")
                    then <article>{ $z/self::article/title,
                                    u(<year>2009</year>),
                                    $z/self::article/author
                          }</article>
                    else $z
              else $z }</v></state>
```

3.5 Hypothetical Queries

A hypothetical XUF update (a transform expression) creates modified copies of XML data. It binds a number of variables to exact copies of XML data that are assigned new node identities and it performs updates against these variables. As we did for regular updates, we construct a state from all these variables:

$$\begin{aligned}&\mathcal{E}[\![\textbf{copy}\,\$v_1 := e_1,\,\ldots,\,\$v_n := e_n\,\textbf{modify}\,e\,\textbf{return}\,e']\!]\,x\\ &= \textbf{let}\,\$s := \mathcal{C}[\![e]\!]\,\sigma\,S\,\textbf{id},\,\$v_1 := \$s/v_1,\,\ldots,\,\$v_n := \$s/v_n\,\textbf{return}\,\mathcal{E}[\![e']\!]\,(\text{error}())\end{aligned}$$

where S is $\text{<state>}<v_1>\{\mathcal{E}[\![e_1]\!]\,x\}</v_1>\ldots<v_n>\{\mathcal{E}[\![e_n]\!]\,x\}</v_n>\text{</state>}$ and σ contains the bindings from each variable $\$v_i$ to

$$\lambda s.\lambda u.\,\text{<state>}\{\,s/v_1,\ldots,<v_i>\{u(s/v_i/\text{node}())\}</v_i>,\ldots,s/v_n\,\}\text{</state>}$$

4 Related Work

Although there are already a number of proposals for XQuery update languages [1,2,3,14], there is now a W3C candidate recommendation, called XQuery Update Facility (XUF) [18]. The work by Fan *et al* [5] implements XQuery transform queries without requiring any change to existing XQuery processors. It uses (among others) a naive method that evaluates XQuery updates using pure XQuery recursive functions. Contrary to our type-guided update translations, recursive functions offer very few opportunities for optimization. The work by Cheney [3] introduces an XML update language similar to XUF, called FLUX, and gives it operational semantics and a sound, decidable static type system. In contrast to XUF, FLUX does not allow aliasing of the mutable store, and thus it avoids the interference problem. The work by Ghelli *et al* [15] gives denotational semantics to XQuery updates, by extending the XQuery data model with stores and store histories, and uses it for a commutativity analysis. The work by Foster *et al* [11] on XQuery view maintenance has similar goals as ours but uses the Galax algebra for the update mappings. Unlike these related approaches that use framework-specific algebras, our work can be incorporated into any existing XQuery engine since it translates XUF queries to plain XQuery.

5 Conclusion

The effectiveness of our translation framework can be attributed to the extensive use of type information. Although state transformations can also be generated from untyped XUF queries using recursive functions, the quality of the generated code would be so low that would offer very few opportunities for optimization. Another characteristic of our approach that makes it different from related work is that it captures node identity explicitly, allowing us to propagate it through state transformations easily, thus satisfying the XUF semantics that expects identity preservation through updates.

In addition to the correctness proof, the extended version of this paper [6] contains various extensions, including handling positional queries (such as, sequence indexing), union types, and reordering the pending updates, as required by the XUF semantics. The most important extension is handling data aliasing during updating by detecting expressions that return replicated XML nodes. These expressions are factored out from the state, while updates to replicas are directed to the original data sources.

All the algorithms described in this paper have already been implemented in Haskell and the presented examples have been tested. The source code is available at `http://lambda.uta.edu/Updates.hs`. This code has yet to be incorporated into our XQuery database management system, HXQ [9].

References

1. Benedikt, M., Bonifati, A., Flesca, S., Vyas, A.: Adding Updates to XQuery: Semantics, Optimization, and Static Analysis. In: XIME-P'05 (2005)
2. Cheney, J.: Lux: A Lightweight, Statically Typed XML Update Language. In: PLAN-X'07 (2007)
3. Cheney, J.: FLUX: FunctionaL Updates for XML. In: ICFP'08 (2008)
4. El-Sayed, M., Wang, L., Ding, L., Rundensteiner, E.A.: An Algebraic Approach for Incremental Maintenance of Materialized XQuery Views. In: WIDM'02 (2002)
5. Fan, W., Cong, G., Bohannon, P.: Querying XML with Update Syntax. In: SIGMOD'08 (2008)
6. Fegaras, L.: A Typed-Guided Translation of XQuery Updates, Extended Paper (2010), `http://lambda.uta.edu/xuf10.pdf`
7. Fegaras, L.: Propagating Updates through XML Views using Lineage Tracing. In: ICDE'10 (2010), `http://lambda.uta.edu/updates09.pdf`
8. Fegaras, L.: Incremental Maintenance of Materialized XML Views (2010), `http://lambda.uta.edu/views10.pdf`
9. Fegaras, L.: HXQ: A Compiler from XQuery to Haskell (2010), `http://lambda.uta.edu/HXQ/`
10. Fernandez, M., Simeon, J., Choi, B., Marian, A., Sur, G.: Implementing XQuery 1.0: the Galax experience. In: VLDB'03 (2003)
11. Foster, J.N., Konuru, R., Simeon, J., Villard, L.: An Algebraic Approach to XQuery View Maintenance. In: PLAN-X'08 (2008)
12. Fourny, G., Pilman, M., Florescu, D., Kossmann, D., Kraska, T., McBeath, D.: XQuery in the Browser. In: WWW'09 (2009)
13. Ghelli, G., Onose, N., Rose, K., Simeon, J.: XML Query Optimization in the Presence of Side Effects. In: SIGMOD'08 (2008)
14. Ghelli, G., Re, C., Simeon, J.: XQuery!: An XML Query Language with Side Effects. In: Grust, T., Höpfner, H., Illarramendi, A., Jablonski, S., Mesiti, M., Müller, S., Patranjan, P.-L., Sattler, K.-U., Spiliopoulou, M., Wijsen, J. (eds.) EDBT 2006. LNCS, vol. 4254, pp. 178–191. Springer, Heidelberg (2006)
15. Ghelli, G., Rose, K., Simeon, J.: Commutativity analysis for XML updates. In: TODS'08, 33(4) (2008)
16. May, N., Helmer, S., Moerkotte, G.: Strategies for query unnesting in XML databases. In: TODS'06, 31(3) (2006)
17. W3C. XQuery 1.0 and XPath 2.0 Formal Semantics (2007), `http://www.w3.org/TR/xquery-semantics/`
18. W3C. XQuery Update Facility 1.0. W3C Candidate Recommendation 1 (June 2009), `http://www.w3.org/TR/xquery-update-10/`

EBSL: Supporting Deleted Node Label Reuse in XML*

Martin F. O'Connor and Mark Roantree

Interoperable Systems Group, School of Computing,
Dublin City University, Dublin 9, Ireland
{moconnor,mark.roantree}@computing.dcu.ie

Abstract. Recently, there has been much research into the specification of dynamic labeling schemes supporting XML updates. The primary design goal of any dynamic labeling scheme is to limit the growth rate in node label size, and consequently increase query performance and reduce update costs. The ability to reuse deleted node labels is a key property in achieving this goal. In this paper, we review the existing dynamic labeling schemes that provide this functionality and identify their shortcomings. We present our own dynamic labeling scheme that guarantees every delete node label can be reused. Further, we provide a deleted node label reuse strategy that best suits the nature of node insertions and deletions in an XML tree.

1 Introduction

In recent years, there has been considerable research on the development of new dynamic labeling schemes capable of supporting XML updates. To date, most of the analysis of such labeling schemes has been limited to the computation complexity of the update cost, the impact on label size under various update scenarios and to comparative performance analysis with other labeling schemes. In our previous work [15], we provided a holistic evaluation framework based on the desirable properties that are characteristic of a *good* dynamic labeling scheme for XML. In this paper, we focus on one such desirable property - the ability to reuse deleted node labels.

Almost all dynamic labeling schemes for XML published to date [16], [20], [2], [21], [11], [19], [4], [5], [9], [1] are not truly dynamic in that they support insertion updates of nodes only. When a node is deleted, the node label is marked as deleted. Subsequently, if we want to insert a new node at the same position in the XML tree as the previously deleted node, a new node label is generated. The deleted node label is not reused and is thus, wasted. In a highly dynamic environment with frequent node insertions and deletions, such as online transaction processing systems of heterogeneous data deployed in XML repositories, the inability to reuse deleted node labels leads to a rapid increase in label sizes. Large

* Funded by Enterprise Ireland Grant No. CFTD/07/201.

M.L. Lee et al. (Eds.): XSym 2010, LNCS 6309, pp. 73–87, 2010.

node label sizes result in slower label comparison operations and consequently to slower query evaluations and slower update performance.

To incorporate deleted node label reuse as a property of a dynamic labeling scheme, is not a trivial task. Between any two consecutive nodes, there may have been an arbitrary number of node deletions. The ability to detect, identify and reclaim a deleted node label must be provided from the information encoded in the label alone. The labeling scheme may not rely on external indices to keep track of nodes as they are deleted and inserted. Furthermore, it is not sufficient to reclaim deleted node labels simply because they exist. A deleted node label may be longer in size than a newly generated label. In such scenarios, it is preferable to generate and insert the smaller node labels first and to only reuse the larger labels when no smaller labels are available. Consequently, it is necessary to identify the deleted label and determine the size of the deleted label in order to determine if it is suitable for reuse in the current scenario. All of this functionality must be provided from the information encoded in the labels alone while maintaining document order and guarantying that all nodes labels are unique throughout the XML tree whether they are newly generated or recently reused.

Contribution. In this paper, we present our new dynamic labeling scheme called Enhanced Binary String Labeling (EBSL) that provides full support for the reuse of deleted node labels during insertion operations. EBSL does not require the relabeling of existing nodes nor the recalculation of any values when inserting new nodes in an XML tree. To the best of our knowledge, EBSL is the only dynamic labeling scheme which guarantees that every deleted node label can be reused. Finally, EBSL supports a deleted label reuse strategy that best suits the nature of node deletions and node insertion in an XML tree.

This paper is structured as follows: in §2, we review the three dynamic labeling schemes that claim to support deleted node label reuse. In §3, we present our new dynamic labeling scheme, namely EBSL, and the underlying properties that facilitate deleted node label reuse. These properties ensure every deleted node label can be reused and the size of the reclaimed label can always be determined from the neighboring labels. In §4, we present our algorithms which perform the detection, identification and selection of the appropriate deleted node label for reuse. Finally in §5, our conclusions are presented.

2 Related Research

Several surveys have been performed that provide an overview and analysis of the principle dynamic labeling schemes for XML proposed to date [17], [6], [18], [15]. To the best of our knowledge, there are only three published dynamic labeling schemes for XML that support the reuse of deleted node labels while maintaining document order [12], [8], [13].

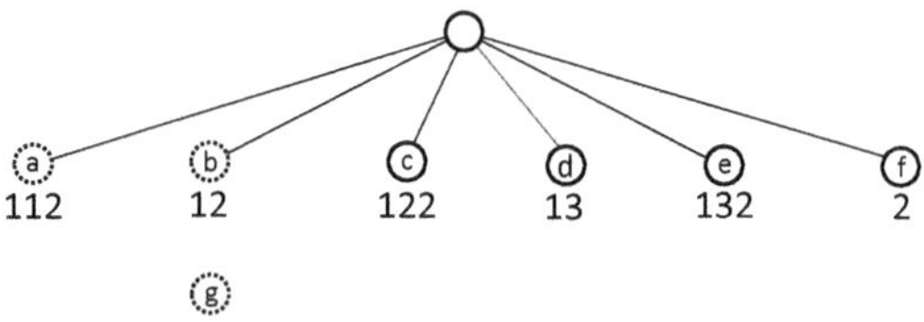

Fig. 1. Reusing a deleted node label in a QED labeled tree

2.1 Extended QED Labeling Scheme

The Extended QED labeling scheme [12] uses a quaternary code to encode node labels. Four numbers 0, 1, 2 and 3 are used in the code and each number is stored with two bits; i.e.: 00, 01, 10, 11. However, the number 0 is reserved as a separator and the remaining numbers 1, 2 and 3 are used to encode the node labels. The authors provide an algorithm `AssignInsertedCodeWithReuse` to extend the QED labeling scheme to support the reuse of deleted node labels and the algorithm has the property of always selecting the smallest deleted node label available.

Consider an XML tree which has been initially labeled with 16 nodes. The first 6 nodes are illustrate in Fig. 1. Now delete the first two nodes *a* and *b*. Insert a new node *g* before the current leftmost node *c*. According to algorithm `AssignInsertedCodeWithReuse`, the new node *g* will be assigned the label 112. The smallest deleted label (12) of node *b* was not reused.

Perhaps a more significant problem with algorithm `AssignInsertedCodeWithReuse` is that the same label is assigned to two different nodes. Consider an XML tree which has been initially labeled with 16 nodes. The first 4 nodes (a, b, c and d) are illustrated in Fig. 2. Insert a new node *g* to the left of the current leftmost node *a*. Then insert a new node *h* between node g and node *a*. The new node *h* will be assigned the label 1112. But this label has already been assigned to node *g*. The assignment of the same node label to two different nodes violates the properties of unique node identity as required by the XPath data model.

2.2 Improved Binary String Labeling Scheme

In [8], the authors propose a dynamic labeling scheme called IBSL (Improved Binary String Labeling) which supports node updates without the need to relabel existing nodes. IBSL, an extension of their earlier work [7], is a binary string

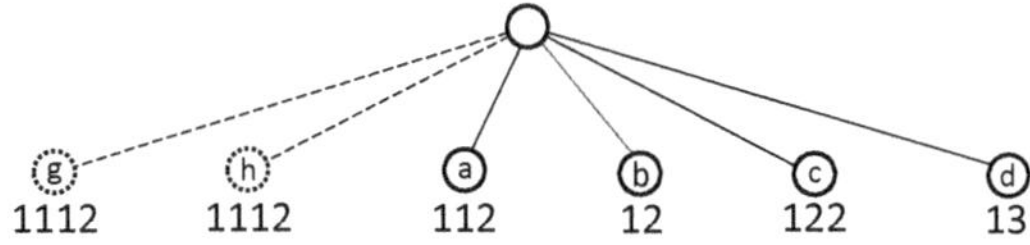

Fig. 2. Duplicate label assignment in a QED labeled tree

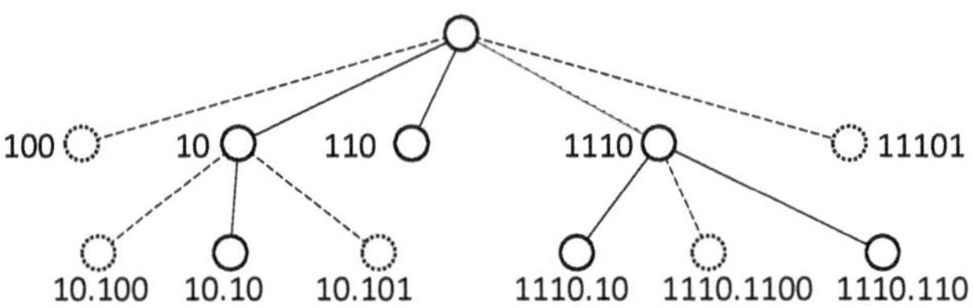

Fig. 3. IBSL Labeled XML tree

prefix-based labeling scheme and introduces new insertion algorithms to permit the reuse of deleted node labels in their original position. Fig. 3 illustrates an IBSL labeled XML Tree, the dotted circles indicating newly inserted nodes in an existing tree.

In [8], the authors present an algorithm (Algorithm 3) to insert a new node label with the smallest length between two adjacent node labels. The algorithm is designed to process three generic cases: inserting a new leftmost node (case 1); inserting a new node between two adjacent nodes (case 2); and finally inserting a new rightmost node (case 3). The second case of inserting a new node between two consecutive nodes is broken down further into 3 subcases. Thus, five distinct case scenarios are presented in all. However, it can be shown that the algorithm fails to reuse deleted labels in four of these scenarios. We will highlight two of these now.

A comment on the convention we use is necessary at this point. Every node insertion is considered to be an insertion between two consecutive nodes. N_{left} is the node label on the left, N_{right} is the node label on the right, and N_{left} is lexicographically less than N_{right}. When inserting a new node to the right of the current rightmost node, N_{left} is said to be not empty and N_{right} is empty. The new node to be inserted is referred to as N_{new}. In our algorithms, we use the symbol $\oplus$ to denote the concatenation of two binary strings.

Case 1: Inserting a new node to the left of the current leftmost node. Consider an XML tree which has been initially labeled with just two nodes a and b. Insert the following new nodes in the order they are listed: node c and node d, as illustrated in Fig. 4. Delete node c (the current leftmost node is now node d). Finally, insert a new node e to the left of the current leftmost node d. Node

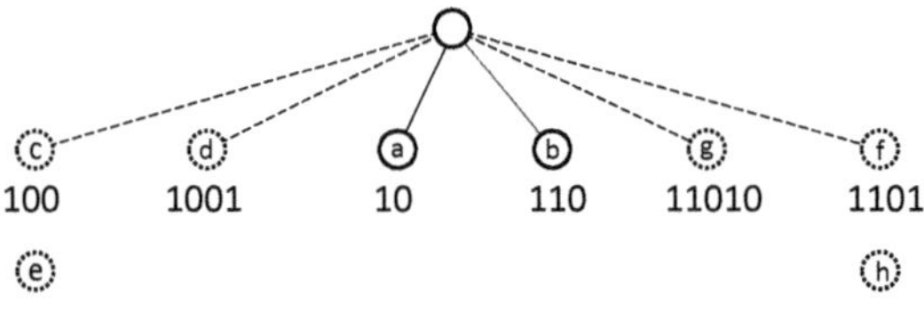

Fig. 4. Case 1 and 3: Inserting a new leftmost node and new rightmost node after a node deletion

label e is assigned the label 10010 and not assigned the deleted label of node c (100). Thus, algorithm 3, case 1 did not reuse the deleted node label.

Case 3: Inserting a new node to the right of the current rightmost node. Consider an XML tree which has been initially labeled with just two nodes a and b. Insert the following new nodes in the order they are listed: node f and node g, as illustrated in Fig. 4. Delete node f (the current rightmost node is now node g). Finally, insert a new node h to the right of the current rightmost node g. Node label h = 110101. There is a typographical error in case 3 [8]. However, there is a clear symmetry between case 1 and case 3 and we surmise the authors meant to write that N_{new} should be lexicographically greater than N_{left}. In either case, N_{new} does not reuse the deleted node label that belonged to node f (1101).

2.3 V-CDBS Labeling Scheme

To the best of our knowledge, there is only one published dynamic labeling scheme, called V-CDBS [13], that supports the reuse of deleted node labels. V-CDBS is a binary string dynamic labeling scheme. Referring to the authors illustrated example of V-CDBS codes in Table 2 in [13] and using their algorithm 3 `AssignMiddleBinaryStringWithSmallestSize` [13], when N_{left}=0001 and N_{right}=001, inserting a new node will result in N_{new}=0001011. The valid label with the smallest size and lexicographically ordered between N_{left} and N_{right} is 00011 and is not reused.

The algorithm `AssignMiddleBinaryStringWithSmallestSize` can never gu arantee to *always* select the middle binary string with the smallest size due to the intrinsic properties of the assign initial labels algorithm employed by the V-CDBS labeling scheme. The V-CDBS assign initial labels algorithm is presented as algorithm 2 in [13]. It adopts a recursive divide-and-conquer approach whereby given N nodes to label, it first identifies and labels the middle node between 0 and N. The middle node is then used to divide the search space and the algorithm continues recursively. The middle node is selected using the formula: middle(start,end) = round(start + (end - start)/2). The first node is assumed to begin at position zero and consequently the round function guarantees that every node from 1 to N will be labeled. For example, middle(0,4) = round(0 + (4-0)/2) = 2. However, middle(0,3) = round(0 + (3-0)/2) = 2 also. The use of the round function introduces an approximation function into the V-CDBS assign initial labels algorithm. Thus, the V-CDBS labels are not assigned in a deterministic manner. In other words, the label value of node n is not and cannot be determined solely from the label values of node n+1 or node n-1. The V-CDBS encoding algorithm can guarantee lexicographical order but cannot guarantee the accurate calculation of the size of a node label n or indeed the label n itself, based solely on the node labels adjacent to node n. It follows that when node n is deleted, the V-CDBS labeling scheme cannot guarantee the accurate calculation of the deleted node label n (and its size), and consequently cannot guarantee that the deleted node label n will be reused.

3 Enhanced Binary String Labeling Scheme (EBSL)

In this section, we introduce our new dynamic labeling scheme for XML called the Enhanced Binary String Labeling scheme (EBSL). EBSL is based on the IBSL labeling scheme. EBSL does not require the relabeling of existing nodes nor the recalculation of any values when inserting new nodes in an XML tree. EBSL fully supports the reuse of deleted node labels when inserting new nodes into positions that previously contained deleted nodes. EBSL guarantees that every deleted node label can be reused. That is to say, there are no (simple or complex) insertion/deletion scenarios that will result in a deleted node label remaining unused when it would be appropriate to reuse that label. EBSL may be deployed using the prefix-based approach and thus, support ancestor-descendant, parent-child and sibling-ordered XPath evaluations. Finally, EBSL supports a deleted label reuse strategy that best suits the nature of node deletions and insertions in an XML tree. Conceptually, the construction of a dynamic labeling scheme for XML (that permits the reuse of deleted nodes labels) may be viewed as a three stage process:

1. The `AssignInitialLabels` stage.
2. The `SimpleInsertion` stage.
3. The `InsertionWithDeletedLabelReuse` stage.

Before we present the algorithms facilitating the construction process, it is necessary to introduce our customized definition of lexicographical order, a key property facilitating the reuse of deleted node labels.

3.1 Lexicographical Order

EBSL compares node labels using lexicographical order and not numerical order. Our customized definition of lexicographical order differs from existing approaches [10], [6], [14], [3], [21], [7], [13] and is also different to the definition employed by the IBSL labeling scheme [8].

Definition 1. *(Lexicographical order $\prec$) Given two consecutive binary strings S_{left} and S_{right} (S_{left} represents the left binary string, S_{right} represents the right binary string), S_{left} is said to be lexicographical equal to S_{right} iff they are exactly the same. S_{left} is said to be lexicographically less than S_{right} ($S_{left} \prec S_{right}$) iff*

1. *the lexicographical comparison of S_{left} and S_{right} is bit by bit from left to right. If the current bit of S_{left} is 0 and the current bit of S_{right} is 1, then $S_{left} \prec S_{right}$ and stop the comparison, or*
2. *$len(S_{left}) < len(S_{right})$, S_{left} is a prefix of S_{right}, the first extra bit of S_{right} = 1 (i.e.: $substring(S_{right}, len(S_{left})+1, len(S_{left})+1) = 1$), then $S_{left} \prec S_{right}$ and stop the comparison, or*
3. *$len(S_{left}) > len(S_{right})$, S_{right} is a prefix of S_{left}, the first extra bit of S_{left} = 0 (i.e.: $substring(S_{left}, len(S_{right})+1, len(S_{right})+1) = 0$), then $S_{left} \prec S_{right}$ and stop the comparison.*

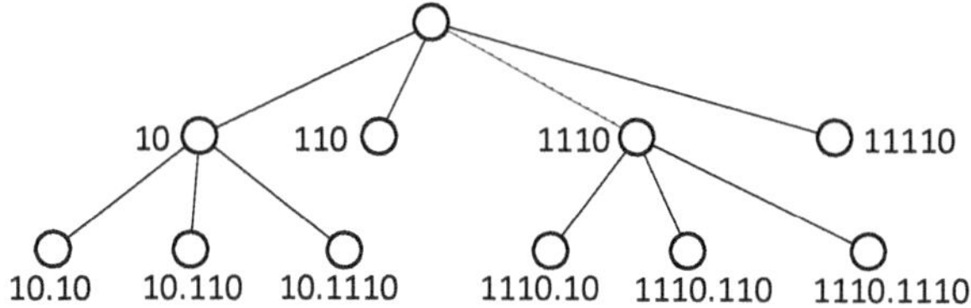

Fig. 5. An EBSL tree labeled using the `AssignInitialLabels` algorithm

The conventional definition of lexicographical order defines a prefix string to be always lexicographically less than the larger string beginning with that prefix (e.g.: 110 $\prec$ 11001). In our definition of lexicographical order, (condition 3) the larger string containing the prefix is lexicographical less than the prefix string if and only if the subsequent bit immediately after the prefix in the larger string is a 0 bit (e.g.: 11001 $\prec$ 110). Conversely, (condition 2) the larger string containing the prefix is lexicographical greater than the prefix string if and only if the subsequent bit immediately after the prefix in the larger string is a 1 bit (e.g.: 110 $\prec$ 11010).

3.2 The Assign Initial Labels Algorithm

The EBSL `AssignInitialLabels` encoding algorithm is the same as the IBSL `AssignInitialLabels` algorithm [8] and thus is not detailed here. The algorithm takes as input a parent node, and assigns a unique label to every child node of the parent. The first child is always assigned the self_label 10. Thereafter, all subsequent children are deterministically labeled such that the self_label of child *i* is the computed as the concatenation of a 1 bit and the self_label of child *i - 1*. The algorithm may be applied recursively to the XML tree to assign labels to every node in the tree. An example of an EBSL labeled tree is illustrated in Fig. 5.

Definition 2. *($\Re$label) A node label with the properties of a label assigned by the* ***AssignInitialLabels*** *algorithm is denoted as an $\Re$label. The properties that uniquely characterize an $\Re$label are:*

1. *The node label begins with a prefix binary string consisting of one or more consecutive 1 bits, and*
2. *The node will contain a single 0 bit and this 0 bit will be the last bit in the node label.*

Every node label assigned by the `AssignInitialLabels` algorithm is an $\Re$*label*. Definition 2 defines the unique characteristics of an $\Re$*label*. Examples of an $\Re$*label* are 10, 110, 1110, 11110, 111110 and so on. All $\Re$*label* node labels are lexicographically greater than the first child label 10. $\Re$*label* node labels will always and only ever be assigned when inserting a new node to the right of the

Algorithm 1. Simple Insertion Algorithm

input : left self_label N_{left}, right self_label N_{right}
output: New self_label N_{new} such that $N_{left} \prec N_{new} \prec N_{right}$
begin
  Case 1: N_{left} is empty but N_{right} is not empty
  `/* Insert a new node before the current leftmost node. */`
  $N_{new} \longleftarrow N_{right} \oplus 0$; `// ⊕ means concatenation.`
  Case 2: N_{left} is not empty but N_{right} is empty
  `/* Insert a new node after the current rightmost node. */`
  $N_{new} \longleftarrow 1 \oplus N_{left}$;
  Case 3: N_{left} is not empty and N_{right} is not empty
  `/* Insert a new node between two existing nodes. */`
  if *($len(N_{left}) \leq len(N_{right})$)* **then** $N_{new} \longleftarrow N_{right} \oplus 0$;
  else if *($len(N_{left}) > len(N_{right})$)* **then** $N_{new} \longleftarrow N_{left} \oplus 1$;
end

current rightmost node. The ability to identify a node label with the properties of an $\Re label$ is a key requirement in order to guarantee that every node label can be reclaimed and reused in the face of arbitrary nodes insertions and node deletions.

3.3 The Simple Insertion Algorithm

Algorithm 1 is the EBSL `SimpleInsertion` label encoding algorithm. The algorithm takes as input two node labels, N_{left} and N_{right}, and generates a new node label N_{new} such that $N_{left} \prec N_{new} \prec N_{right}$. The `SimpleInsertion` algorithm assumes no nodes have been deleted in the XML tree. This assumption is important so as to permit the clear specification of the rules governing the creation of a new node label when inserted between two existing consecutive node labels (and when no deleted labels are available to be reused).

It should also be noted that although cases 1 and 3 of our `SimpleInsertion` algorithm is the same as the IBSL simple insertion algorithm, case 2 is different. Concerning case 2, the IBSL simple insertion algorithm assigns $N_{new} = N_{left} \oplus 1$. Our `SimpleInsertion` algorithm case 2 assigns $N_{new} = 1 \oplus N_{new}$. This change fundamentally distinguishes the EBSL labeling scheme from the IBSL labeling scheme in a dynamic scenario, because new node insertions to the right of the current rightmost node will now end in a 0 bit, and not a 1 bit. This will directly influence lexicographical order evaluations and consequently the label values of new node inserted after the rightmost node. Algorithm 1 case 1 introduces a new category of labels called $\ell label$.

Definition 3. *($\ell label$) A node label with the properties of a label assigned by Case 1 of the `SimpleInsertion` algorithm (algorithm 1) is denoted as an $\ell label$. The properties that uniquely characterize an $\ell label$ are:*

1. *The node label begins with a single 1 bit, and*
2. *All subsequent bits in the node label consists of a sequence of two or more consecutive 0 bits.*

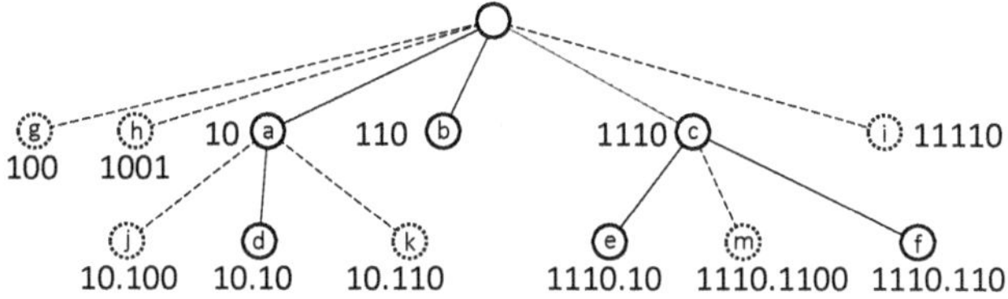

Fig. 6. An EBSL labeled tree with new nodes inserted (dotted circles) using the `SimpleInsertion` algorithm (algorithm 1)

Examples of an $\ell label$ are 100, 1000, 10000, 100000, 1000000 and so on. All $\ell label$ node labels are lexicographically less than the first child node 10. $\ell label$ node labels will only ever be assigned when inserting a new node to the left of the current leftmost node. The ability to identify a node label with the properties of an $\ell label$ is a key requirement in order to guarantee that every node label can be reused.

We provide an illustration of an EBSL labeled tree in Fig. 6 with nodes a through f assigned by the `AssignInitialLabels` algorithm and nodes g through m inserted in alphabetical order using the `SimpleInsertion` algorithm. The `SimpleInsertion` algorithm case 3 can never generate a new node label that has the characteristics of either an $\Re label$ or an $\ell label$. It should be observed that an arbitrary EBSL node label will be an $\Re label$ label or an $\ell label$ label or neither of the two. The three cases in the `SimpleInsertion` algorithm are closed (i.e.: both N_{left} and N_{right} cannot be empty).

4 Reusing Deleted Node Labels

In this section, we present our algorithms to facilitate the insertion of a new node into an XML tree while permitting the reuse of deleted node labels. Before we present these algorithms, it is good to summarize what we know thus far so as to identify the conditions in which these algorithms must operate.

An arbitrary node label in an EBSL labeled tree will always fall into one and only one of the following three lexicographical categories:

1. The node label will be lexicographically greater than ($\succ$) the node label 10.
2. The node label will be lexicographically less than ($\prec$) the node label 10.
3. The node label will be lexicographically equal to the node label 10.

When we consider a node insertion algorithm, there are always three high level scenarios to be processed:

1. Insertion of a new node after the current rightmost node.
2. Insertion of a new node before the current leftmost node.
3. Insertion of a new node between two existing nodes with non-empty labels.

In our EBSL deterministic labeling scheme, case 1 is the most important scenario and case 3 will always rely on case 1 to identify and reclaim a deleted node label.

Algorithm 2. Insert New Node After Rightmost Node

```
/* This algorithm inserts a new node after the current rightmost node N_right and, if
   it exists, reuses the deleted node label to the right of N_right that was originally
   used to create N_right.                                                          */
input  : left self_label N_left is not empty
output: New self_label N_new such that N_left ≺ N_new
begin
    if (N_left == 10) then
        N_new ⟵ 1 ⊕ N_left ;           // Apply SimpleInsertion algorithm, Case 2
        return N_new;

    /* The Following IF statement is processed when N_left ≺ 10.                    */
    else if (prefix of N_left == 100) then
        N_new ⟵ SelectNewRightmostNodeLessThan10(N_left);
        label_found ⟵ true;
        return N_new;

    /* The Following IF statement is processed when 10 ≺ N_left.                    */
    else if (prefix of N_left == 11) then
        N_new ⟵ SelectNewRightmostNodeGreaterThan10(N_left);
        label_found ⟵ true;
        return N_new;
    end
end
```

Case 2 has a natural symmetry with case 1. Due to space restrictions, case 2 is not included in this paper. We first present the algorithms for case 1, followed by the algorithm for case 3.

4.1 Inserting a New Node after the Rightmost Node

Algorithm 2 is the EBSL `InsertNewNodeAfterRightmostNode` encoding algorithm that supports the reuse of deleted node labels. Algorithm 2 takes one node label as input, the non-empty left self_label N_{left}. This algorithm will output a new node label N_{new} such that N_{new} will be the reclaimed deleted node label to the right of N_{left} that was originally used to create N_{left} or a newly generated node label if there is no deleted node label available to be reused.

Essentially, the purpose of algorithm 2 is to determine the prefix of N_{left}, and based on the prefix, to call a function which will determine exactly what the new node label should be. If the node label N_{left} has the prefix 100, the function `SelectNewRightmostNodeLessThan10` will be invoked and will identify and reclaim a deleted node label if one exists, otherwise it will generate a new node label. If the node label N_{left} has the prefix 11, the function `SelectNewRightmostNodeGreaterThan10` will be invoked and will identify and reclaim a deleted node label if one exists, otherwise it will generate a new node label. The details of these functions will be presented later in this section.

4.2 Function SelectNewRightmostNodeLessThan10

Algorithm 3 contains the pseudocode of the function `SelectNewRightmostNode LessThan10`. This function receives as input the current rightmost node label

Algorithm 3. SelectNewRightmostNodeLessThan10

```
/* This algorithm takes as input the current rightmost node N_left such that N_left ≺
   10, and selects a deleted node label lexicographically greater than N_left. We are
   certain there exists at least one deleted node label to the right of N_left because
   the first self_label assigned by the AssignInitialLabels algorithm is always 10 and
   the current rightmost node N_left ≺ 10, therefore label 10 has been deleted.      */
input  : left self_label N_left, N_left is not empty, N_left ≺ 10
output: New self_label N_new such that N_left ≺ N_new
begin
    /* Remember N_left has prefix 100.                                               */
    if (lastbit of N_left == '0') then
        N_new ⟵ substring(N_left, 1, len(N_left) - 1);

    else if (lastbit of N_left == '1') then
        N_temp ⟵ N_left;
        while (lastbit of N_temp == '1') do
            /* Remove all consecutive 1 bits from the end of label.                  */
            N_temp ⟵ substring(N_temp, 1, len(N_temp) - 1);
        end
        N_new ⟵ substring(N_temp, 1, len(N_temp) - 1);
        /* Reclaim the deleted node label on RHS originally used to create N_left.   */
    end
end
```

N_{left} with a non-empty self_label such that $N_{left} \prec 10$. The purpose of this function is to identify and reclaim the deleted node label (if it exists) to the right of N_{left} that was originally used to create N_{left}. If a deleted node label is not available to be reused, the function should generate a new node label. From a high level point of view, there are just two cases to consider when inserting a new node to the right of the current rightmost node N_{left} when $N_{left} \prec 10$:

1. The first case is when the node label N_{left} was itself created as a result of an insertion operation to the left of a leftmost *ℓlabel* node and therefore N_{left} also has the properties of an *ℓlabel* (e.g.: 100, 1000, 10000, 100000). In this case, N_{new} will be selected such that N_{new} is the *ℓlabel* lexicographically greater than N_{left} where length(N_{left}) = *m* and length(N_{new}) = *m-1*. For example, if the current rightmost node label N_{left} = 1000, then N_{new} = 100.
2. The second case exploits the fact that all other node labels $\prec 10$ must have resulted from an insertion operation between two existing nodes with non-empty labels. Therefore, if N_{left} is the current rightmost node, and N_{left} was created as the result of an insertion operation between two nodes with non-empty labels, then we know for certain at least one deleted node label exist to the right of N_{left} (i.e.: the deleted node label to the right of N_{left} that was original used to create N_{left}). In this second case, we will reuse the deleted node label to the right of N_{left} that was originally used to create N_{left}.

Algorithm 4. SelectNewRightmostNodeGreaterThan10

```
   /* This algorithm takes as input the current rightmost node N_left such that 10 ≺
      N_left.                                                                   */
   input : left self_label N_left, N_left is not empty, 10 ≺ N_left
   output: New self_label N_new such that N_left ≺ N_new
1  begin
      /* Remember N_left has prefix 11.                                        */
2     if (lastbit of N_left == '0') then
3        N_temp ⟵ substring(N_left, 1, len(N_left) - 1);
         /* Remove the last 0 bit from the label N_left.                        */
4        if (AllBitsAreOne (N_temp)) then
            /* Confirms N_left is an ℜlabel.                                     */
5           N_new ⟵ N_temp ⊕ 10;
            /* Insert new label according to simple insertion rules, Case 2.    */
6        else
7           N_new ⟵ N_temp;
            /* Otherwise, reclaim deleted node label on RHS originally used to create
               N_left by simply removing the last 0 bit (line 3).               */
8        end
9
10    else if (lastbit of N_left == '1') then
         /* In this case, the N_left label was originally created by appending a 1 bit
            to a label on the LHS of N_left. However, we want to find the deleted node
            label on the RHS that was originally used to create N_left. Therefore we mus
            first remove all consecutive 1 bits, and then finally remove the last 0 bit
            to obtain the deleted node label.                                    */
11       N_temp ⟵ N_left;
12       while (lastbit of N_temp == '1') do
            /* Remove all consecutive 1 bits from the end of label.             */
13          N_temp ⟵ substring(N_temp, 1, len(N_temp) - 1);
14       end
15       N_new ⟵ substring(N_temp, 1, len(N_temp) - 1);
         /* Remove the last 0 bit to reclaim the deleted node label on RHS originally
            used to create N_left.                                               */
16    end
17 end
```

4.3 Function SelectNewRightmostNodeGreaterThan10

Algorithm 4 contains the pseudocode of the function `SelectNewRightmostNode GreaterThan10`. This function receives as input the current rightmost node label N_{left} with a non-empty self_label such that $10 \prec N_{left}$. The purpose of this function is to identify and reclaim the deleted node label to the right of N_{left} that was originally used to create N_{left}. If a deleted node label is not available to be reused, the function generates a new node label. From a high level point of view, there are just two cases to consider when inserting a new node to the right of the current rightmost node N_{left} when $10 \prec N_{left}$:

1. The first case is when the node label N_{left} was itself created as a result of an insertion operation to the right of a rightmost $\Re label$ and therefore N_{left} also has the properties of an $\Re label$ (e.g.: 110, 1110, 11110, 111110). In this case, N_{new} will be selected such that N_{new} is the smallest $\Re label$ lexicographically greater than N_{left}. For example, if the current rightmost node label $N_{left} = 110$, then $N_{new} = 1110$.

Algorithm 5. Insert New Node Between Two Existing Nodes (Reuse)

```
/* This algorithm inserts a new node between two existing consecutive nodes with
   non-empty labels.                                                              */
input  : left self_label N_left is not empty, right self_label N_right is not empty
output: New self_label N_new such that N_left ≺ N_new ≺ N_right
begin
    N_temp ⟵ InsertNewNodeAfterRightmostNode (N_left);
    if (N_temp ≺ N_right) then
        N_new ⟵ N_temp;
    else
        N_new ⟵ SimpleInsertion (N_left, N_right);
    end
    return N_new
end
```

2. The second case exploits the fact that all other node labels $\succ$ 10 must have resulted from an insertion operation between two existing nodes with non-empty labels. Therefore, if N_{left} is the current rightmost node, and N_{left} was created as the result of an insertion operation between two nodes with non-empty labels, then we know for certain there must be at least one deleted node label available to the right of N_{left} (i.e.: the deleted node label to the right of N_{left} that was originally used to create N_{left}). In this second case, we will reuse the deleted node label to the right of N_{left} that was originally used to create N_{left}.

4.4 Inserting a New Node between Two Existing Nodes with Non-empty Labels

Algorithm 5 is the EBSL `InsertNewNodeBetweenTwoExistingNodes` encoding algorithm that supports the reuse of deleted node labels. Algorithm 5 initially invokes the function `InsertNewNodeAfterRightmostNode` passing the node label N_{left} as a parameter and returns a temporary node label N_{temp}. If N_{left} is an $\Re label$, then N_{temp} will be assigned the smallest $\Re label$ lexicographically greater than N_{left} (e.g.: if N_{left} = 110, then N_{temp} = 1110). If N_{left} is an $\ell label$, then N_{temp} will be assigned the $\ell label$ lexicographically greater than N_{left} such that length(N_{left}) = m and length(N_{temp}) = m-1 (e.g.: if N_{left} = 1000, then N_{temp} = 100). If N_{left} is neither an $\Re label$ nor an $\ell label$, then N_{temp} will be assigned the node label to the right of N_{left} that was originally used to create N_{left} (e.g.: if N_{left} = 11001, then N_{temp} = 110). Finally, the node label N_{temp} will fall under one of three lexicographic conditions:

1. If the N_{temp} label is lexicographically less than N_{right}, then N_{temp} is a deleted node label and is available for reuse. Therefore, N_{new} is assigned the label of N_{temp}.
2. If the N_{temp} label is lexicographically equal to N_{right}, then the N_{temp} label is already in use and assigned to N_{right}. Therefore, N_{new} is assigned a new node label generated by the `SimpleInsertion` algorithm.

3. If the N_{temp} label is lexicographically greater than N_{right}, then there are no deleted node labels available between N_{left} and N_{right}. Therefore, N_{new} is assigned a new node label generated by the `SimpleInsertion` algorithm.

It may be observed that the `InsertNewNodeBetweenTwoExistingNodes` algorithm does not select the smallest deleted node label available between two given consecutive node labels. In an XML tree, when given κ nodes to insert, the κ nodes must be inserted in document order. The labeling scheme cannot arbitrarily decide the order in which to insert the nodes. By initially selecting the shortest deleted node label available, the V-CDBS labeling scheme ensures the node labels between N_{left} and the shortest deleted node label will remain unused when inserting a contiguous sequence of nodes between two consecutive node labels. Due to the deterministic labeling property of our EBSL labeling scheme, the `InsertNewNodeBetweenTwoExistingNodes` algorithm will always select the deleted node label immediately to the right of N_{left} if it exists. Otherwise, it will always select the $\Re label$ or $\ell label$ to the immediate right of N_{left} when N_{left} is an $\Re label$ or $\ell label$ respectively. Consequently the deterministic property of the EBSL labeling scheme always guarantees that every deleted node label can be reused. Holistically, the EBSL labeling scheme will always select the shortest deleted node labels available when inserting a sequence of nodes between two given nodes that contain a sequence of deleted node labels.

5 Conclusions

In this paper, we presented our Enhanced Binary String Labeling scheme (EBSL) supporting XML updates. EBSL does not require the relabeling of existing nodes nor the recalculation of any values when inserting new nodes in an XML tree. EBSL guarantees every deleted node label can be reused, all assigned nodes labels are unique and document order is maintained. EBSL supports a deleted label reuse strategy that best suits the nature of node insertions and node deletions in an XML tree.

As part of our future work, we will perform an analysis of the label size under various update scenarios and evaluate the computational complexity of our algorithms. We will also attempt to extract the underlying principles facilitating the reuse of deleted node label in our EBSL labeling scheme with the goal of specifying the core properties such that any binary string dynamic labeling scheme can support deleted node label reuse if they adapt their labeling scheme to encapsulate these properties. We will investigate the specification of an update operator to efficiently process bulk node insertions. This should be possible as every node is deterministically created based on the labels of the adjacent nodes. We will also investigate various label reuse strategies for the bulk update operator.

References

1. Alkhatib, R., Scholl, M.H.: Compacting XML Structures Using a Dynamic Labeling Scheme. In: BNCOD, pp. 158–170 (2009)
2. Amagasa, T., Yoshikawa, M., Uemura, S.: QRS: A Robust Numbering Scheme for XML Documents. In: ICDE, pp. 705–707 (2003)
3. An, D.C., Park, S.M., Park, S.: Efficient Secure Labeling Method under Dynamic XML Data Streams. In: Matsuura, K., Fujisaki, E. (eds.) IWSEC 2008. LNCS, vol. 5312, pp. 246–260. Springer, Heidelberg (2008)
4. Böhme, T., Rahm, E.: Supporting Efficient Streaming and Insertion of XML Data in RDBMS. In: DIWeb, pp. 70–81 (2004)
5. Duong, M., Zhang, Y.: LSDX: A New Labelling Scheme for Dynamically Updating XML Data. In: ADC, pp. 185–193 (2005)
6. Härder, T., Haustein, M.P., Mathis, C., Wagner, M.: Node Labeling Schemes for Dynamic XML Documents Reconsidered. Data Knowl. Eng. 60(1), 126–149 (2007)
7. Ko, H.K., Lee, S.: An Efficient Scheme to Completely Avoid Re-labeling in XML Updates. In: Aberer, K., Peng, Z., Rundensteiner, E.A., Zhang, Y., Li, X. (eds.) WISE 2006. LNCS, vol. 4255, pp. 259–264. Springer, Heidelberg (2006)
8. Ko, H.K., Lee, S.: A Binary String Approach for Updates in Dynamic Ordered XML Data. IEEE Trans. Knowl. Data Eng. 22(4), 602–607 (2010)
9. Kobayashi, K., Liang, W., Kobayashi, D., Watanabe, A., Yokota, H.: VLEI code: An Efficient Labeling Method for Handling XML Documents in an RDB. In: ICDE, pp. 386–387 (2005)
10. Li, C., Ling, T.W.: An Improved Prefix Labeling Scheme: A Binary String Approach for Dynamic Ordered XML. In: Zhou, L.-z., Ooi, B.-C., Meng, X. (eds.) DASFAA 2005. LNCS, vol. 3453, pp. 125–137. Springer, Heidelberg (2005)
11. Li, C., Ling, T.W.: QED: A Novel Quaternary Encoding to Completely Avoid Re-labeling in XML Updates. In: CIKM, pp. 501–508 (2005)
12. Li, C., Ling, T.W., Hu, M.: Reuse or Never Reuse the Deleted Labels in XML Query Processing Based on Labeling Schemes. In: Li Lee, M., Tan, K.-L., Wuwongse, V. (eds.) DASFAA 2006. LNCS, vol. 3882, pp. 659–673. Springer, Heidelberg (2006)
13. Li, C., Ling, T.W., Hu, M.: Efficient Updates in Dynamic XML Data: from Binary String to Quaternary String. VLDB Journal 17(3), 573–601 (2008)
14. Min, J.K., Lee, J., Chung, C.W.: An Efficient XML Encoding and Labeling Method for Query Processing and Updating on Dynamic XML Data. Journal of Systems and Software 82(3), 503–515 (2009)
15. O'Connor, M.F., Roantree, M.: Desirable Properties for XML Update Mechanisms. In: EDBT/ICDT Workshops (2010)
16. O'Neil, P.E., O'Neil, E.J., Pal, S., Cseri, I., Schaller, G., Westbury, N.: ORDPATHs: Insert-Friendly XML Node Labels. In: SIGMOD Conference, pp. 903–908 (2004)
17. Sans, V., Laurent, D.: Prefix based Numbering Schemes for XML: Techniques, Applications and Performances. PVLDB 1(2), 1564–1573 (2008)
18. Su-Cheng, H., Chien-Sing, L.: Node Labeling Schemes in XML Query Optimization: A Survey and Trends. IETE Technical Review 26, 88–100 (2009)
19. Thonangi, R.: A Concise Labeling Scheme for XML Data. In: International Conference on Management of Data (COMAD '06), Computer Society of India (December 2006)
20. Wu, X., Lee, M.L., Hsu, W.: A Prime Number Labeling Scheme for Dynamic Ordered XML Trees. In: ICDE, pp. 66–78 (2004)
21. Xu, L., Ling, T.W., Wu, H., Bao, Z.: DDE: From Dewey to a Fully Dynamic XML Labeling Scheme. In: SIGMOD Conference, pp. 719–730 (2009)

Lessons Learned from DB2 pureXML Applications: A Practitioner's Perspective

Matthias Nicola

IBM Silicon Valley Lab.
555 Bailey Ave, San Jose, CA 95123, USA
mnicola@us.ibm.com

Abstract. Beyond using XML as a message format, more and more companies are storing XML data permanently in a database. Database researchers and vendors alike have spent a lot of effort on designing, studying, and implementing XML database technology. In this paper we report our experiences from working with a broad variety of companies that have developed and deployed XML applications on top of DB2. We discuss three real-world XML database scenarios and their design considerations, and describe recurring patterns in XML applications. We highlight common concepts and observations, and document challenges that point to future work for the database community.

Keywords: XML, database systems, experiences, XQuery, SQL/XML.

1 Introduction

XML has become the de-facto standard format for information exchange between organizations, business processes, and applications. Companies in virtually all commercial and industrial sectors have defined XML formats to standardize and streamline information management within their industry. The main reasons include that XML is extensible, flexible, self-describing, and suitable for combining structured, unstructured and semi-structured information. XML has become the fabric of Service-Oriented Architectures (SOA), which are prevalent in today's IT world.

Beyond XML as a message format, there is a continuous need to store XML permanently: sometimes for auditing and compliance reasons, sometimes because XML is a more flexible and suitable data format than a rigid relational database schema, and sometimes because using XML can simplify applications and improve their efficiency. When companies keep XML in persistent storage, they typically want to insert, index, query, and update XML with the same performance, scalability, and ACID properties as traditional data in relational databases.

In response to this trend, the research community has developed a range of XQuery processors and XML database systems such as Galax, Lore, MonetDB/XQuery, Natix, Pathfinder, Timber, and others [1]. On the commercial side, the major database vendors have added XML capabilities to their products [12][15][19] and several XML-only databases have emerged [8]. The SQL standard has been extended with an XML data type and XML-specific functions, collectively known as SQL/XML [6].

M.L. Lee et al. (Eds.): XSym 2010, LNCS 6309, pp. 88–102, 2010.

The SQL/XML functions XMLQUERY and XMLTABLE as well as the predicate XMLEXISTS enable users to include XPath, XQuery, or XQuery Updates in SQL statements. SQL/XML also allows users to construct XML from relational tables, using functions such as XMLELEMENT, XMLATTRIBUTES, and XMLAGG. All of these advances have enabled an increasing number of companies to manage XML in a database effectively.

Over several years we have worked with companies in various industries to assist them in their design and implementation of XML applications on DB2. This includes applications in retail, government, health care, finance, and others [9]. Our work with these applications allowed us to expand our understanding of their characteristics and requirements, and to assess the success of XML technologies and languages in the real-world.

After a brief summary of DB2's XML capabilities in Section 2, the main contributions of this paper are the following:

- We describe three real XML database applications, including their motivation and requirements for using XML, the database design decisions, performance trade-offs, and the benefits received from the XML database (Section 3).
- We identify a set of findings as well as recurring challenges and design patterns in XML applications (Section 4).
- Based on our findings we identify future work for the XML database community (Section 5).

2 Overview of DB2 pureXML

This section provides a brief overview of the XML support in DB2 9.7. Further details can be found in [5] and [15]. DB2 pureXML comprises a set of XML features in the DB2 database management system. At the core of pureXML is the XML data type, which can be used to define XML columns in tables and views. XML columns store XML documents in a parsed tree format that corresponds to the XQuery Data Model [24]. Each node in the tree has a pointer to its parent and pointers to all its children. If the tree is larger than a single page in a DB2 table space, DB2 automatically splits the tree into multiple *regions* and each region is stored on a separate page [15]. Multiple regions can reside on the same page.

When XML documents are parsed and stored, tag names are internally replaced with unique integer numbers. This reduces the space consumption and improves navigation performance through integer-based node comparisons. Additionally, DB2's table compression can reduce XML storage consumption by another 60% to 80%.

The use of XML Schemas in DB2 is optional and does not impact the hierarchical storage format. Users can choose to validate all inserted or updated documents in an XML column against the same schema or to validate different documents against different schemas. This schema flexibility is critical for many XML applications.

To improve search performance, users can define *full-text indexes* or path-specific *XML value indexes*. DB2's text indexing capabilities are based on Lucene [10] and commonly used in content-centric XML applications. In contrast, data-centric XML applications typically use XML value indexes (Fig. 1). An XML value index is a

B-Tree that maps path/value pairs to a nodeID and a rowID. The rowID points to the relational row that contains the matching XML document. The nodeID points to the matching node and region. The index contains zero, one, or multiple index entries per document, depending on the number of nodes that match the XMLPATTERN.

```
CREATE TABLE customer (cid INTEGER, info XML);

CREATE INDEX idx1 ON customer(info) GENERATE KEYS USING
XMLPATTERN '/customerinfo/addr/zip' AS SQL VARCHAR(5);
```

Fig. 1. Sample table with XML column and XML value index

DB2 offers SQL/XML and XQuery. SQL/XML constructs such as XMLQUERY and XMLEXISTS can use XML column names as a context ($INFO) for XPath or XQuery expressions (Fig. 2, top). Applications can also use XQuery as a stand-alone language (Fig. 2, middle). The function db2-fn:xmlcolumn takes an XML column name as input and returns the sequence of all documents in that column. Fig. 2 (bottom) shows an XQuery transform expression [23] in an SQL Update statement to modify one or more existing XML documents in an XML column.

```
SELECT cid, XMLQUERY('$INFO/customer/name')
FROM customer
WHERE cid > 1234 AND
      XMLEXISTS('$INFO/customer/addr[zip = 95123]');

for $i in db2-fn:xmlcolumn("CUSTOMER.INFO")/customer
where $i/addr/city = "Singapore"
return <myresult>{$i/name}</myresult> ;

UPDATE customer
SET INFO = XMLQUERY('copy $new := $INFO
                     modify do replace
                     value of $new/customer/addr/zip with 95141
                     return  $new')
WHERE ...;
```

Fig. 2. Sample SQL/XML query, XQuery, and XML Update in DB2

SQL stored procedures and user-defined functions that manipulate XML with SQL/XML or XQuery can declare parameters and variables of type XML. This enables XML application development with the existing concepts for procedures and functions that many users are familiar with. For the same reason, existing database APIs such as JDBC, .NET, and CLI/ODBC, are enhanced for XML. For example, DB2 supports the new SQLXML interface that is defined in the JDBC 4.0 standard.

3 Examples of XML Database Applications: Requirements and Design Considerations

This section describes three commercial XML database applications. We explain why XML was chosen as a data storage format and how the known access patterns were critical input to important database design decisions.

3.1 Forms Processing at a Government Tax Agency

Background: The responsibility of this tax agency is to handle all tax processing for one of the fifty states in the US. Every year, this agency collects and processes approximately 11 million personal income tax returns, 1.3 million corporate tax returns, and 2 million sales and highway use tax filings. Additionally, about 20 miscellaneous types of taxes are collected and processed. The total tax collection exceeds $80 billion per year. The agency needs to validate all tax returns with business rules, collect payments or pay refunds as appropriate, and perform tax audits.

Business Objects/Data Characteristics: Traditionally, tax processing is a paper-based business. For each *tax return*, known as a *tax filing*, a tax payer fills out several forms. Processing paper forms is expensive due to the cost of buying and printing the paper, and the cost to physically ship, sort, route, and store the paper. To reduce this cost, paper forms submitted by tax payers are converted to electronic records as early in the process as possible. Also, an increasing number of tax payers use electronic tax filing systems. Both paper forms and electronic forms share important characteristics:

1. *Schema diversity*: Given the complexity of US tax laws, there are many distinct types of tax forms. This agency deals with over 3000 distinct forms. Each type of forms has a distinct set of fields and calculation rules.
2. *Sparse data*: Most tax forms contain many fields for optional information. These fields are left blank if they don't apply to a given tax payer.
3. *Schema evolution*: A significant number of tax forms change from one tax year to the next, typically due to changes in tax laws. Fields on a form might get added, removed, or modified.

Challenges: The agency's experience with processing forms has shown that these characteristics make a relational representation difficult. To handle the schema diversity, a normalized relational schema would require one or multiple tables for each form type, leading to thousands of tables. Since the number and types of forms per tax filing can vary widely, it is hard to determine which tables to join to obtain all forms for one filing. Additional lookup tables and application logic would be required. These are costly to maintain over time, especially during schema evolution, which can require existing tables to be further normalized. The high sparsity of the tax data causes 70% to 80% of the cells in such a relational database schema to be NULL.

Alternative relational schemas can be considered, such as name/value pair tables, also called entity-attribute-value model (EAV). In its basic form, an EAV table has three columns (`id`, `name`, `value`) so that field names are not represented as column *names*, but as *values* in the column `name`. This approach has inherent drawbacks:

- It's very hard to define constraints for EAV tables, because the logical meaning of the column `value` changes from row to row. Data quality is hard to enforce.
- Column statistics that usually aid relational optimizers in the selection of good access plans do not always work well for EAV tables.
- Writing business queries against EAV tables is complex and often requires many self-joins. Reporting queries with many predicates were found to be particularly difficult and inefficient.

Novel approaches to overcome these problems in relational databases are being investigated [4], but have not yet found their way into commercial products.

Why XML: Contrary to a relational design, representing tax forms and filings in XML is very natural. First, XML is a good choice for sparse data because optional elements or attributes can be omitted if they don't contain a value in a form instance. Second, a collection of XML documents does not need to follow a single fixed schema. Thus, all tax forms and filings can be stored in a single XML column, despite the inherent schema diversity and schema evolution.

Database Design Considerations: Given that one tax filing consists of multiple tax forms, a key design issue was to choose the most suitable XML document granularity. Intuitive options are (a) to use one XML document per tax *form*, or (b) one document per *filing* with all forms for one filing combined in a single document. To make this decision, one must analyze:

- What are the logical business objects from an application and users' point of view – forms or filings?
- What is the predominant granularity of access for read/write operations?

We found that the logical data unit from a business perspective is one tax filing at a time, and most typically the tax application reads or writes a full filing rather than individual forms. The reason is that individual tax forms cannot be interpreted in a meaningful way without the context of all other forms in the same filing.

Fig. 3 shows the basic DDL for the main table in the tax processing database at this agency. The columns `taxpayer_id` and `filingdate` serve as a primary key and support a frequent access paths, i.e. finding a filing for a given tax payer at a certain time. The `taxpayer_id` column also serves in referential integrity constraints since cross-table constraints cannot be expressed on XML columns. Secondary indexes are defined on select elements in the XML column to support more advanced search patterns. Most queries are SQL/XML statements with relational and/or XML predicates. They typically use XPath and do not require the full power of XQuery.

```
create table filings(
    taxpayer_id INTEGER   NOT NULL,
    filingdate  TIMESTAMP NOT NULL,
    filing      XML,      PRIMARY KEY (taxpayer_id,filingdate))
```

Fig. 3. Table definition for tax filings

Benefits: The table in Fig. 3 is used by a workflow application that validates and processes tax filings based on business rules. The components of this application interact in a service-oriented manner, exchanging tax filings as XML documents. The XML-based database design enables a desirable property that would be missing in a fully relational database schema: *the representation of the logical business objects (tax filings) is the same in the application as in the database.* The agency perceives this as a major benefit because it simplifies application development and significantly reduces the cost of application maintenance during schema evolution. An XML schema change for tax filings does not change the schema of the `filings` table.

The same design principles have enabled the tax agency to rapidly develop other applications, including one that serves and captures online forms on the web. The forms are represented in XFDL (eXtensible Forms Description Language) [21] which supports the XForms standard [22]. Every form captured in the web server is stored as-is in a database table with an XML column, similar to Fig. 3. The ease of this XML-based database design allows new forms applications to be prototyped (and sometimes productized) in weeks or days instead of months or years.

3.2 Order Processing at a Telecommunication Company

Background: This company serves private and business customers in more than 150 countries. It offers over 100 categories of products and services, including data, voice, and IP services, internet access, security solutions, networks, IT hosting, conferencing and call center solutions. The portfolio of products and services is very diverse. Most products and services are customizable, subject to a high degree of *variability* and *complexity*. Due to the fast pace of innovation (*evolution*) in the telecommunication sector, the company frequently enhances existing products and introduces new ones.

Business Objects/Data Characteristics: Orders are business objects that are created by customers or sales personnel through order entry systems. Orders describe the requested product and service options in detail, and directly reflect the diversity, complexity, and evolution of the company's offerings.

Challenges: Mapping the diverse and complex orders to a relational schema is difficult and scatters the details of each order over dozens of tables, for some orders more than 100 tables. Since a normalized relational schema is a very artificial representation of these orders, application code to insert or read them is complicated and error-prone. Such code is also CPU- and network-intensive, requiring many calls to the database to read/write a single order. When products are modified or added, adjusting the database schema and application code is complex and time consuming.

Why XML: The company decided to represent each order as an XML document based on the Open Applications Group Integration Specification (OAGIS) [16]. This format is highly flexible to handle data variability efficiently, and it interconnects various order management applications in a service-oriented fashion.

The OAGIS standard defines a cross-industry XML-based business language that describes business processes, messages, and information integration. It covers common business scenarios such as logistics, supply-chain management, customer relationship management, payments, manufacturing, and order management. OAGIS enables companies to design service-oriented architectures based on standardized but very flexible and extensible models. OAGIS also simplifies business-to-business and application-to-application integration via web services or an enterprise service bus.

OAGIS represents each message and business object as an *XML business object document* (BOD). The design and usage of BODs follow an object-oriented approach. Each BOD consists of a noun (object) and a verb (method) that defines the action that is to be performed on the object. Fig. 4 shows the core structure of a ProcessPurchaseOrder BOD. In this BOD, the noun is `<PurchaseOrder>` and the verb is `<Process>`. The `<ApplicationArea>` contains meta information such as the origin, business event, or timestamp associated with the BOD. The `<DataArea>` holds the actual business information (payload) of the BOD.

While a discussion of the full XML structure of this BOD is beyond the scope of this paper [18][16], note that a single ProcessPurchaseOrder BOD can contain multiple line items (`PurchaseOrderLine/Item` in Fig. 4). Each line item is an XML fragment that describes a product or service that is part of the order. Although a ProcessPurchaseOrder BOD contains a lot of other information in addition to the items, such as status, payment, and contact information, the line items are of key interest to the order fulfillment applications.

```
<ProcessPurchaseOrder>
  <ApplicationArea>...</ApplicationArea>
  <DataArea>
    <Process>...</Process>
    <PurchaseOrder>
      <PurchaseOrderHeader>...</PurchaseOrderHeader>
      <PurchaseOrderLine>
        <Item>...</Item>
      <PurchaseOrderLine>
      <PurchaseOrderLine>
        <Item>...</Item>
      <PurchaseOrderLine>
      (...)
    </PurchaseOrder>
  </DataArea>
</ProcessPurchaseOrder>
```

Fig. 4. Simplified structure of a ProcessPurchaseOrder BOD (namespaces omitted)

The structure of the company's order documents follows the OAGIS standard ProcessPurchaseOrder BODs in Fig. 4, but contains a variety of modifications and extensions. Most order BODs are 15KB to 300KB in size. Occasionally large BODs are up to 10MB with 50 or more line items.

Database Design Considerations: Orders contain a variable number of line items much like the tax filings described in section 3.1 contain a variable number of forms. Again, it was critical to determine the logical business objects from an application point of view (orders or items?), and the predominant granularity of access. We found that some steps in the order management process operate on one order at a time, while others operate on one item at a time. *On aggregate, however, both the number of* *reads and the number of updates of individual items are an order of magnitude larger than the number of reads or writes of a full order.* Therefore, database schema and access methods must make the manipulation of individual items simple and efficient.

Several design options were prototyped and compared. One option was to use a single table with one row per BOD, similar to the tax filing table in Fig. 3. However, given the frequent access to items as individual objects, it was decided to use two tables (Fig. 5). The `order` table contains one row per BOD with key XML values extracted into relational columns, such as `doc_id`, `doc_id_version`, and a few others omitted in Fig. 5. In each row, the XML column `orderbod` contains a BOD in which the item fragments have been removed at insert time. These item fragments are inserted into the `item` table (one per row) and a foreign key relates each item to its order. A few key fields from each item are extracted into relational columns.

```
CREATE TABLE order(oid BIGINT NOT NULL PRIMARY KEY,
                   doc_id VARCHAR(64), doc_id_version INTEGER
                   ,..., orderbod XML);

CREATE TABLE item(oid BIGINT NOT NULL, seq_number INTEGER,
                  item__id VARCHAR(64), item_id_version INTEGER,
                  line_number VARCHAR(32), upc_id VARCHAR(32)
                  ,..., lineitem XML,
                  FOREIGN KEY (oid) REFERENCES order(oid));
```

Fig. 5. Core tables of the order management database

Fig. 7 shows a SQL/XML stored procedure in DB2 that applications call to insert a new BOD into the tables in Fig. 5. The BOD is received as a parameter of type XML and immediately parsed, so that repeated XML parsing in the procedure is avoided. Then the procedure generates a new `orderID` as a primary key. The remainder of the procedure consists of two INSERT statements, one for each target table. Both INSERTs contain a sub-select with an XMLTABLE function [6] that takes the new BOD as input and extracts the required values for the columns of the respective table.

In the first INSERT, the XMLTABLE function also applies an XQuery update expression to the original BOD to delete all line items. The XMLTABLE function in the second INSERT produces one row for each of these items and uses the clause `FOR ORDINALITY` to number them sequentially [6]. The XQuery constructor `document{}` creates a new document node, so that correct item documents are inserted (Fig. 7).

Fig. 7 shows a SELECT statement that reads a *complete* order, inserting the item fragments back into the correct position in the BOD. The variables `$ORDERBOD` and `$OID` implicitly refer to the respective columns in the `order` table.

Benefits: At first sight, this approach of "cutting holes" into the BODs and splitting out the items into separate documents may seem contrary to the idea of storing XML "as-is". But, the granularity of information that should constitute an XML document really depends on the application that processes the information. A single order BOD containing all items is useful for order transmittal and other parts of the business

```
CREATE PROCEDURE INSERT_BOD (IN bod XML)  LANGUAGE SQL
BEGIN
  DECLARE orderID BIGINT;
  SET orderID = NEXTVAL FOR order_id_sequence;
              -- SQL sequence object to generate unique IDs
  INSERT INTO order
    SELECT orderID, T.doc_id, T.doc_id_version,...,T.xmldoc,
    FROM XMLTABLE('$doc' PASSING bod AS "doc"
         COLUMNS
          doc_id            VARCHAR(64)
           PATH '//PurchaseOrderHeader/DocumentID/ID',
          doc_id_version    INTEGER
           PATH '//PurchaseOrderHeader/DocumentID/RevisionID',
          (...)
          xmldoc            XML
           PATH 'copy $new := .
       modify do delete $new//PurchaseOrder/PurchaseOrderLine
                 return $new'    ) AS T;

  INSERT INTO item
   SELECT orderID, T.*   FROM
   XMLTABLE('$doc//DataArea/PurchaseOrder/PurchaseOrderLine'
            PASSING bod AS "doc"
    COLUMNS
     sequence_number FOR ORDINALITY,
     item_id         VARCHAR(64) PATH 'Item/ItemID/ID',
     item_id_version INTEGER     PATH 'Item/ItemID/ RevisionID',
     line_number     VARCHAR(32) PATH 'LineNumber',
     upc_id          VARCHAR(32) PATH 'Item/UPCID',
     (...)
     lineitem        XML         PATH 'document{.}') AS T;
END%
```

Fig. 6. Stored procedure to insert a BOD into the tables in Fig. 5

```
SELECT XMLQUERY('copy $new := $ORDERBOD
              modify do insert
                   db2-fn:sqlquery("SELECT lineitem
                                    FROM item i
                                    WHERE i.oid = parameter(1)
                                   ORDER BY seq_number", $OID)
              after $new$doc//PurchaseOrder/PurchaseOrderHeader'
              return $new')
FROM order WHERE...;
```

Fig. 7. SQL/XML statement to reconstruct original BODs

process. However, order fulfillment applications that frequently read and update individual items prefer to treat items as individual objects and individual documents.

This 2-table design does not enable any more operations than a 1-table design that stores the complete BOD as a single intact XML document. But, it allows many operations to be *simpler* and/or more *efficient*, for the following reasons:

- Reading and replacing an item based on its `item_id` are two of the most frequent operations and can often be expressed without any XPath:

```
SELECT * FROM item WHERE oid = ? and item_id = ?
UPDATE item SET lineitem = ? WHERE oid = ? and item_id = ?
```

  Corporate database application developers with a strong relational background but little experience with SQL/XML, perceive this simplicity as a significant benefit, which is critical for the adoption of new XML database technology. (While some of the order management applications use the XQuery Update Facility in the SET clause of the UPDATE, others simply replace the full item, as in this example.)
- Currently, an XML update in DB2 locks the entire row and document. The smaller granularity of the item documents implies that less data is locked and allows for greater concurrency, esp. when multiple items of the same order are processed.
- Out of approximately 200,000 possible paths in the BOD schema, less than 20 are replicated into relational columns, leading to a hybrid XML/relational database schema. The relational columns hold data that is known to be read-only and frequently queried or aggregated across orders or items. These columns can be:
  - o easily accessed by third-party software that is not fully XML-aware.
  - o referenced in foreign key constraints to other relational tables in the database.
  - o used to define a table with hash partitioning, range partitioning, or multi-dimensional clustering, which cannot be defined based on XML columns.

The hybrid design is not meant to avoid the use of XPath or XQuery as much as possible. With 200,000 possible paths in the data, XPath embedded in SQL is a critical part of the solution to deal with the variability and complexity of the BODs. Keeping the majority of the data in XML columns allows the application to evolve and new products to be introduced without impacting the database schema.

3.3 Event Logging at a Financial Services Company

Background: The internet banking system at a European banking group logs every event in any of their web applications. Events include clicks that take a user to a new web page or dialog, entry of user data, as well as clicks that initiate banking transactions. The event logging happens across a set of diverse applications such as checking accounts, loan applications, investment banking, and others. The event logging at this bank supports troubleshooting and technical problem resolution as well as auditing and compliance regulations for certain applications.

Business Objects/Data Characteristics: Events are represented as small XML documents (2kb to 15kb) because the information captured varies widely from one event to the next. The large number of event types and the diversity of the banking applications lead to thousands of possible attributes that can occur in an event. However, each *instance* of an event only carries a few dozen attributes.

Challenges/Why XML: The body of each event is variable and application-dependent, and cannot be mapped easily to a relational schema. Different applications require autonomy and flexibility in deciding what information to include in the event records. Application developers must be able to change and extend existing applications or introduce new applications at any time without causing schema changes in the event logging infrastructure or database. The event logging workload is very insert intensive. There are 10M to 20M inserts in a 24-hour day, with peak insert rates of 1000 events per second. There is no offline maintenance window for this system since the internet applications run 24x7.

Database Design Considerations: Each event contains a fixed set of header fields, such as user ID, application ID, session ID, date, and timestamp. These exist for every event and are stored in fixed relational columns. Event bodies are stored in an XML column. Insert performance is given priority over query performance to ensure that writing the events does not impact the performance or progress of the web applications. Query rates are significantly lower than the insert rates. While some queries simply search on the header fields, others include unpredictable XML predicates on the event body. Due to the variability of events, more than 100 XML indexes are defined, mostly on optional elements. Many of the indexes are very small because XML indexes in DB2 contain index entries only for those documents that contain the indexed path. Hence, only a subset of the indexes needs to be maintained per insert, which is critical to sustain high rates of concurrent XML inserts.

Benefits: XML columns allow variable data to be captured at very high rates. More than 10,000 XML inserts per second are possible on a mid-size database server [13].

Event logging is a very common XML database scenario that we have also seen at other financial companies in various flavors. For example, an insurance company in the UK exchanges XML messages via web services with external business partners such as insurance brokers. The messages follow the Origo standard [17] and contain insurance quote requests, quote responses, insurance applications, and so on. Each XML message constitutes a business event, and is validated against the Origo schema and stored intact in DB2 to meet compliance and legal requirements. This database serves not only as an audit log but also uses SQL/XML to extract and convert a subset of the XML elements to relational rows to feed legacy applications at the firm.

A North American investment bank captures the details of each derivative trade in a separate XML document in FpML format [7]. FpML 5.0 consists of 76 XML schema documents and defines more than 7000 elements and attributes, most of them optional. The data complexity was found to preclude a reasonable relational representation. Each trade is a business event and stored in an XML column in DB2. When a trade is modified, a new version of its XML document is inserted. The database acts as an audit log and uses SQL/XML to extract data for down-stream applications such as risk management, compliance management, and business reporting.

3.4 Summary of the Three Case Studies

The applications discussed in sections 3.1-3.3 have several characteristics in common:

- Each XML document represents a single business object: one document per tax filing, one document per order and item, and one document per event.
- Data sparsity is prevalent: blank fields in tax forms, product options that are not chosen, and optional event properties.
- Schema diversity/variability is a key reason for using XML: many different tax forms, many complex products, many different events/no fixed schema per event.

- Schema evolution is another reason for using XML: evolving tax laws and forms, innovation of communication products, and autonomy to change or add events.
- XML is chosen over a fully relational solution to simplify database design and application code, and to reduce the cost of system maintenance over time.
- Although each application could have chosen an XML-only design, a hybrid XML/relational solution was used to integrate well with existing relational data, and to achieve a good mix of simplicity, performance, flexibility, and skill match.
- Except for the Origo application, document validation with XML Schemas already happens in the middle tier to detect errors early and is not repeated in DB2.

4 Findings and Lessons Learned

The XML applications in section 3 are examples from a larger range of companies that we assisted in their design and implementation of XML applications on DB2. Our work with these companies allows us to note several findings. We are aware that each of our findings has exceptions. Despite the variety of companies that we worked with, we do not claim to have done a representative survey of all XML database use cases. Our findings apply predominantly to data-oriented enterprise business applications.

1. **Most XML applications use many small XML documents.** We have not seen any applications that keep all data in a single large XML document. Also, applications with millions or billions of small documents (<100kb) are much more common than applications with very few large documents (>10MB per document). When we have encountered large documents, we often found that they are an artificial concatenation of independent business objects, e.g. to simplify downloads or ftp transfer. Exceptions include certain content-centric and bio-medical applications that can have genuinely large documents. Yet, even for them the size of a single document is small compared to the total volume of all documents managed in a single collection [8].
2. **XML volumes grow in the number rather than in the size of the documents.** Although some applications add elements to existing documents, the predominant growth stems from increasing numbers of documents. Findings 1 and 2 stand in contrast to the popular use of a single large XML document (typically XMark [3]) for evaluating XML research prototypes [2]. Benchmarks such as XMach, XBench, and TPoX use large collections of small documents, trying to resemble real-world XML applications [3].
3. **XML document structures are often non-negotiable.** Many applications cannot design their own XML document structure but are forced to consume a given XML format. Commonly, an XML format is predefined by an enterprise-wide or even industry-wide standard (such as OAGIS, FpML, and Origo mentioned in section 3) or by the fact that an existing XML producer cannot be changed.
4. **XML-only environments tend to be rare.** Most enterprises that manage large amounts of XML also manage large amounts of data in relational format or in legacy hierarchical and network databases (IMS, IDMS, Adabas). Since there is often some business relationship between XML and other enterprise data, many application scenarios eventually need to query or combine both types of data. As an example, the

tax agency described in section 3.1 stores tax filings in XML, but the related account and payment information are a perfect fit for, and will remain in, relational tables.

5. **Tight integration of XML and relational data management is valuable.** This finding follows from the previous one. Although XML-only databases can be suitable for certain use-cases, their use should avoid the creation of "information silos" within an enterprise and not require costly data integration projects.

6. **SQL/XML has broader adoption than XQuery without SQL.** This finding may seem natural, given that DB2 is a hybrid XML/relational DBMS. But, the preference for SQL/XML is rooted much deeper than that. First there is the aforementioned need to integrate XML with existing relational investments. Another reason is that many companies require a gradual adoption of new technology rather than a radical switch (evolution, not revolution). Gradual adoption reduces risk and eases the integration into an enterprise IT landscape. For example, many mature tools that surround today's databases still have limited XML or XQuery capabilities, e.g. ETL, data mining, or business reporting tools. Furthermore, today's database administrators and database application developers typically have a strong relational background. They often perceive XQuery as difficult to learn, partially due to the differences between the XML data model and the relational model. Adding XML columns to a familiar relational database environment, and adding XPath to the familiar concepts of SQL statements and SQL stored procedures, *significantly* eases XML adoption for many database professionals. As mentioned in section 3.2, this can be critical for success.

7. **Hybrid XML/relational database schemas are common.** This follows from the previous finding. A hybrid approach allows applications to get "the best of both worlds" to meet their requirements for data integration, usability, performance, flexibility, and ease of application development. Examples include the hybrid schemas for order management and event logging in sections 3.2 and 3.3.

8. **Choosing the "right" document granularity is important.** As shown in section 3, a suitable document granularity can simplify application development, increase concurrency, and improve performance. Where possible, documents should match the logical business objects of the application and the predominant granularity of access.

9. **XML is effective to achieve denormalization without redundancy.** Normalized relational tables can require applications to issue complex joins or dozens of separate SQL queries to retrieve all data fields for one logical business object. Relational denormalization is often inadequate to mitigate this problem because it introduces redundancy. In contrast, the tree structure of XML represents 1-to-many relationships without redundancy, because a parent node is not repeated for each of its child nodes. Thus, XML can represent business objects in a single denormalized document without incurring the redundancy. This allows business objects to be inserted and retrieved in a *single* statement and without joins. This reduces the number of database API calls, application complexity, CPU cost, and network traffic. This is true for all scenarios in section 3, and a significant benefit over a normalized relational representation.

10. **Moving XML processing from the application to the database is valuable.** Many applications still use custom code to perform XML manipulation, such as extracting elements from stored documents, splitting documents into smaller fragments, or converting XML to relational format. A database with parsed XML storage can perform these tasks without extra XML parsing. Hence, pushing these operations to SQL/XML or XQuery in the database reduces CPU and memory

consumption and number of required database calls. It also simplifies application code and reduces the cost of maintaining applications over time. The order application in section 3.2 previously performed element extraction with an XML parser in Java, and realized significant performance gains from moving this to SQL/XML in DB2.

5 Conclusion and Future Work

In this paper we discussed real-world XML database applications, their motivation for storing XML, their requirements and access patterns, and some of their database design considerations. From these and other DB2 XML applications we derived a set of findings. We see that schema variability and complexity are some of the key drivers for XML database adoption. The majority of XML applications in a business setting such as banking, insurance, retail, health care, or manufacturing manage large numbers of small XML documents and often need to combine XML and relational data. SQL/XML and hybrid database schemas are gaining increasing popularity among corporate database professionals to integrate XML and relational data.

The *design of hybrid XML/relational database schemas* is a manual process that requires good knowledge of the business data and typical access patterns. A well-defined and generalized design methodology is lacking. In contrast, the design of relational database schemas is well understood and supported by tools and algorithms, such as normalization. These relational methods cannot be immediately applied to the design of hybrid schemas. The reason is that XML is inherently denormalized and adds more hierarchical structures, sparsely populated objects, and variability to the relational world. More work in the spirit of [11] is required to develop design methods for hybrid database schemas, and to verify them through experimental studies.

As companies accumulate increasing amounts of XML, there is a growing demand for *business reporting, OLAP, and data mining over XML*. Most commercial software in this space has only limited XML capabilities or requires XML to be mapped to relational structures. However, due to the complexity and variability that is inherent in many real-world XML formats [7][16][17], only a fraction of the XML elements and attributes can be reasonably mapped. More work such as [20] is needed to develop methods and prototypes for XML reporting, analytics, and data mining.

More effort is also required to improve the *usability of XML, XQuery, and SQL/XML* for database application developers. One problem is a lack of easy to understand meta data that describes persisted XML documents, especially when an XML Schema is very complex or absent. We continue our work in [14] which creates a mapping from logical data items to the corresponding XPaths, and translates SQL over logical data items into SQL/XML statements. Another problem is the integration of XML and XML query languages in widespread relational mapping frameworks such as Hibernate and iBatis. Many users need solutions that augment existing applications with XML rather new XML-only solutions.

The *SQL/XML standard is currently lacking referential integrity constraints across XML columns and across XML and relational columns*. Defining the semantics of such constraints is not trivial, given that XML can be schema-less and nodes referenced in such constraints can be optional, repeating, or variable in their data type. This is another important area for future work.

References

1. Abdel Kader, R., van Keulen, M.: Overview of query optimization in XML database systems, Technical Report TR-CTIT-07-39, University of Twente, Enschede
2. Afanasiev, L., Marx, M.: An analysis of XQuery benchmarks. Inf. Syst. 33(2) (2008)
3. Barbosa, D., et al.: XML Benchmarks. In: Encyclopedia of Database Systems (2009)
4. Beckmann, J., et al.: Extending RDBMSs To Support Sparse Datasets Using An Interpreted Attribute Storage Format. In: ICDE 2006 (2006)
5. Beyer, K., et al.: System RX: One Part Relational, One Part XML. In: SIGMOD 2005 (2005)
6. Eisenberg, A., Melton, J.: Advancements in SQL/XML. SIGMOD Record 33(2) (2004)
7. FpML (Financial Products Markup Language), http://www.fpml.org/
8. Holstege, M.: Big, Fast, XQuery: Enabling Content Applications. IEEE Data Engineering Bulletin 31(4) (2008), http://sites.computer.org/debull/A08dec/marklogic.pdf
9. IBM, DB2 pureXML Case Studies, http://www.ibm.com/developerworks/wikis/display/db2xml/DB2+pureXML+Case+Studies
10. Lucene, http://lucene.apache.org/
11. Moro, M., et al.: Schema advisor for hybrid relational-XML DBMS. In: SIGMOD 2007 (2007)
12. Murthy, R., et al.: Towards an enterprise XML architecture. In: SIGMOD 2005 (2005)
13. Nicola, M., Gonzalez, A.: Taming a Terabyte of XML Data. IBM Data Management Magazine 14(1) (2009)
14. Nicola, M., Kiefer, T.: Generating SQL/XML Query and Update Statements. In: 18th Intl. Conference on Information and Knowledge Management, CIKM 2009 (2009)
15. Nicola, M., Kumar-Chatterjee, P.: DB2 pureXML Cookbook. IBM Press Books (2009) ISBN 0138150478
16. Open Applications Group Integration Specification (OAGIS), http://www.oagi.org/
17. Origo Standard, http://www.origoservices.com/
18. Rowell, M.: The Open Applications Group Integration Specification. Developer Works (2003), http://www.ibm.com/developerworks/xml/library/x-oagis/
19. Rys, M.: XML and Relational Database Management Systems: Inside Microsoft SQL Server. In: SIGMOD 2005 (2005)
20. Wiwatwattana, N., et al.: X^3: A Cube Operator for XML OLAP. In: ICDE 2007 (2007)
21. XFDL (eXtensible Forms Description Language), http://www.w3.org/TR/NOTE-XFDL
22. XForms 1.1, http://www.w3.org/TR/2009/REC-xforms-20091020/
23. XQuery Update Facility, http://www.w3.org/TR/2006/WD-xqupdate-20060711/
24. XQuery 1.0 and XPath 2.0 Data Model (XDM), http://www.w3.org/TR/xpath-datamodel/

Searchable Compression of Office Documents by XML Schema Subtraction

Stefan Böttcher, Rita Hartel, and Christian Messinger

University of Paderborn, Computer Science, Fürstenallee 11, 33102 Paderborn, Germany
stb@uni-paderborn.de, rst@uni-paderborn.de,
michri@uni-paderborn.de

Abstract. Starting with Microsoft Office 2007, the Office Open XML file formats have become the default file format of Microsoft Office. As each day a lot of office documents have to be stored and transferred, reducing the document size will yield a benefit when storing and transferring these files. We present a compressed format for XML-based office documents that omits that data from an office document that is already defined by the Office Open XML format. Our evaluation shows that our compressed format reduces the – already compressed – office documents to a data size down to 41% of the original document size. Furthermore, for search operations tested in our evaluation, searching is faster on our compressed office documents than it is on the original documents.

Keywords: XML compression, Microsoft Office document compression, efficient search on compressed Open Office XML documents.

1 Introduction

1.1 Motivation

With Office 2007, Microsoft introduced a new storage format called Office Open XML (ISO/IEC 29500, ECMA-376), also called OOXML, for its office products Word, PowerPoint and Excel. The OOXML format stores the office document in form of a zipped (i.e., already compressed) archive that contains several XML files plus some additional media files (e.g. pictures embedded in the document).

Although OOXML files are already compressed and yield documents sizes that are significantly smaller than those of comparable documents produced by prior office versions, single documents can still reach sizes of several Megabytes and many companies store and exchange huge numbers of these documents. Whenever storing these documents, exchanging these documents, or full text search in these documents is a bottleneck, we consider a stronger and still searchable compression for the OOXML data format to be a significant advantage.

1.2 Contributions

We present an approach to compressing the XML structure of Office 2007 documents into a data format that is significantly smaller than the document size of Microsoft's

M.L. Lee et al. (Eds.): XSym 2010, LNCS 6309, pp. 103–112, 2010.

compressed documents stored in OOXML data format. Furthermore, our compressed data format allows performing a fast full text search on the compressed documents.

Our compression approach is based on a technique called XML Schema subtraction (XSDS), which removes data from an MS office document that is defined by the MS Office XML Schema. Thus, using XSDS-compressed Office documents instead of original Office documents allows on the one hand saving storage costs and energy costs while archiving the documents and on the other hand reducing the amount of data to be processed while searching for certain content.

1.3 Paper Organization

The remainder of this paper is organized as follows. Section 2 describes how XSDS can be used for removing schema information from an OOXML document. Section 3 gives an overview of how full text search can be executed directly on the compressed data, i.e., without prior total decompression. Section 4 evaluates the compression ratio of XSDS and the search on XSDS compressed MS Office documents. Section 5 compares XSDS to related work. Finally, Section 6 summarizes our contributions.

2 The Concept

2.1 Office Open XML Format

Office Open XML documents are stored as ZIP files containing XML and other data files (e.g. embedded figures), along with a specification of the relationships between them. Depending on the type of the document, the packages have different internal directory structures and names.

Each of the formats (docx, pptx and xlsx) contains a single (docx) or several XML files containing the textual content of the office document.

The internal format of the XML files is specified by ISO/IEC 29500 and ECMA-376, which specify a set of XML schemata that define the data formats.

Some parts of each Office XML file are strictly determined by the Office Open XML standard, e.g., that each Word document starts with the tag <document>. Other parts are variable and vary from document to document (e.g. whether or not a paragraph (<p>) contains paragraphProperties (<pPr>)).

2.2 The Basic Idea

OOXML compression by XML schema subtraction (XSDS) relies on the following main ideas. XSDS stores only those parts of the XML document that can vary according to the XML Schema in the compressed format and omits all information that is strictly defined by the XML schema information. A similar idea is followed by the approaches XCQ [19] and DTD subtraction [4] both of which generate a compressed document by deleting information provided by a DTD from a given XML document. However, in contrast to these approaches, XSDS considers arbitrary XML schemas, which is significantly more complex than just considering DTDs. This paper reports about XSDS, but focuses on the advantages of applying XSDS to XML-based office documents as an application standard which is significant for office users.

In our compressed format all XML documents contained in the MS Office file are compressed via XSDS. The remaining files contained in the MS Office file (e.g. media files) remain compressed via gzip.

2.3 This Paper's Example

As the whole Office Open XML standard is too huge to be discussed within this paper, we only have a detailed look on a small excerpt of OOXML documents

Figure 1(a) shows an example of a paragraph containing the text "Hello World!".

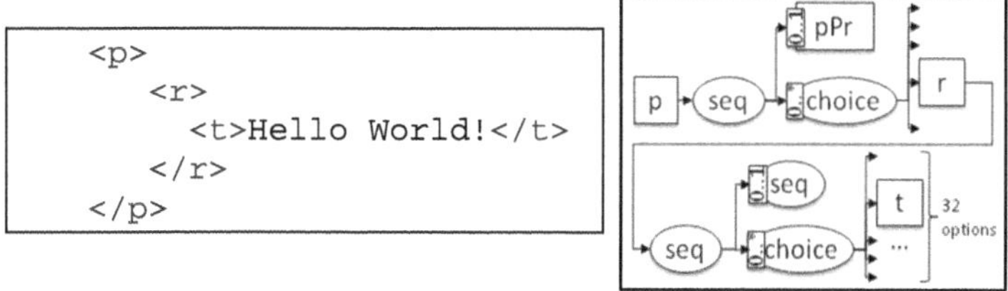

Fig. 1. (a) docx-representation of a paragraph (b) Excerpt of the Office Open XML Schema

Each paragraph contains a sequence of 0 or 1 paragraph properties (<pPr>) followed by a choice of 5 options, the fourth of which is the element <r> that defines a text run (each paragraph is split into any number of text runs, where a text run may even end inside a word). Each text run consists of 0 or 1 sequences of other elements followed by a sequence of any number (0..*) of choices of 32 options. The second option is the element <t> representing a text and containing the string data.

Figure 1(b) shows a visualization of the paragraph element <p> and its definition.

2.4 Removing Schema Information from the Document Structure in XSDS

For each sub-tree of the XML document, there exists a set of rules within the XSD that specify the structure of the XML sub-tree. Some of these specification rules are strict, i.e. the sub-tree corresponding to these XSD specification rules is uniquely predefined by the XSD. Other specification rules allow for different sub-trees. Altogether, XML schema definitions contain three operators that allow for variant parts within the XML document specified by the given schema: First, the XSD operator 'choice' requires choosing one out of a set of given options. Second, the XSD operator 'all' requires that all elements declared by children of the 'all' element appear once but in any order within the XML document. Third, XSD operators (like minOccurs and maxOccurs) requiring a repetition of elements usually allow for a varying number of elements (including the sub-trees beneath these elements).

The compression of the non-variant parts of an XML document, i.e. of the nodes that are fixed by the XSD for the current position in the XML document, is simple. We can omit these nodes from our compressed format, as these nodes can be reconstructed for the given position from the XSD.

The compression of the variant parts within an XML document works as follows. During each compression step, we consider one element of the XML document and the XSD rule that defines the content of this element and that allows for variant parts. For each content of an element in the XML document for which the XSD allows a choice, we only store the option chosen at the current position. This requires log(n) bits, if there are n different options. For each element in the document the content of which is specified with the help of the XSD operator 'all', we only encode the order of those elements occurring in the XML document, the XSD type definitions of which are children of the 'all' element in the XSD. This requires less than n*log(n) bits, if there are n elements within the scope of the 'all' operator. Finally, for each element in the document the content of which is specified with the help of a repetition of elements in the XML schema, we only store the number of occurrences found in the XML document. (We calculated a frequency distribution on the values encoded for repetition operators for a set of test documents and computed a Huffman encoder based on that distribution for the values 0..24. All other numbers are stored by a dynamic integer encoding).

When applying the compression by removing schema information given from the Office Open XML excerpt shown in Figure 1(b) we compress the variant parts of the XML structure of the docx-fragment shown in Figure 1(a) to the bit sequence

0 10 011 0 10 00001

This bit sequence contains: first, a single bit '0' stating that there is no <pPr>-element, then, the integer value '1' (Huffman-encoded as '10') stating that there is one occurrence of the 'choice' sub-tree, next, the bits '011' stating that we have chosen the 4th of 5 options of the 'choice' element, then, a single bit '0' stating that there is no sequence 'seq', then, the integer value '1' (Huffman-encoded as '10') which states that there is one occurrence of the 'choice' sub-tree, finally, the bit sequence '00001' stating that we have chosen the 2nd of 32 options of the choice element.

The remaining parts of an XML fragment for this Office Open XML excerpt are fixed by the Office Open XML standard, i.e., they need not to be stored in the compressed format. This includes all element names found in the XML fragment.

Therefore, we need 10 bits and 2 integers to store the structure of the docx-fragment given in Figure 1(a), or 14 bits if we Huffman-encode the 2 integers based on our frequency distribution. In contrast, the structure of the docx-fragment consists of 21 characters to be stored.

2.5 Compressing the Textual Data

Besides the XML structure, an office document contains textual data. While the schema of Open Office XML documents strictly defines large parts of the structure of a given document, it provides less information on the textual data. Nevertheless, we follow an approach presented by XMill [16] that groups together textual data that is included by the same parent elements. For these purposes, for each parent element of textual data, a single container is provided that stores the textual data in document order. Storing the textual data in different containers provides two advantages:

When performing a full text search on office documents, not the whole XML document, but only that container that contains the textual data has to be searched.

As each container stores data of the same domain (e.g., textual data, distinct values for certain properties), calculating a compressed representation of each container separately from the other containers yields a stronger compression ratio than compressing all the textual data of one document together.

XSDS mainly distinguishes three different types of textual data: String data, Integer data and data enumerations that only allow selecting a value out of a given enumeration of possible values. In our implementation, we compress each container that contains String data via the generic text compressor gzip or via the text compressor bzip2. Dependent on the application requirements, any other generic text compressor could be used (e.g. a searchable text compressor, if an even more efficient search is needed). We store each entry of an Integer container via a variable-length Integer encoding storing 1-5 bytes per Integer value depending on the concrete value.

Finally, we store each value within an enumeration container analogously to a choice within the structure: If an enumeration container allows n different values, we store the position of the current value within the n alternatives. Each value is represented by an encoding with size log(n) bits.

3 Searching

In contrast to other compressors like gzip, bzip2, or XMill [16] that are mainly used for archiving, XSDS allows searching the compressed data, i.e., without prior decompression. A task often to be done on Word documents (docx) is a full text search that returns from a collection of documents those documents that contain a given String (e.g. all documents containing the String “Scott”).

Whereas for docx files, performing a full text search means to unzip the XML file containing the document content and parsing that file in order to identify those tags representing the textual content, XSDS compressed data provides a small, simple index to the textual data itself. As the constant data of the XML document is stored into several different compressed containers, only that container that contains the textual content of the office document has to be unzipped and searched, i.e., the amount of data to be unzipped is significantly smaller than when searching in the original docx file. Furthermore, in our approach, exact search for string constant in the text represented by the original docx file only requires a simple string search in a string container. In comparison, exact search for string constants in the text represented by the original docx file requires to navigate through and search in the original docx file XML documents which is significantly less efficient.

4 Evaluation

4.1 Compression Ratio

In order to evaluate our office storage format, we assorted an office data collection containing books from the project Gutenberg (plus the bible) in Word format, OECD statistics in Excel format and PowerPoint presentations collected randomly via Google.

Figure 2 shows the results of our evaluation. Although the Microsoft Office format is already compressed via gzip, our format yields even smaller documents. The size of our compressed data is given in percent of the size of the Microsoft's compressed data format (i.e., docx, xlsx or pptx).

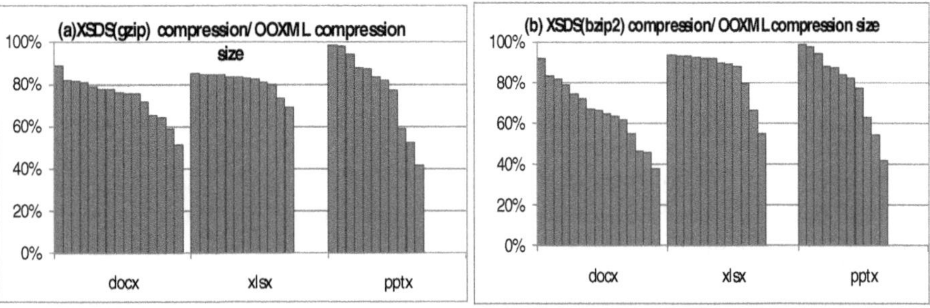

Fig. 2. Evaluation of our compressed data format for (a) gzip-based XSDS and (b) bzip2-based XSDS in comparison to Microsoft's Office format

The Word documents – the sizes of which vary from 26kB to 1951kB – are compressed to ratios of 89% to 51% of the docx file size (avg: 74%) using gzip as constant compressor or to ratios of 92% to 38% of the docx file size (avg: 66%) using bzip2. Furthermore, the Excel documents – the sizes of which vary from 15kB to 152kB – are compressed to ratios of 85% to 69% of the xlsx file size (avg: 81%) using gzip as constant compressor or to ratios of 94% to 55% of the xlsx file size (avg: 85%) using bzip2. The PowerPoint documents – the sizes of which vary from 56 kB to 6.1MB – are compressed to ratios of 99% to 41% of the pptx file size (avg: 78%) using gzip as constant compressor or to ratios of 99% to 42% of the pptx file size (avg: 79%) using bzip2.

Many operations on the documents do not require a complete decompression, as they can be performed as navigation or update operations on the compressed data directly. But whenever a document needs to be decompressed, this can be performed in decent time. E.g. it takes 1.3 seconds to decompress a word document with more than 200 pages and less than 20 seconds to decompress the bible with 1186 pages.

How strong an office document can be compressed by using XSDS mainly depends on the format of the office document – independent of whether it is a Word, an Excel, or a PowerPoint document. The less external media files (as e.g. pictures) a document contains, the better the document is compressed. This is caused by the fact that XSDS only compresses the parts stored in form of an XML document whereas the 'external' parts are compressed via gzip (similar as in the original office format).

4.2 Search Time

In order to test the full text search performance, we have searched the docx-files of our test data for whether or not they contain the non-existing String "xyz".

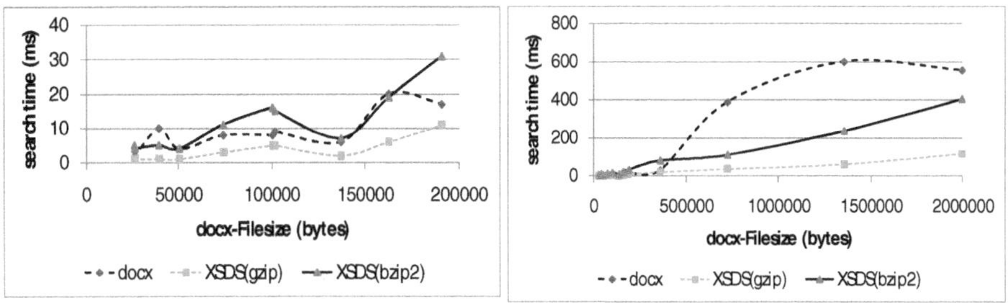

Fig. 3. Search on (compressed) office documents for documents up to (a) 200kB and (b) 2MB

When searching the XSDS-compressed office documents, we can directly navigate to the container containing the textual data – that is compressed either via gzip of via bzip – and search with the help of the Knuth-Morris-Pratt algorithm for the given String. Our text search is exact, i.e. it finds also text constants in a docx-file that are split into different text runs that are separated by XML tags.

To simulate the search on the original document, we opened the zip entry word/document.xml of each Word document via a zip-capable input stream and searched the XML file with the help of the Knuth-Morris-Pratt algorithm for the given String. This simulation is just a lower bound for the real text search in the docx document for the following reason. In order to perform an exact search, a simple String search is not suitable but would have to be replaced by XML parsing and navigation, which takes more time than just String search that has been used in this evaluation. This simulation leads to both, to false positives (as the searched string could be found in the structure of the XML file or in other text-data of the XML file) and to false negatives (as the searched string could be split into different text runs and therefore would not be contained as a consecutive String within the XML file).

Although the simulation of full text search on the original compressed docx document is tuned for speed by ignoring text that is split into different runs thereby being less exact than our XSDS full text search, our XSDS full text search is more time efficient. In Figure 3(a), the search times are shown for small documents up to 200 kB. Gzip-based XSDS (XSDS(gzip)) always performs best, whereas bzip2-based XSDS (XSDS(bzip2) performs similar to original fulltext search (docx) – the difference (XSDS(bzip2) – docx) ranges between -5 and 14 ms. Figure 3(b) shows the search times for larger documents up to 2MB. As full text search on XSDS-compressed documents appears to scale better than original full text search, for large documents, XSDS(gzip) performs best yielding a speed up factor of up to 10.5 in comparison to docx followed by XSDS(bzip2) yielding a speed up factor of up to 3.5 in comparison to docx. For example, the whole bible (1186 pages) compressed by XSDS(gzip) can be searched in 116 ms, whereas it can be searched in 405 ms if it is compressed by XSDS(bzip). However, the simulated search of the original docx file takes 555 ms.

5 Related Work

As the OOXML format already contains a gzip compression, the most obvious step to reduce the size of the documents is to exchange the compression technique.

As the mayor part of the content of the OOXML zip archive are XML files, compressing them with a special, XML conscious compressor appears to be evident.

There exist several approaches to XML structure compression, which can be mainly divided into three categories: grammar-based compressors, encoding-based compressors, and schema-based compressors. Similar as for text compressors, some XML compressors do not generate compressed data that supports evaluating queries or full text search, i.e., query processing on the compressed data needs prior decompression.

Grammar-based compressors share repeated occurrences of identical or similar sub-trees. Examples for grammar-based compressors are [6], [1], XQzip [9] and BPLEX [7]. These approaches allow querying compressed data.

The encoding-based compressors encode the XML elements in a shorter way. They allow for a faster compression speed than the other compressors, as only local data has to be considered in the compression as opposed to considering different sub-trees as e.g. in grammar-based compressors. Examples for encoding based compressors are [13], XMill [16], [8], XGrind [21], XPRESS [18], [3], [25], and XQueC [2]. As XMill does not preserve the XML structure while compressing, XMill compressed data cannot be queried without prior total decompression, whereas all the other encoding-based approaches allow query evaluation on the compressed data directly.

Schema-based compressors subtract the given schema information from the structural information of an XML document. Instead of a complete XML structure stream or tree, they only generate and output information not already contained in the schema information. Schema-based compression includes approaches as XCQ [19], XAUST [20], Xenia [23] and DTD subtraction [4], which all are queryable.

XSDS follows the same basic idea to delete information which is redundant because of a given schema. In contrast to XCQ, XAUST and DTD subtraction that can only remove schema information if it is given by a DTD, XSDS works on XML schema. Therefore, XSDS is significantly more complex than DTDs, as it allows e.g. for extending and restricting types, defining enumerations and the 'all'-operator. Furthermore, XSDS uses a counting schema for repetitions that compresses stronger than e.g. the compression techniques used in XCQ or Xenia. Furthermore, XSDS is not restricted to compressing OOXML, as it has been used e.g. for SEPA too [5].

For generic, lossless text compression there exist several approaches that differ in reached compression ratio and in the ability to be searched without total decompression. Lossless text compressors can be mainly divided into the following categories.

Entropy coders, e.g. Huffman [15], Golomb [14], Range coding [17], Arithmetic coding [24] and Fibonacci [12], try to assign a minimum number of bits per byte of the original text. Huffman, Golomb, Range coding and Arithmetic coding are not searchable, as reading them requires parsing of the compressed data from the beginning, but Fibonacci allows for accessing any letter of the compressed data directly.

Dictionary coders, e.g. LZ77 [26], LZ78 [27], and LZW [22], search for repeated occurrences of subtexts in the text and substitute them with a reference to the dictionary of already read subtexts. As the dictionary is rebuilt during the decoding process, these coders require total decompression when searching for a given subtext.

Statistical compressors are based on context models and prediction. Examples for statistical compressors are PPM [10] and DMC [11]. These compressors require total decompression when searching for a given subtext.

In comparison to all other approaches, XSDS is the only approach that combines the following advantageous properties: XSDS removes XML data nodes that are fixed by the given XML schema, it encodes choices, repetitions, and 'all'-groups in an efficient manner, and it allows for efficient query processing on the compressed XML data.

To the best of our knowledge, no other XML compression technique combines such a compression performance for Office Open XML documents with such search speed on compressed data.

6 Conclusions

We have presented a compression technique for Microsoft Office documents which is based on XSDS (XML schema subtraction) – an XML compressor that generates a strongly compressed data format that is at the same time efficiently searchable.

Our compressed data format stores only those parts of the XML structure of the internal representation of a Microsoft Office document that are variant according to the given schema information, and it omits all data that is strictly defined by the given schema information. Thereby, our compressed data format provides two major advantages: First, the strongly compressed document representation produced by XSDS may save costs and energy by saving main memory required to process data, by saving secondary storage needed to archive compressed XML data, and by saving bandwidth for data transfer. Second, XSDS supports a fast full text search on the compressed document without prior total decompression.

This is supported by our experiments which demonstrate that XSDS compresses the already compressed Microsoft Office documents to a size of down to 41% of the original document size. Furthermore, full text search directly on the compressed Microsoft Office documents is not only possible, but in our experiments, full text search performs even faster on our XSDS compressed Microsoft Office formats than on the original docx documents. Therefore, we consider our XSDS-based compression technique for Microsoft Office documents to be highly beneficial in all Microsoft Office applications for which the data volume or the search time is a bottleneck.

Finally, our approach is not restricted to OOXML documents [5], but can be applied to compress all XML data that obeys a given XML schema.

References

1. Adiego, J., Navarro, G., de la Fuente, P.: Lempel-Ziv Compression of Structured Text. In: Data Compression Conference (2004)
2. Arion, Bonifati, A., Manolescu, I., Pugliese, A.: XQueC: A Query-Conscious Compressed XML Database. ACM Transactions on Internet Technology (2007)
3. Bayardo, R.J., Gruhl, D., Josifovski, V., Myllymaki, J.: An evaluation of binary xml encoding optimizations for fast stream based XML processing. In: Proc. of the 13th International Conference on World Wide Web (2004)
4. Böttcher, S., Steinmetz, R., Klein, N.: XML Index Compression by DTD Subtraction. In: 9th International Conference on Enterprise Information Systems, ICEIS (2007)

5. Böttcher, S., Hartel, R., Messinger, C.: SEPA. Queryable SEPA Message Compression by XML Schema Subtraction. In: 12th International Conference on Enterprise Information Systems, ICEIS (2010)
6. Buneman, P., Grohe, M., Koch, C.: Path Queries on Compressed XML. In: VLDB (2003)
7. Busatto, G., Lohrey, M., Maneth, S.: Efficient Memory Representation of XML Dokuments. In: Bierman, G., Koch, C. (eds.) DBPL 2005. LNCS, vol. 3774, pp. 199–216. Springer, Heidelberg (2005)
8. Cheney, J.: Compressing XML with multiplexed hierarchical models. In: Proceedings of the 2001 IEEE Data Compression Conference, DCC 2001 (2001)
9. Cheng, J., Ng, W.: XQzip, Querying Compressed XML Using Structural Indexing. In: Bertino, E., Christodoulakis, S., Plexousakis, D., Christophides, V., Koubarakis, M., Böhm, K., Ferrari, E. (eds.) EDBT 2004. LNCS, vol. 2992, pp. 219–236. Springer, Heidelberg (2004)
10. Cleary, J., Witten, I.: Data compression using adaptive coding and partial string matching. IEEE Transactions on Communications 32(4), 396–402 (1984)
11. Cormack, G., Horspool, N.: Data compression using adaptive coding and partial string matching. Computer Journal 30(6) (1987)
12. Fraenkel, A., Klein, S.: Robust universal complete codes for transmission and compresion. Discrete Applied Mathematics 64, 31–55 (1996)
13. Girardot, M., Sundaresan, N., Millau: An Encod¬ing Format for Efficient Representation and Exchange of XML over the Web. In: Proceedings of the 9th International WWW Conference (2000)
14. Golomb, S.W.: Run-length encodings. IEEE Trans Info Theory 12(3), 399 (1966)
15. Huffman, D.A.: A method for the construction of minimum-redundancy codes. In: Proc. of the I.R.E. (1952)
16. Liefke, H., Suciu, D.: XMill: An Efficient Compressor for XML Data. In: Proc. of ACM SIGMOD (2000)
17. Martin, G.N.N.: Range encoding: an algorithm for removing redundancy from a digitized message. In: Video and Data Recording Conference, Southampton (1979)
18. Min, J.K., Park, M.J., Chung, C.W.: XPRESS: A Queriable Compression for XML Data. In: Proceedings of SIGMOD (2003)
19. Ng, W., Lam, W.Y., Wood, P.T., Levene, M.: XCQ: A queriable XML compression system. Knowledge and Information Systems (2006)
20. Subramanian, H., Shankar, P.: Compressing XML Documents Using Recursive Finite State Automata. In: Farré, J., Litovsky, I., Schmitz, S. (eds.) CIAA 2005. LNCS, vol. 3845, pp. 282–293. Springer, Heidelberg (2006)
21. Tolani, P.M., Hartisa, J.R.: XGRIND: A query-friendly XML compressor. In: Proc. ICDE (2002)
22. Welch, T.A.: A technique for high-performance data compression. Computer Journal 17(6), 8–19 (1984)
23. Werner, C., Buschmann, C., Brandt, Y., Fischer, S.: Compressing SOAP Messages by using Pushdown Automata. In: ICWS (2006)
24. Witten, H., Neal, R.M., Cleary, J.G.: Arithmetic coding for data compression. Communcations of the ACM 30(6), 520–540 (1987)
25. Zhang, N., Kacholia, V., Özsu, M.T.: A Succinct Physical Storage Scheme for Efficient Evaluation of Path Queries in XML. In: ICDE (2004)
26. Ziv, Lempel, A.: A Universal Algorithm for Sequential Data Compression. IEEE Transactions on Information Theory 23(3), 337–343 (1977)
27. Ziv, Lempel, A.: Compression on individual sequences via variable-rate coding. IEEE Transactions on Information Theory (1978)

Fast Detection of Functional Dependencies in XML Data

Hang Shi[1], Toshiyuki Amagasa[2], and Hiroyuki Kitagawa[2]

[1] Department of Computer Science,
Graduate School of Systems and Information Engineering
[2] Center for Computational Sciences,
University of Tsukuba,
1–1–1 Tennodai, Tsukuba 305–8573, Japan
eric_shi@kde.cs.tsukuba.ac.jp, {amagasa,kitagawa}@cs.tsukuba.ac.jp

Abstract. In this paper we discuss a scheme for efficiently detecting functional dependency in XML data (XFD). The ability to detect XFD in XML data is useful in many real-life applications, such as XML schema design, relational schema design based on XML data, and redundancy detection in XML data. However, detection of XFD is an expensive task, and an efficient algorithm is essential in order to deal with large XML data collection. For this reason, we propose an efficient way to detect XFD in XML data. We assume that XML data being processed are represented as hierarchically organized relational tables. Given such data, we attempt to detect XFDs existing within and among the tables. Our basic idea is to adopt the PipeSort algorithm, which has been successfully used in OLAP, to detect XFDs within a table. We modify the basic PipeSort algorithm by incorporating a pruning mechanism by taking the features of XFDs into account, thereby making the whole process even faster. Having obtained a set of XFDs existing in tables, we attempt to detect XFDs existing among tables. In this process, we also make use of the features of XFDs for pruning. We show the feasibility of our scheme by some experiments.

1 Introduction

A functional dependency (FD) [1] is a kind of constraints between two sets of attributes in a relation from a database; a set of attributes, called determinant attributes, functionally determine another (dependent) attribute, if and only if each value in the determinant attributes is associated with precisely one value in the determinant attribute. FD plays a crucial role in defining the normal forms (NFs) in relational databases, by which we can capture and/or control the redundancy existing in a relational database, thereby making it possible to keep the consistency and integrity of the database.

In an analogy to the FD in relational database, functional dependencies in XML data (XFD) have been proposed [2] owing to the recent rapid diffusion of XML [3]. The objective of XFD is to describe dependency relations among XML

M.L. Lee et al. (Eds.): XSym 2010, LNCS 6309, pp. 113–127, 2010.

elements, thereby defining the concept of normal forms in XML data (XNFs). It is worth to mention that, unlike relational databases, XML data can be flexible and hierarchical. For this reason, defining XFD (and XNF as well) is not a trivial task, and there have been many proposals depending on the way how data items (in XML data) and the keys are defined, consequently. Specifically, XFDs that have been proposed so far can roughly be categorized into the following two approaches: path-based approaches [4] and tree-tuple based approaches [2,5,6]. In the former, target elements are identified in terms of path expressions, whereas, in the latter approach, tree tuples are extracted for the subsequent functional dependency description.

Those having said, in real-life applications, XFDs may not be specified in many cases. However, there is a demand for detecting XFDs from a given set of XML data for several reasons: 1) one may wish to detect redundancies existing in the XML data for saving storage space and/or improving updatability; 2) one may want to enhance the existing XML schema, written in DTD, W3C XML Schema, or RELAX NG, by incorporating XFDs; and 3) one may want to refer to XFDs extracted from an existing XML data collection as a hint to design a new XML schema. When doing so, efficiency on the detection process is another important concern due to the growing volume of XML data, that is, give a large XML data, fast detection of XFDs is quite important.

However, most of the existing studies on XFDs focus on the definition of functional dependencies in XML data, and the efficiency in the detection is out of their scopes. Yu and Jagadish [5,6] proposed the generalized tree tuple based XML functional dependency and algorithms for detecting XML data redundancies in XML data. In their approach, XML data are converted into a set of hierarchically linked relational tables. Given such tables, XFDs are detected if the grouping over the determinant attributes and the grouping over determinant and dependent attributes result in the same group. This fact implicates that the more the attributes and/or the relations exist, the more we need to perform grouping operations, which leads to the poor performance against a large XML data.

To cope with this problem, we adopt the PipeSort algorithm [7], which has been successfully used in OLAP [8], to detect XFDs within a table. We modify the basic PipeSort algorithm by incorporating a pruning mechanism by taking the features of XFD into account, thereby making the whole process even faster. Having obtained a set of XFDs existing in tables, we attempt to detect XFDs existing among tables. In this process, we also make use of the features of XFD for pruning. We show the feasibility of our scheme by some experiments.

The rest of this paper is organized as follows. Section 2 introduces the definition of XFD and the detection algorithm proposed by Yu and Jagadish [5,6]. Section 3 introduces the proposed scheme, followed by experimental evaluation in Section 4. Section 5 briefly reviews the related work. And Section 6 concludes this paper.

2 Preliminaries

In this section, we briefly review the definitions of XFDs, XML data redundancies, and detection algorithm by Yu and Jagadish [5,6]. The reason why we are based on this approach is that it is powerful enough to capture XFDs proposed by other researches.

2.1 Generalized Tree Tuple Based XML Functional Dependency

At first, we formally define schema, XML data, path expression, and equality of XML data fragments before defining XML functional dependency (XFD). Most of the definitions are based on [5,6], but are simplified for brevity.

Definition 1 (Schema). *A schema is defined to be $S = \langle E, T, r \rangle$, where:*

- *E is a finite set of element labels.*
- *T is a finite set of element types. Each $e \in E$ is associated with a $\tau \in T$ (written as $(e : \tau)$) of the form:*

$$\tau ::= \mathsf{str}|\mathsf{int}|\mathsf{float}|\mathsf{SetOf}\,\tau|\mathsf{Rcd}[e_1 : \tau_1, \ldots, e_n : \tau_n]|\mathsf{Choice}[e_1 : \tau_1, \ldots, e_n : \tau_n]$$

- *$r \in E$ is called the element type of the root. We assume that r does not appear in T for any $\tau \in E$.*

This definition corresponds to the core part of W3C XML Schema [9], i.e., str, int, and float are simple types, and SetOf, Rcd and Choice are complex types. Specifically, SetOf corresponds to a complex type whose `maxOccurs` value is greater than 1. Rcd and Choice correspond to `sequence` and `choice` complex types, respectively. Figure 1 shows a schema used as a running example.

```
university: Rcd
  department: SetOf Rcd
    name: str
    course: SetOf Rcd
      cid: str
      cname: str
      student: SetOf Rcd
        sid: str
        sname: str
        gender: str
        score: str
        addr: SetOf Rcd
```

Fig. 1. An example of schema

A schema element e_k is identified by a path expression, $path(e_k) = /e_1/e_2/\ldots/e_k$, where $e_1 = r$ and e_i is a label in $\mathcal{V}$. A schema element e_k is a set of elements, it is called *repeatable*.

An XML data instance is then modeled as a rooted labeled tree.

Definition 2 (XML tree). *An XML tree is defined to be $T = \langle N, P, V, r \rangle$, where:*

- *N is a set of labeled date nodes.*
- *$P \subset N \times N$ is a set of parent-child edges. For each $n \in N$ except for r, there exists an exactly one $n' \in N$ such that (n', n) and $n \neq n'$. n' is called n's parent.*

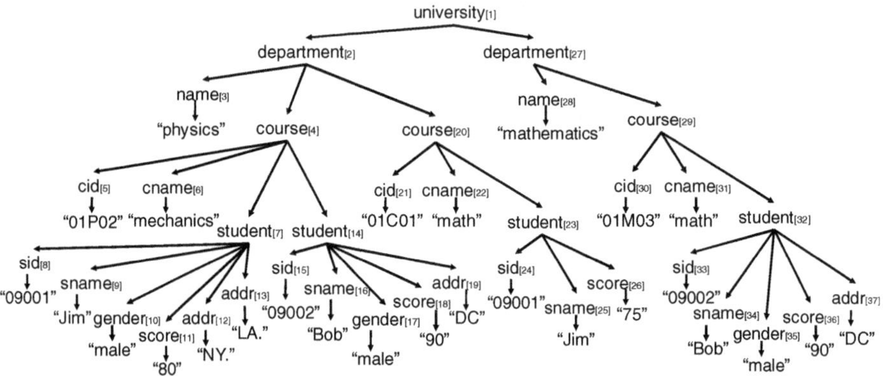

Fig. 2. An example of XML data

- *V is a set of value assignments. For each leaf node $v \in N$, there is exactly one $(v, s) \in V$ that assigns v to the simple value s.*
- *$r \in N$ is the distinguished root node.*

In an analogy to schema elements, data nodes can be addressed using a path expression. A data element is said to be *repeatable*, if its corresponding schema element is repeatable. Figure 2 shows an example of XML data that conforms to the schema in Figure 1. Note that each node is annotated by its node ID, which is the pre-order number of the node.

In Definition 3, we discuss the equality between two XML nodes.

Definition 3 (XML data equality). *Given two nodes n_1 in $T_1 = \langle N_1, P_1, V_1, r_1, \rangle$ and n_2 in $T_2 = \langle N_2, P_2, V_2, r_2, \rangle$, they are* node-value equal, *denoted as $n_1 =_{nv} n_2$, iff:*

- *n_1 and n_2 exist and have the same label.*
- *There is a one-to-one mapping between the child nodes of n_1 and n_2, such that $n_1' =_{nv} n_2'$, where n_1' and n_2' are child nodes of n_1 and n_2, respectively.*
- *$(n_1, s) \in V_1$ iff $(n_2, s) \in V_2$, where s is a simple value.*

This definition intuitively states that two data nodes are node-value equal iff the subtrees rooted at the two nodes are identical without considering the order among sibling nodes. For example, `student` nodes 14 and 32 in Figure 2 are node-value equal.

2.2 XML Functional Dependency (XFD)

We are now ready to define XML functional dependency (XFD).

Definition 4 (Generalized tree tuple). *A generalized tree tuple (GTT) of data tree $T = \langle N, P, V, n_r \rangle$, with regard to a particular data node n_p (pivot node), is a tree $t^T_{n_p} = \langle N^t, P^t, V^t, n_r \rangle$, where:*

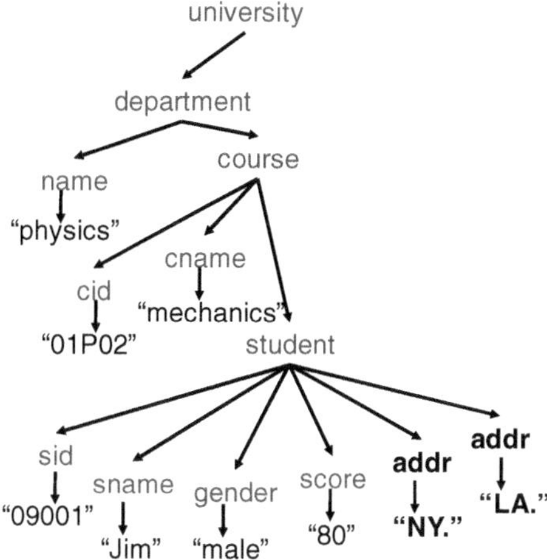

Fig. 3. An example of generalized tree tuple with student as the pivot node

- $N^t \subseteq N$ *such that* $n_p \in N^t$;
- $P^t \subseteq P$;
- $V^t \subseteq V$;
- $n \in N^t$ *iff 1)* n *is a descendant or an ancestor of* n_p, *or 2)* n *is a non-repeatable direct descendant of an ancestor of* n_p;
- $(n_1, n_2) \in P^t$ *iff* $(n_1, n_2) \in P$ *and both* n_1 *and* n_2 *are in* N^t; *and*
- $(n, s) \in V^t$ *iff* $(n, s) \in V$ *and* $n \in N^t$.

Intuitively, a GTT is a data tree constructed around a pivot data node (n_p), that is, the separation is done only at subtree rooted above the pivot node. So, both the entire subtree rooted at n_p and all ancestors of n_p are kept. Figure 3 illustrates an example of generalized tree tuple with student as the pivot node. Note that both addr nodes of the student are preserved in GTT. A *tuple class* C_p is the set of all GTTs, whose pivot nodes share the same path p (called *pivot path*).

Definition 5 (XML functional dependency (XFD)). *An XFD is a triple* $\langle C_p, LHS, RHS\rangle$, *written as* $LHS \rightarrow RHS$ *w.r.t.* C_p, *where* C_p *is a tuple class,* LHS *is a set of paths* ($P_{l_i}, i = \{1, 2, \ldots, n\}$) *relative to* p, *and* RHS *is a path* (P_r) *relative to* p. *An XFD holds on a data tree* T, *iff any two GTTs* $t_1, t_2 \in C_p$ *satisfy the following conditions:*

- $\exists i \in \{1, 2, \ldots, n\}, t_1.P_{l_i} = \perp$ *or* $t_2.P_{l_i} = \perp$, *or*
- *If* $\forall i \in \{1, 2, \ldots, n\}, t_1.P_{l_i} =_{pv} t_2.P_{l_i}$, *then* $t_1.P_r \neq \perp$, $t_2.P_r \neq \perp$, *and* $t_1.P_r =_{pv} t_2.P_r$.

where $t.P$ *denotes the set of node(s) identified by following path* P *from the pivot node of* t, *and* $\perp$ *denotes a null value.*

An XFD states that, for any two GTTs t1, t2 in C_p, if they share the same LHS, they have the same RHS.

Examples of XFD. The followings are examples of XML data redundancies, that can be found in the previous example, and how they are captured in terms of XFD.

1. Any two students with the same `sid`, e.g., nodes 14 and 32, must have the same `sname`.
$$\{sid\} \to sname \text{ w.r.t. } C_{student}$$
2. Any two students with the same `sid` must have the same set of addresses.
$$\{sid\} \to addr \text{ w.r.t. } C_{student}$$
3. For a student, his/her `score` is determined by the *course* that he/she is enrolled.
$$\{cid, sid\} \to score \text{ w.r.t. } C_{course}$$

2.3 Detecting XML Data Redundancies

Having defined XFD, the next problem is how to detect XML data redundancies.

XML data representation. First, we need an efficient representation of XML data. In [5,6], they represent XML as a set of hierarchically-linked relational tables. Figure 4 depicts a storage example that corresponds to Figure 2. We are not able to explain the detail due to the space limitation, but the main idea is to represent *essential tuple classes*, which are tuple classes with pivot paths that correspond to repeatable schema elements, as a set of relational tables, and represent their hierarchical relationships using foreign key references. In the example, `department`, `course`, `student`, and `addr` elements are represented as relational tables, because they are repeatable (see Figure 1)[1]. All non-repeatable nodes are represented as relational attributes, and parent-child relationships are represented as foreign key references (`parent` attribute). A GTT can be retrieved by joining those tables using the keys.

Note that, although we are based on the relational XML storage in this paper, the proposed scheme is not necessarily limited to the storage structure; it can easily be applied to other storage schemes, such as native XML storage, if we extract necessary information from the stored XML data.

XFD detection strategy. Because GTTs are stored in separated relational tables, the process to detect XFD becomes complicated, i.e., we need to find both *intra-relation* and *inter-relation* functional dependencies. Specifically, at each relation, we perform the following process:

1. Detect intra-relation FDs.
2. Detect inter-relation FDs involving descendant relations.
3. Generate candidate inter-relation FDs for subsequent detection at the parent level.

[1] Note that `university` is the exception due to being the root.

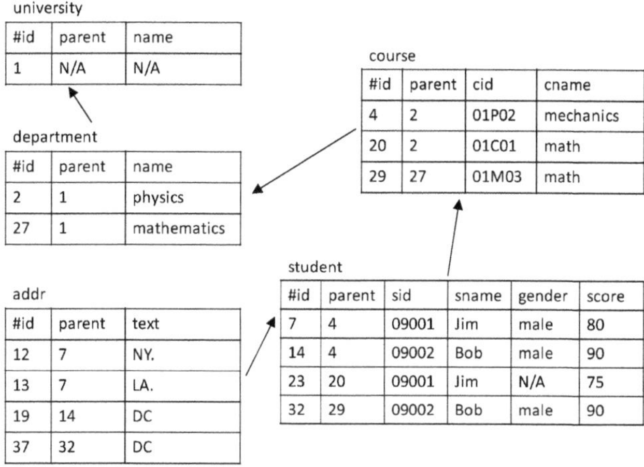

university

#id	parent	name
1	N/A	N/A

department

#id	parent	name
2	1	physics
27	1	mathematics

course

#id	parent	cid	cname
4	2	01P02	mechanics
20	2	01C01	math
29	27	01M03	math

student

#id	parent	sid	sname	gender	score
7	4	09001	Jim	male	80
14	4	09002	Bob	male	90
23	20	09001	Jim	N/A	75
32	29	09002	Bob	male	90

addr

#id	parent	text
12	7	NY.
13	7	LA.
19	14	DC
37	32	DC

Fig. 4. A relational representation of XML

Intra-relation FD detection. The algorithm for detecting intra-relation FD is based on well-known partition-based algorithms, e.g, TANE [10]. An*attribute partition* of a set of attributes $X(\Pi_X)$ is a set of partition groups, where each group contains all tuples sharing the same X value. For example, in $R_{student}$, $\Pi_{sid,sname} = \{\{7, 23\}, \{14, 32\}\}$. An important fact here is that an XFD ($LHS \rightarrow RHS$ w.r.t. C_p) holds iff $\Pi_{LHS \cup RHS} = \Pi_{LHS}$ in R_p. In fact, we can easily observe that $\Pi_{sid,sname} = \Pi_{sid}$. So, we conclude that an XFD, $\{sid\} \rightarrow sname$ w.r.t. $C_student$ holds.

Utilizing this feature, we can detect intra-relation FD in a bottom-up manner (Figure 5). I, N, G, S stands for SID, SName, Gender and Score, respectively. It illustrates a lattice structure over the student table shown in Figure 4. Each node represents an attribute set, and each edge (X, Y) corresponds to an XFD. Let $Y = X \cup \{A\}$, then edge (X, Y) corresponds to an XFD $X \rightarrow A$ w.r.t. C_p . Starting from the smallest attribute sets, the algorithm finds intra-relation FDs by following the lattice. It is important to mention that, having detected an XFD, we may be able to prune away some edges without checking partitions. In the above example, from (I, IN) (thick edge), we can infer such XFDs that can be derived by adding the same set of attributes to both LHS and RHS, i.e., (IG, ING), (IS, INS), and $(IGS, INGS)$ (dotted edges) are pruned away, and there is no need to check them, consequently.

Inter-relation FD detection. Having detected intra-relation FDs, the next task is to detect inter-relation XFDs by using the results of intra-relation FDs. The key concept is *candidate inter-relation FD generation*. Let P' be a parent relation of P, an XFD is a candidate inter-relation FD if it satisfies the following properties: 1) for $LHS \cup X \rightarrow RHS$ w.r.t. C_P to hold for any attribute set X in relation P', $LHS \cup \{./parent\} \rightarrow RHS$ w.r.t. C_P must hold; and 2) for

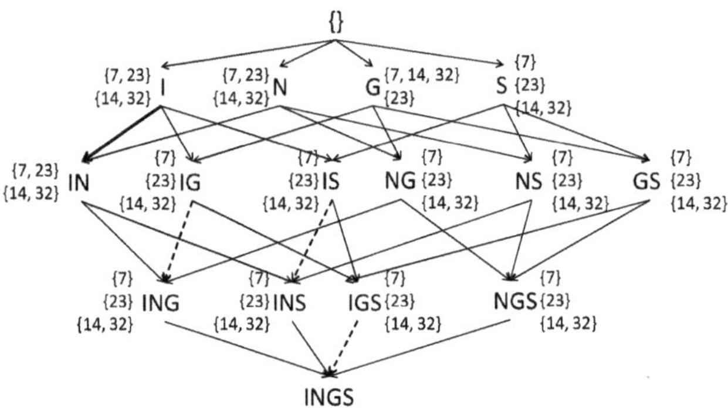

Fig. 5. Intra-relation FD detection ($R_{student}$)

$LHS \cup X \rightarrow RHS$ *w.r.t.* C_P to be a non-trivial XFD for any attribute set X in relation P', $LHS \rightarrow RHS$ w.r.t. C_P must *not* hold.

Taking R_{course} for example, by adding `parent` attribute, we can check non-trivial candidates of inter-relation FD by $\Pi_{parent,sid} = \Pi_{parent,sid,score}$. As a result, two non-trivial candidates of inter-relation FDs can be found:

$$\{cid, sid\} \rightarrow score \text{ w.r.t. } C_{course}$$
$$\{cname, sid\} \rightarrow score \text{ w.r.t. } C_{course}$$

2.4 Problems

Although the above approach successfully detects XFDs, it contains several problems. First, for intra-relation FD detection, it requires a large number of grouping operations according to the size of attribute lattice, which leads to the poor performance against a large XML data. Second, for inter-relation FD detection, more aggressive pruning of XFDs can be considered by taking into account the axioms of FDs.

3 The Proposed Scheme

As defined above, the procedure to detect XFDs is consisting of two subtasks, namely, intra- and inter-relation FD discovery. Actually, each subtask potentially contains unnecessary grouping or comparison operations. So, we attempt to eliminate those inefficiencies by introducing an optimized algorithm taking the feature of functional dependency.

3.1 PipeSort for Intra-relation FD Detection

Our idea is to exploit PipeSort [7] for intra-relation FD detection. PipeSort was originally proposed for optimizing the computation of multiple GROUP-BYs in

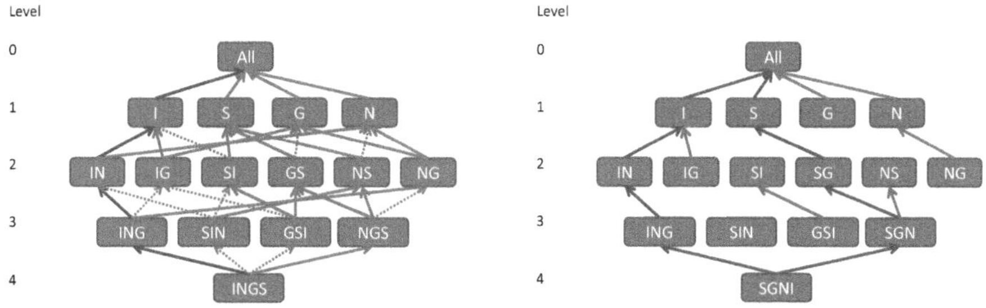

Fig. 6. PipeSort applied to $R_{student}$ (before (left) and after pruning (right))

OLAP systems. The computation of attribute partitions is essentially the same with GROUP BY. So, we try to minimize the number of sort operations.

The PipeSort algorithm is based on sort operation and incorporates the cache result, amortize scan, and share sorts to reduce the disk I/O cost. Suppose that there is a relational table with four attributes, A, B, C, and D, and sort this table using the all attributes ($ABCD$) as the sort key in this order. As a consequence, not only the sorted relation $ABCD$, but also ABC, AB, and A can be obtained by just disregarding attributes with lower-priorities. This is called a *pipeline*. An important notice here is it does not require any additional sort operation.

When applying PipeSort to intra-relation FD detection, we firstly construct an attribute lattice. Unlike the original intra-relation FD detection algorithm in which the process proceeds in a bottom-up manner, our approach proceeds in a top-down fashion. We decide the priority of all attributes, and sort the relation according to the priority. We then try to detect intra-relation FDs within the pipeline.

Notice that, for R_p, as soon as we know $X \rightarrow Y$ w.r.t. C_p does *not* hold, we also know that any intra-relation FDs having subsets of X as its LHS and Y as its RHS can not hold, respectively. Meanwhile, if we get $X \rightarrow Y$ w.r.t. C_p, which means X determines Y. We can presume that any superset of X can also determine Y. In this way, we can perform pruning on the attribute lattice.

Let us take a look at an example in Figure 6. First, we sort the relation according to `sid`, `sname`, `gender`, and `score` in this order (written as $INGS$), and form the first pipeline (Figure 6 (left)). We then get some intermediate results as follows: $ING \rightarrow S$[2] does not hold (written as $ING \nrightarrow S$), but $IN \rightarrow G$ and $I \rightarrow N$ hold. From $ING \nrightarrow S$, we can infer that any subset of ING can not determine S, so immediately we know the following results:

$$IN \nrightarrow S,\ IG \nrightarrow S,\ NG \nrightarrow S,\ I \nrightarrow S,\ N \nrightarrow S,\ G \nrightarrow S$$

In addition, we know that any superset of IN can determine G, and any super set of I can determine N:

$$IN \rightarrow G,\ INS \rightarrow G,\ I \rightarrow N,\ IG \rightarrow N,\ IS \rightarrow N,\ IGS \rightarrow N$$

[2] This is a shorthand of $\{sid, sname, gender\} \rightarrow score$.

Having inferred those additional results, the corresponding edges in the attribute lattice are removed (dotted edges in Figure 6 (left)).

In the next step, we choose another pipeline so that its length is as long as possible. Consequently, we form $SGNI$, and do the same process. In this way. based on the intermediate results, we can prune some unnecessary edges. The process is kept doing till we handle all the pipelines. Finally, we get the results in Figure 6 (right), in that there are only 14 edges left.

The following is the pseudo-code for detecting intra-relation FDs by using PipeSort.

Algorithm. DiscoverFdWithPipeSort

Input: R_p with attributes $a_1, \ldots, a_n$

$FDs \leftarrow \emptyset$

Generate the attribute lattice (LAT) containing all potential FDs over $a_1, \ldots, a_n$.

repeat

  Generate the longest pipeline (*pipe*) from LAT.

  Detect FDs (fds) from *pipe* using attribute partitions.

  Generate inferred FDs ($ifds$) from fds.

  Generate non-FDs ($nfds$) from fds and *pipe*.

  $FDs \leftarrow FDs \cup fds \cup ifds$

  Remove edges corresponding to $fds \cup ifds \cup nfds$ from LAT.

until $LAT \neq \emptyset$

return FDs

3.2 Further Optimization

When comparing attribute partitions, in a naive implementation, we need multiple scans over the table. Suppose that we try to process the pipeline, $ABCD$, ABC, AB, and A. We first compare $ABCD$ and ABC, then compare ABC and AB, and so on. In fact, this process can be done in a single scan over the $ABCD$ partition by checking multiple combinations of attributes. This has a significant impact on the process, and we will demonstrate it in the experiments.

3.3 Enhancing Inter-relation FD Discovery

XFDs exist not only in a relation but also across relations. Our objective here is to make the process of inter-relation FDs detection more efficient. The potential target for this stage is the attributes that are not determined by intra-relation FDs. Such attributes may be determined by combining attributes outside of the relation. In the previous example, we found that `score` is not determined by any attributes inside the relation. We also found that the following FDs hold:

$$\{sid\} \rightarrow sname \text{ w.r.t. } C_{student}$$
$$\{sid\} \rightarrow gender \text{ w.r.t. } C_{student}$$
$$\{cid\} \rightarrow cname \text{ w.r.t. } C_{course}$$

In principle, we need to check all possible combinations as follows:

(1) $\{sname, cid\} \rightarrow score$, $\{sname, cname\} \rightarrow score$, $\{sname, cid, cname\} \rightarrow score$
(2) $\{gender, cid\} \rightarrow score$, $\{gender, cname\} \rightarrow score$, $\{gender, cid, cname\} \rightarrow score$
(3) $\{cname, sid\} \rightarrow score$, $\{cname, sname\} \rightarrow score$, $\{cname, gender\} \rightarrow score$, $\{cname, sid, sname\} \rightarrow score$, $\{cname, sid, gender\} \rightarrow score$, $\{cname, sname, gender\} \rightarrow score$, $\{cname, sid, sname, gender\} \rightarrow score$
(4) $\{sid, cid\} \rightarrow score$
(5) $\{sname, gender, cname\} \rightarrow score$

Now, we know that $sid \rightarrow sname$. This indicates that if `sid` with the parent attribute cannot determine `score`, then `sname` combined with this parent attribute cannot determine `score` either. So, we consider `sid` as a candidate for determining `score`, and we do not need to check any combination of `sname` with parent attribute (1). As a consequence, we only need to check the combinations of `sid` with attributes in its parent relation.

The same discussion applies to `gender` (2). In R_{course}, $\{cid\} \rightarrow cname$ holds. As for (3), combinations of `cname` with attributes in $R_{student}$ need not to be checked. So cid is considered as another candidate for determining score.

In summary, instead of checking all the combinations, first we only need to check the combination of the candidates. Particularly in this case, we check combination of `sid` in $R_{student}$ and `cid` in R_{course} (4). In order to cover all the situations, we also check the combination of `sname`, `gender`, and `cname` (5) which turned out to be much fewer than exhaustive combinations. Finally we have

$$\{sid, cid\} \rightarrow score \text{ w.r.t. } C_{course}$$

4 Experimental Evaluation

We implemented the proposed scheme on top of Microsoft SQL Server 2008 using C#. We converted the XML file into hierarchically linked tables and stored them on disk. All experiments were conducted on a PC with a 2.0GHz P4 CPU and 2GB RAM, running Windows XP (SP2) and .NET3.5. For timing measurements, each experiment was run three times and the average reading was recorded.

In order to show the efficiency, we implement our approach by applying PipeSort in two ways: one is naive implementation and the other one is using the technique of single scan.

4.1 Real-Life Datasets

To show the effectiveness of our proposed algorithms, we discover XFDs on two available real-life data sources. One is the Mondial [11] geography dataset and the other is DBLP [12] bibliography dataset. To examine its practicality and to verify the existence of data redundancies in real world datasets, we conducted some experiments to perform comparative analysis on the proposed algorithm.

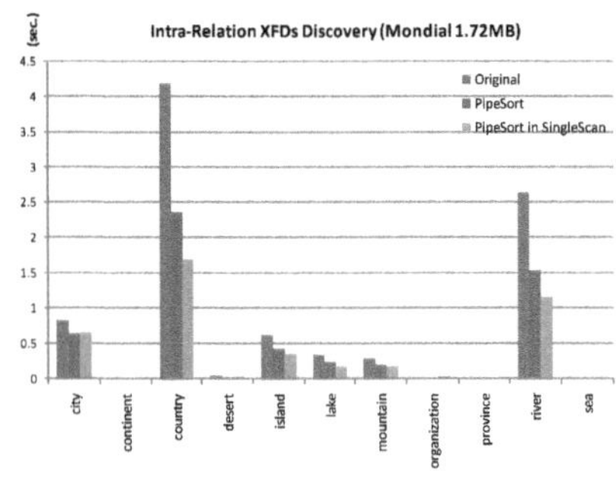

Fig. 7. Intra-Relation XFDs Discovery on Mondial

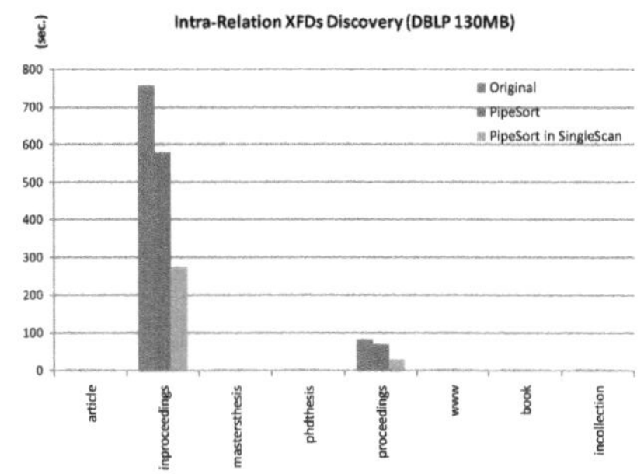

Fig. 8. Intra-Relation XFDs Discovery on DBLP

4.2 Experimental Results

Figure 7 to Figure 10 show the experimental results of the time cost when discovering XFDs in intra-relation and inter-relation.

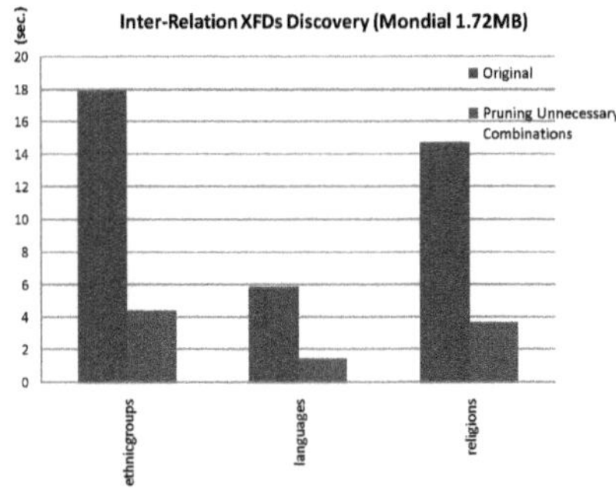

Fig. 9. Inter-Relation XFDs Discovery on Mondial

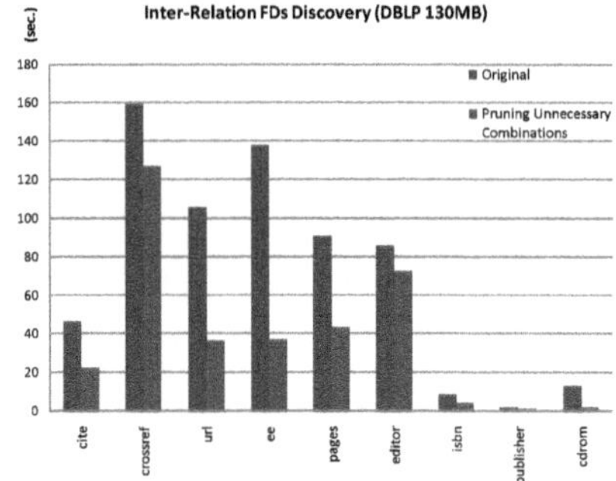

Fig. 10. Inter-Relation XFDs Discovery on DBLP

In Figure 7 and Figure 8 the X axis stands for the table name while Y axis is the time cost. We can see clearly that by applying the PipeSort method, the time cost of finding XFDs is much less than the original algorithm. Meanwhile, the degree of loops can be reduced largely in one single-scan so that we can make the discovery faster. Especially when the table size is really large or contains many attributes, like the relations "country", "river" and "inproceedings", then the PipeSort is much faster according to Figure 7 and Figure 8.

Figure 9 and Figure 10 show the time cost of inter-relation XFDs discovery. The X axis is the attribute cannot be determined during the intra-relation while Y axis also stands for the time cost. Since we prune some unnecessary combinations by using the properties of functional dependency. The discovery has been processed fast. The performance is shown in Figure 9 and Figure 10.

5 Related Work

XML data is usually described as a "schema-less" labeled tree, which means that there is no pre-designed schema. The problem with this is that it is so flexible that it only presents syntax without any constraints. To address this problem, a number of constraint specifications have been proposed recently including the notion of XML Keys [13,14], XML Functional Dependencis [15,16,17,18,19,20,21], and XML Normal Forms [22,2,23,24], among which undoubtedly XFD is the foundation of XML constraints and also plays the important role in defining normal forms.

XFDs, which have been proposed so far, can roughly be categorized into the following two main approaches: path-based approach [16,4,19,20,21] and tree-tuple based approaches [2,5]. In the former, the authors define the XFDs by specifying the target element of the constraint. But, in reality, it is often difficult. In the latter approach, instead of specifying target elements, the authors use tree tuples, each of which is a XML sub-tree by picking up each schema element and projecting away all the other nodes.

However, this approach can not handle set and multi-valued dependencies. In order to cope with this problem, C. Yu and H. V. Jagadish proposed generalized tree tuple based XFDs definition. The approach they developed can not only be used for the previous definitions of XFDs, but also capable of detecting XFDs involve set elements while maintaining clear semantics [5].

One of the major drawbacks of [5] is its efficiency in finding XFDs. In the first place, it needs to make many partitions of each table, followed by comparisons among those partitions, Obviously, this process contains some unnecessary combinations and there is not an effective way to deal with the comparisons.

In [25] the authors present a scalable and efficient algorithm to discover the composite keys in large database. The main idea is based on a cube operation to find all non-keys. This is similar to our work because we all apply some cube operations to detect constraints existing in data collection. In our PipeSort algorithm, group-by is the foundational operation, while in [25] slicing and group-by are proposed as the primary method. Also, in both approaches some necessary pruning has been done to speed up the discovery process. However, generally speaking, rather than detecting the non-FD, which means that functional dependencies do not hold (like discovery of non-keys). We think that it is important and interesting to discover the relationship of one attribute set can determine another (functional dependency).

In the paper, so naive implementation of this process is quite time-consuming. To speed up this process, we apply PipeSort method [7], which was originally developed for OLAP computation [8,26]. This process incorporates the cache-result, amortize-scan, and share-sorts to reduce the disk I/O cost, and based on the intermediate results we can prune some unnecessary combinations and this can make our system efficiently.

6 Conclusions

XML data redundancies are greatly existing and have a richer semantic. And functional dependency is playing an important role in avoiding data redundancies. Many definitions are given on XML functional dependency, but there is not an efficient way to discover XML functional dependencies(XFDs).

In our paper, based on the notion given in [5], we propose an efficient way to discover XFDs. We apply the PipeSort method to speed up the XFDs discovery process, and also based on the XFD properties many combinations can be pruned.

In order to see the effectiveness of our proposal, we did the implementation and experimentation using the data source from the real world. Based on the experimental results, we can verify that our proposal is useful and effective. As a part of our future work, we plan to build the system without transforming XML document into relational databases.

Acknowledgments

This study has been partly supported by the Grant-in-Aid for Scientific Research in Priority Areas (#21013004) and Grant-in-Aid for Young Scientists (B) (#21700093).

References

1. Codd, E.F.: Further normalization of the data base relational model. IBM Research Report, San Jose, California RJ909 (1971)
2. Arenas, M., Libkin, L.: A normal form for XML documents. In: Proc. PODS 2002, pp. 85–96 (2002)
3. W3C: Extensible Markup Language (XML) 1.0, 5th edn., Recommendation (November 2008), `http://www.w3.org/TR/xml/`
4. Vincent, M.W., Liu, J., Liu, C.: Strong functional dependencies and their application to normal forms in XML. ACM Trans. Database Syst. 29(3), 445–462 (2004)
5. Yu, C., Jagadish, H.V.: Efficient discovery of XML data redundancies. In: Proc. VLDB 2006, pp. 103–114 (2006)
6. Yu, C., Jagadish, H.V.: XML schema refinement through redundancy detection and normalization. VLDB J. 17(2), 203–223 (2008)
7. Agarwal, S., Agrawal, R., Deshpande, P., Gupta, A., Naughton, J.F., Ramakrishnan, R., Sarawagi, S.: On the computation of multidimensional aggregates. In: Proc. VLDB 1996, pp. 506–521 (1996)
8. Gray, J., Chaudhuri, S., Bosworth, A., Layman, A., Reichart, D., Venkatrao, M., Pellow, F., Pirahesh, H.: Data Cube: A relational aggregation operator generalizing group-by, cross-tab, and sub totals. Data Min. Knowl. Discov. 1(1), 29–53 (1997)
9. W3C: XML Schema Part 2: Datatypes, 2nd edn., Recommendation (October 2004), `http://www.w3.org/TR/xmlschema-2/`
10. Huhtala, Y., Kärkkäinen, J., Porkka, P., Toivonen, H.: TANE: An efficient algorithm for discovering functional and approximate dependencies. Comput. J. 42(2), 100–111 (1999)

11. May, W.: Information Extraction and Integration with Florid: The Mondial Case Study, http://www.dbis.informatik.uni-goettingen.de/lopix/lopixmondial.html
12. Ley, M.: DBLP Bibliography, http://www.informatik.uni-trier.de/~ley/db/
13. Grahne, G., Zhu, J.: Discovering approximate keys in XML data. In: Proc. CIKM 2002, pp. 453–460 (2002)
14. Hartmann, S., Link, S.: Unlocking keys for XML trees. In: Schwentick, T., Suciu, D. (eds.) ICDT 2007. LNCS, vol. 4353, pp. 104–118. Springer, Heidelberg (2006)
15. Lee, M.L., Ling, T.W., Low, W.L.: Designing functional dependencies for XML. In: Jensen, C.S., Jeffery, K., Pokorný, J., Šaltenis, S., Bertino, E., Böhm, K., Jarke, M. (eds.) EDBT 2002. LNCS, vol. 2287, pp. 124–141. Springer, Heidelberg (2002)
16. Liu, J., Vincent, M.W., Liu, C.: Functional dependencies, from relational to XML. In: Broy, M., Zamulin, A.V. (eds.) PSI 2003. LNCS, vol. 2890, pp. 531–538. Springer, Heidelberg (2004)
17. Hartmann, S., Link, S.: More functional dependencies for XML. In: Kalinichenko, L.A., Manthey, R., Thalheim, B., Wloka, U. (eds.) ADBIS 2003. LNCS, vol. 2798, pp. 355–369. Springer, Heidelberg (2003)
18. Lv, T., Yan, P.: A survey study on XML functional dependencies. In: Proc. ISDPE 2007, pp. 143–145 (2007)
19. Fassetti, F., Fazzinga, B.: Approximate functional dependencies for XML data. In: Ioannidis, Y., Novikov, B., Rachev, B. (eds.) ADBIS 2007. LNCS, vol. 4690, pp. 86–95. Springer, Heidelberg (2007)
20. Shahriar, M.S., Liu, J.: On defining functional dependency for XML. In: Proc. IEEE ICSC 2009, pp. 595–600 (2009)
21. Zhao, X., Xin, J., Zhang, E.: XML functional dependency and schema normalization. In: Proc. HIS 2009, pp. 307–312 (2009)
22. Mok, W.Y., Ng, Y.-K., Embley, D.W.: A normal form for precisely characterizing redundancy in nested relations. ACM Trans. Database Syst. 21(1), 77–106 (1996)
23. Arenas, M., Libkin, L.: An information-theoretic approach to normal forms for relational and XML data. In: Proc. PODS 2003, pp. 15–26 (2003)
24. Pankowski, T., Pilka, T.: Transformation of XML data into XML normal form. Informatica 33(4), 417–430 (2009)
25. Sismanis, Y., Brown, P., Haas, P.J., Reinwald, B.: GORDIAN: Efficient and scalable discovery of composite keys. In: Proc. VLDB 2006, pp. 691–702 (2006)
26. Sarawagi, S., Agrawal, R., Gupta, A.: Research report on computing the data cube. Technical report, IBM Almaden Research Center

TP+Output: Modeling Complex Output Information in XML Twig Pattern Query

Huayu Wu[1], Tok Wang Ling[1], and Gillian Dobbie[2]

[1] School of Computing, National University of Singapore
{wuhuayu,lingtw}@comp.nus.edu.sg
[2] Department of Computer Science, The University of Auckland, New Zealand
gill@cs.auckland.ac.nz

Abstract. Twig pattern is considered a core pattern for XML queries. However, due to the limited expressivity of twig pattern expressions, many queries that aim to find complex output information under one object cannot be expressed in a single twig pattern. Instead, they have to be expressed as XQuery expression, which is transformed into several twig patterns linked by joins. To process such an XQuery query, we need to match multiple twig patterns to the XML document, even though they are all centered on the same object. In this paper we analyze the characteristics of each query node, i.e. the purpose, optionality and occurrence, and define four types of nodes in a twig pattern query to express output information, namely, *output node*, *optional-output node*, *predicated-output node*, and *optional-predicated-output node*. Then we propose the *TP+Output* expression to extend twig pattern queries, to model complex output information based on the semantics of different node types. With TP+Output, queries with the four output types can be expressed in one TP+Output expression and processed more efficiently. We extend our previously proposed twig pattern query processing algorithm, *VERT*, to process the TP+Output query, and demonstrate the performance improvement of using TP+Output to represent queries.

1 Introduction

As XML becomes a standard data format for information storage and exchange, the efficient processing of queries on XML data attracts a lot of research interest. In this paper, we explain how a particular class of queries can be processed more efficiently.

We start by defining the problem that we address in this paper. An XML document is normally modeled as a tree, without considering ID references. Fig. 1 shows an example XML document modeled as a tree with positional labels. Similarly, the core query pattern in most XML query languages (e.g. XPath[5] and XQuery[6]) is also a tree, or several trees linked by joins or other post-processing operations. In particular, an XPath query expression is modeled as a small tree, whereas an XQuery expression corresponds to several trees linked by joins or other post-processing operations. Such a tree pattern query structure is called a

M.L. Lee et al. (Eds.): XSym 2010, LNCS 6309, pp. 128–143, 2010.

twig pattern query. Matching a twig pattern query to an XML document tree to return all occurrences of the twig pattern in the document tree is considered the main operation for XML query processing. This process is called *twig pattern matching.* Transforming a general XQuery query into several twig patterns with joins or other post-processing operations, and optimizing pattern matching for multiple twigs are not included in this paper. We only focus on how the rich semantics of a query pattern impacts on the efficiency of query processing, as discussed below.

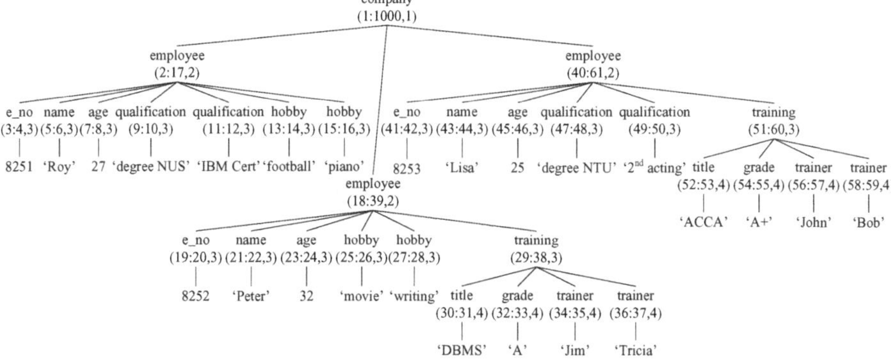

Fig. 1. *Company* document in tree representation

Q1: Find the employees who have at least one qualification, and output their name, as well as hobbies if they have any.
Q2: Find the employees who have football as a hobby, and output their name, and this hobby.
Q3: Find the employees who have football as a hobby, and output their name, and all their hobbies.
Q4: Find all the employees, and output their name, as well as their hobby if it is football.
Q5: Find all the employees, and output their name, and all their hobbies if one of them is football.

Fig. 2. Example queries

A single twig pattern query can express only simple queries, which is the same as the queries that can be expressed in XPath. To express a complex query, one has to use XQuery which builds on XPath by introducing FLWOR constructs to enhance expressivity. A typical XQuery processor normally analyzes the query expression to model it as a set of linked twig patterns for processing [12]. Thus processing an XQuery query may involve matching several twig patterns to the document. There is a class of queries, which finds a particular object based on certain predicates, and outputs complex information about that object. Such queries cannot be expressed by a single XPath or twig pattern expression, because of the complexity of the output. This class of queries have to be expressed using XQuery expressions which match with more than one twig pattern. Fig. 2 shows some example queries with complex output information from a unique object. All of them have simple, or in some cases no predicate applied to the target object, but none of these queries can be expressed in a single twig pattern. Take Q1 as an example, in which *hobby* is optional. Although some employees may not have a hobby, we still output their name. If we attempt to write this query as a single XPath or twig pattern expression, *hobby* will be a required node to qualify employee, which violates the query purpose. Instead to express this query we have to use an XQuery expression, which is shown in Fig. 3(a). To process this query, we need to match two twig patterns and perform an outer join, as shown in Fig. 3(b). Intuitively one pass of pattern matching should be enough because both the predicate and the output information are centered around the same object.

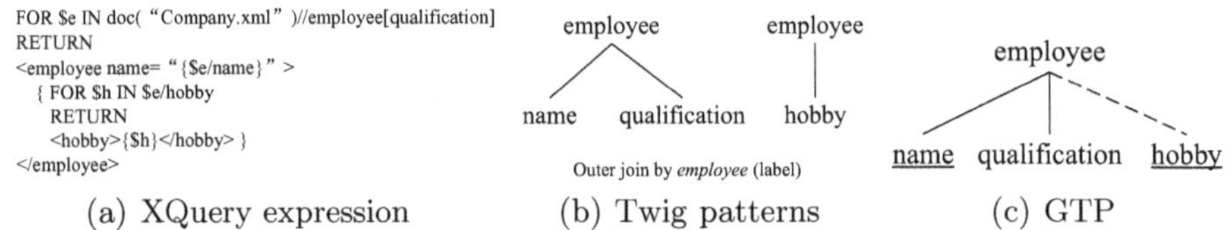

(a) XQuery expression (b) Twig patterns (c) GTP

Fig. 3. Query expressions for Q1 in Fig. 2

The generalized tree pattern (GTP) [10] is an important extension to twig pattern that enhances expressivity, which explicitly marks all output nodes in the twig structure, and introduces a dotted edge to represent optional output nodes. Q1 can be expressed by GTP as one twig pattern with output nodes underlined and optional edges dotted, as shown in Fig. 3(c). Using certain algorithms (e.g. [8]), matching a single GTP pattern is naturally more efficient than matching several twig patterns and joining results, to process queries like Q1.

Although optional output can be expressed by GTP, some other output information can be even more complex and no existing twig pattern extensions can express them. For example, the queries Q3 and Q5 are similar to Q2 and Q4 respectively in Fig. 2. They only differ in the occurrence of the output node *hobby*, i.e. Q2 and Q4 return one hobby, but Q3 and Q5 return all hobbies. Unfortunately, neither twig pattern nor GTP can express Q3 and Q5 precisely. We have to use XQuery to express them, and again as a consequence match different twig patterns even though they are all centered at *employee*.

In this paper we aim to extend the expressivity of twig pattern queries so that a class of queries which involves complex output information under the same output object can be modeled in a single twig pattern, and thus be processed using one pass of pattern matching. We first investigate different types of nodes in an XML query, and then extend twig pattern query by introducing additional notation to model different output types. The contributions of this paper can be summarized as follows:

– Analyze the characteristics of query nodes, which leads to the definition of query nodes to express output information: *output nodes*, *optional-output nodes*, *predicated-output nodes* and *optional-predicated-output nodes*.

- Extend twig pattern queries with notation to explicitly mark different types of output nodes. We call the extended twig pattern *TP+Output*.
- Extend our previous query processing algorithm, *VERT*, to process TP+Output queries.
- Conduct experiments to compare the query processing performance between TP+Output, the original twig pattern representation, and two typical XQuery processors, to verify the performance improvement of using TP+Output.

The rest of this paper is arranged as follows. Section 2 briefly revisits some related work. Section 3 analyzes the characteristics of query nodes and Section 4 presents TP+Output, our extension to the twig pattern query. Section 5 provides our extension to the query processing algorithm *VERT*, to process TP+Output queries. Finally, Section 6 describes our experimental results and Section 7 concludes this paper.

2 Related Work

XML query processing has been widely studied. Initially, since the relational database model (RDBMS) dominated database management systems, many approaches that store and query XML data using RDBMS were proposed ([11][20][21] [17][16]). Most of these approaches shred XML documents into relational tables and translate XML queries into SQL to query the database. However, relational approaches to query XML data suffer from problems, such as inefficiency to answer "//"-axis queries (i.e. the queries with ancestor-descendant edges). Later querying XML data natively attracted a lot of research interest. Since an XML query can be expressed as a twig pattern or several join-linked twig patterns, efficiently matching a twig pattern to an XML document became a core part of XML query processing. Al-Khalifa et al. [4] propose a stack-based structural join algorithm, in which a twig pattern query is decomposed into a set of binary relationships to match the document, and the query result built on the combination of these binary matches. The main problem is that there are too many useless intermediate results. To overcome this limitation, Bruno et al. [7] propose a holistic twig join algorithm, *TwigStack*, which avoids producing a large number of intermediate results. There are also many subsequent works [9][14][13][15] that either optimize *TwigStack* or extend *TwigStack* to solve different problems. Because these twig pattern matching algorithms could not efficiently handle content search and content extraction, Wu et al. [19] proposed a semantic approach, which complements the twig pattern algorithms, to handle content problems.

Since XML queries represented by twig patterns are not expressive enough to meet users' demands, another direction is to extend the expressivity of XML twig pattern queries. Particularly, Chen et al. [10] proposed a more expressive structure called generalized tree pattern (GTP) to represent XML queries. Using GTP, optional nodes can be explicitly expressed. Theodoratos et al. [18] introduced a partial tree pattern query semantics which offers a flexible way for users to query XML documents with partially specified query patterns. There has also been a lot of work in keyword-based unstructured XML querying.

3 Query Output Characteristics

In this section, we analyze the characteristics of each node in a twig pattern query. We focus on output query nodes, which is central to our twig pattern extension in the next section.

3.1 Purpose of Query Nodes

Normally an XML query aims to return some information based on certain conditions. As a result, in an XML twig pattern query, some nodes represent conditions, while some nodes represent information to be returned. In a twig pattern query, if a query node specifies some constraints to filter the results, we say this node is for predicate purpose. Contrarily, if a query node specifies what information the query needs to return, we say this node is for output purpose.

Consider the query Q1 in GTP representation in Figure 3(c). Nodes *employee* and *qualification* are used to specify the structural constraint of the query, so they are for predicate purpose, while nodes *name* and *hobby* are for output purpose. However, there is a case that some query nodes are for both predicate and output purposes. Consider a query to find the names of all employees with age greater than 30, and also output the age. In this query, *age* plays a predicate role, as it specifies a selection condition; and it also plays an output role, as we need to return its value. Finally, we classify the purpose of nodes in a twig pattern query into *predicate*, *output* and *predicated-output*.

3.2 Optionality of Different Types of Output Nodes

A predicate node specifying selection condition of a query is normally *required*. For example in Q1, the predicate node *qualification* must be matched in every qualified answer. In some cases, predicate node can also be *optional*. Suppose we change the condition of Q1 to be the employee whose qualification is "IBM Cert" if he has any (i.e. either have no qualification or have qualification of "IBM Cert"). Now the qualification node becomes an optional predicate node. We do not investigate the optionality of predicate, but focus on output information. Optional predicate can be similarly expressed as that in GTP.

The existence of output node and predicated-output node can be either *required* or *optional*. In Q1 *name* is required output information, but *hobby* is optional. If a qualified employee has certain hobbies, we output them alongside his name; otherwise, we just output his name with an empty set of hobbies.

Similarly, the predicated-output node is either required or optional. The query Q2 and Q4 in Fig. 2 both involve predicated-output nodes, but differ on the optionality of the predicated-output node. In Q2, *hobby* is required to qualify an employee. However in Q4, *hobby* is optional, i.e. we do not qualify an employee based on *hobby*. If the *hobby* football exists for a qualified employee, we will output it; otherwise no hobby is output for the qualified employee.

3.3 Occurrence of Different Types of Output Nodes

In an XML document, an element or attribute can be either single-valued or multi-valued with respect to its parent element. For example, in the *Company* document, *e_no*, *name* and *age* are single-valued with respect to *employee*, but *qualification* and *hobby* are multi-valued with respect to *employee*.

The occurrence of an output node depends on whether the corresponding document node is single-valued or multi-valued. For example, if both *name* and *hobby* are output nodes, for each qualified employee one name and all hobbies he/she has are returned. However, the occurrence of a predicated-output node is not as trivial. Comparing the query Q2 and Q3 in Fig. 2, we notice that *hobby* corresponds to a multi-valued element, but unlike Q3, Q2 does not return all the hobbies under a qualified employee. It only returns the satisfied hobby. To summarize, if a predicated-output node corresponds to a multi-valued element, the occurrence of the output information can be either one or many.

4 TP+Output: An Extension of Twig Pattern

As summarized in the last section, a node to express output information in a twig pattern query can be either output node or predicated-output node, either required or optional, and its occurrence is either one or many if it corresponds a multi-valued property. By integrating such information, we classify the query nodes to express output information in a twig pattern query into four types, namely *output node*, *optional-output node*, *predicated-output node* and *optional-predicated-output node*, and the occurrence of *predicated-output node* and *optional-predicated-output node* can be either one or many. Now we formally define each type of query node, and extend the existing twig pattern query to express different types of query node explicitly, by introducing new notation. We call the extended twig pattern *TP+Output*.

4.1 Output Node

Definition 1. In a twig pattern query, if the purpose of a node is for output, and the existence of these nodes is required to qualify an answer, then these query nodes are called *output nodes*.

In Q1 in Fig. 4(a), node *name* is an output node because its purpose is for output and it must exist in each matching answer. We underline the output nodes in a TP+Output query.

4.2 Optional-Output Node

Definition 2. In a twig pattern query, if the purpose of certain nodes is for output, but the existence of these nodes is not required to qualify an answer, then these query nodes are called *optional-output nodes*.

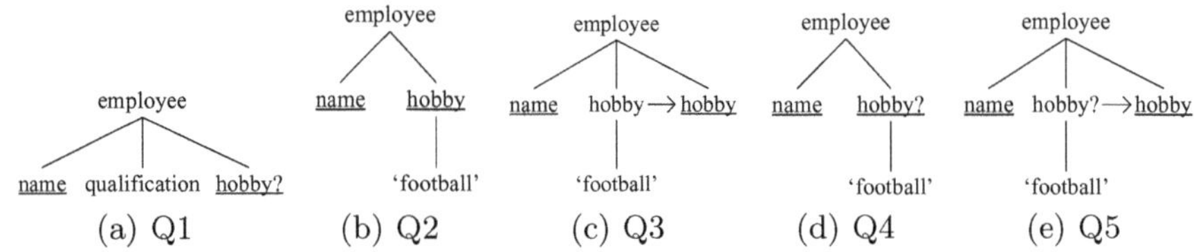

(a) Q1 (b) Q2 (c) Q3 (d) Q4 (e) Q5

Fig. 4. TP+Output expressions for the examples queries in Fig. 2

Consider again the query Q1 in Fig. 4(a). *Hobby* is an optional-output node, because it will be output, and although some employee may not have a hobby, he/she still qualifies as a solution. We underline the node and append a "?" to represent optional-output nodes.

4.3 Predicated-Output Node

Definition 3. In a twig pattern query, if certain nodes are for both predicate and output purposes, and the existence of these nodes is required to qualify an answer, then these query nodes are called *predicated-output nodes.*

There are two cases for predicated-output node: (1) the node corresponds to a single-valued element, and (2) the node corresponds to a multi-valued element in the document. We illustrate why we need to distinguish the occurrence of a predicated-output node.

Recall the example given in Section 3.1, which finds the names of all employees with age greater than 30, and also output their age. In this query, *age* acts as both a predicate and an output role, so this node is a predicated-output node. From the document, we can see *age* is a single-valued property for each *employee.* In our extension, such single-valued predicated-output nodes are simply underlined, and the child value comparison can be used to differentiate predicated-output nodes from output nodes.

However, as mentioned earlier, a predicated-output node may correspond to a multi-valued element in the XML document. In such a case, this notation is insufficient to differentiate some query intentions. Consider the query Q2 and Q3 in Fig. 2. The two queries have exactly the same query predicate, but differ on the occurrence of the predicated-output node *hobby*, i.e. Q2 outputs the employee's name together with his/her hobby that satisfies the predicate, while Q3 outputs the employee's name with ALL his/her hobbies as long as one of them satisfies the predicate. Nevertheless, the notation introduced above for predicated-output node is not able to differentiate the two query purposes. To differentiate the two queries, we introduce an additional query node with the same name as the multi-valued predicated-output node, and an arrow ("$\longrightarrow$") starting from the original node, to indicate the case in which the output occurrence is *many*. The $\longrightarrow$ can be interpreted as "if then" (i.e. in Q3 if one hobby satisfies the predicate, all hobbies are output), so the additional query node pointed to by $\longrightarrow$ is not matched during pattern matching. Now the query Q2 is represented as in Fig. 4(b), and Q3 is represented as in Fig. 4(c).

4.4 Optional-Predicated-Output Node

Definition 4. In a twig pattern query, if certain nodes are for both predicate and output purposes, but the existence of these nodes is not required to qualify an answer, then these query nodes are called *optional-predicated-output nodes.*

Predicated-output node can also be optional, and this leads to the optional-predicated-output node. In the TP+Output extension, we simply append a "?" to the predicated-output node to indicate its optionality. Similarly, if the node corresponds to a multi-valued element, we express the different output occurrences by introducing additional node and arrow ("⟶"). The queries Q4 and Q5 in Fig. 4(d) and 4(e) demonstrate this concept.

Original twig pattern queries cannot express complex output information. If a query contains, e.g. optional-output nodes, predicated-output nodes or optional-predicated-output nodes, the original twig pattern query has to rely on XQuery semantics to translate the complex output information into several twigs linked by joins. Using our extension, all such queries can be expressed in a single twig. In the next section, we will introduce how we extend previous algorithm, *VERT*, to evaluate the TP+Output queries.

5 VERT Extension

We proposed *VERT* to complement the state-of-the-art pattern matching algorithms to handle output and other content problems [19]. In this section, we extend *VERT* to support the TP+Output query. Note that, most structural join based pattern matching algorithms are compatible with *VERT*, thus they are compatible with our extension as well. We start with a brief review of *VERT*.

5.1 VERT Algorithm

VERT introduces both inverted lists and relational tables to index tags and data values in XML documents. In our first approach, we consider the parent node of each value as a property, and construct property tables to store each value and the label of its associated property. Two property tables are shown in Fig. 5(a).

XML query processing with *VERT* is composed of three steps. In the first step, *VERT* performs a content search for value comparisons in query predicates and rewrites the twig pattern query. During this step, the query is simplified, and the inverted list size for relevant query nodes is reduced by the value constraints. Then in the second step, it adopts an existing twig pattern matching algorithm such as *TwigStack* to perform a structural search for the rewritten query with new inverted lists on relevant query nodes. The result of twig pattern matching is raw tuples of labels, rather than values. In the last step, *VERT* extracts values from relational tables to replace labels of properties in the raw result.

We use an example to walk through the process of twig pattern query processing by *VERT* in Fig. 5(b). Node *name* is restricted to value 'Roy', thus this twig pattern is rewritten by collapsing 'Roy' onto the *name* node, which is then renamed as $name_{Roy}$. The content of the inverted list for $name_{Roy}$ will be a selection of labels from table R_{name} where *Value* equals 'Roy', thus obtaining only one label (5:6,3). The rewritten query, which reduces the number of query nodes and the number of structural joins by 1, is then processed using an existing structural join algorithm such as *TwigStack* to obtain a set of labels. Finally *VERT* returns R_{hobby} to retrieve the values of these labels. The column *employee* and *name* may be omitted as they are not required in the output.

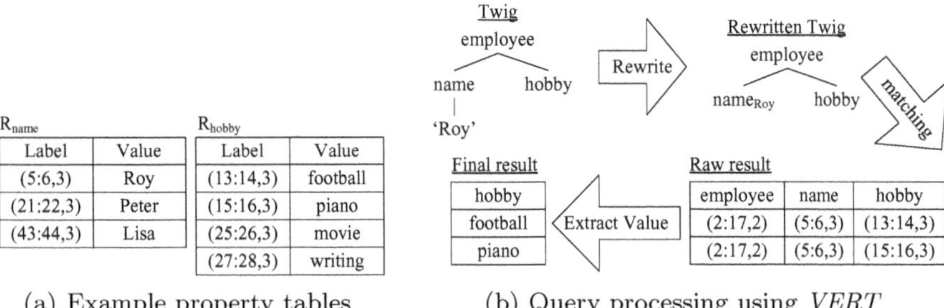

R_{name}

Label	Value
(5:6,3)	Roy
(21:22,3)	Peter
(43:44,3)	Lisa

R_{hobby}

Label	Value
(13:14,3)	football
(15:16,3)	piano
(25:26,3)	movie
(27:28,3)	writing

Final result

hobby
football
piano

Raw result

employee	name	hobby
(2:17,2)	(5:6,3)	(13:14,3)
(2:17,2)	(5:6,3)	(15:16,3)

(a) Example property tables (b) Query processing using *VERT*

Fig. 5. Property tables and query processing using *VERT*

There are also two optimizations to table index proposed for *VERT*. We only refer to the second optimization in this paper since the second optimization is built on the first optimization and includes all its advantages. In the optimization, property tables are replaced by object tables, in which the labels of each object, together with the value of all its single-valued properties, are stored. For multi-valued properties, there will be object/property tables. The inference of object information is discussed in [19]. The tables for *employee* under *VERT* optimization is shown in Fig. 6(a). Using *VERT* optimization, the original twig pattern query can be rewritten to a new twig pattern shown in Fig. 6(b), in which the number of query nodes and number of structural joins are further reduced. The inverted list for the new *employee* node is constructed by selecting the labels in $R_{employee}$ where the corresponding *Name* is "Roy". Since there is only one such label, (2:17,2), the inverted list size is also limited to 1 label, which saves inverted list searching time for *employee* node.

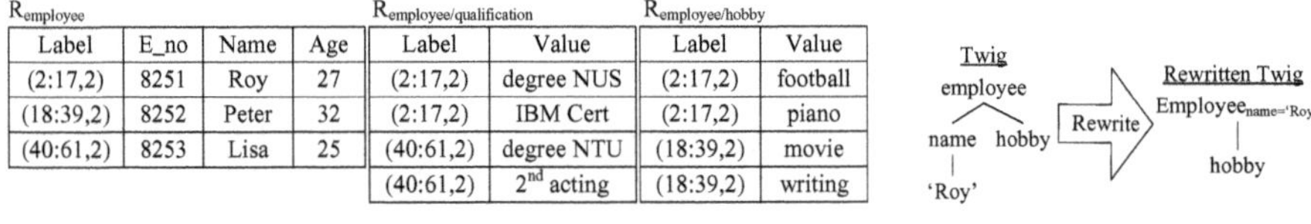

$R_{employee}$

Label	E_no	Name	Age
(2:17,2)	8251	Roy	27
(18:39,2)	8252	Peter	32
(40:61,2)	8253	Lisa	25

$R_{employee/qualification}$

Label	Value
(2:17,2)	degree NUS
(2:17,2)	IBM Cert
(40:61,2)	degree NTU
(40:61,2)	2nd acting

$R_{employee/hobby}$

Label	Value
(2:17,2)	football
(2:17,2)	piano
(18:39,2)	movie
(18:39,2)	writing

(a) Object tables for *employee* (b) Query rewritten

Fig. 6. Object tables for *employee* and query written for Q1 under *VERT* optimization

5.2 VERT Extension

In this section, we present how we extend the VERT algorithm to process the TP+Output queries with the new notations. We build the extension on VERT with optimization, and name the extended algorithm $VERT_{ext}$.

Predicate node: All the query nodes in a TP+Output query which are not underlined are predicate nodes. [8] proposes an efficient pattern matching technique for both required and optional predicate nodes. $VERT_{ext}$ can adopt any pattern matching algorithm, including [8] to perform pattern matching for predicate nodes. Especially to be mentioned is $VERT_{ext}$ can solve the predicate nodes without value comparison, which appear as a leaf in a TP+Output query, in a more efficient way rather than pattern matching. Once we encounter such a predicate node p, we create a new inverted list for its parent object node o, whose content is a selection of labels from the object table R_o based on the condition that p is not null. If p is a multi-valued property of o, values for p are stored in object/property table $R_{o/p}$, as shown in the last section. Hence, the selection is done in $R_{o/p}$ and *distinct* labels are returned. After that the predicate node in the twig pattern query can be removed.

Output node: Output nodes in a TP+Output query are underlined and appear as a leaf query node. We maintain an output list L for all output nodes, together with the objects to which they belong in the query, so that after twig pattern matching we know the value of the nodes that need to be extracted.

Optional-output node: When we encounter an underlined leaf query node with "?" in the TP+Output query, we know that it is an optional-output node. We use a list OL to store all the optional-output nodes. Concretely, for each optional-output node p, we identify the object to which it belongs o, and store o/p in OL. Since optional-output nodes are not required to qualify each solution in the document, these nodes can be omitted during twig pattern matching.

Predicated-output node: Predicated-output nodes are also underlined in the TP+Output query. The constraint to differentiate between predicated-output node and output node is that predicated-output node has a child value comparison whereas the output node is a leaf node. We maintain a predicated-output node list PL to store predicate-output nodes. If the predicated-output node is a single-valued property, we put it along with the object to which it belongs into PL. When the predicated-output node is a multi-valued property, we have two cases as mentioned in Section 4. In the first case we only need to return the value of the property satisfying the predicate, and in the second case, we need to find all values of the multi-valued property, as long as one of them satisfies the predicate. If we have the first case of a predicated-output node p, we store p with the object to which it belongs o (in the form of o/p), along with the associated predicate in PL. If it is in the second case, we only store o/p.

Optional-predicated-output node: Optional-predicated-output nodes are marked by "?" and underlined, and contain child value comparisons. Similar to optional-output nodes, optional-predicated-output nodes are not involved in pattern matching as they are not required to qualify solutions. We use an optional-predicated-output list *OPL* to store such query nodes. Similarly for multi-valued properties, we have two cases: one is outputting the values satisfying the predicate only, while the other is outputting all values as long as one of them satisfies the predicate. So in *OPL*, for each optional-predicated-output node p we store the o/p pair with its object o, the associated predicate, and also a flag which is either *self* or *all*, to indicate whether $\longrightarrow$ is involved for this node.

After handling all the enhanced notations, the TP+Output query is rewritten as a normal twig pattern by removing notations and relevant query nodes as described above, and is matched using *VERT*. Using the output of pattern matching, which is in terms of node labels, we can extract values for the property nodes in L, OL, PL and OPL in relevant tables separately. In more detail, for each o/p in L, we do a selection in object table R_o based on o's labels that are returned by pattern matching. The optional-output nodes in OL are also extracted in a similar way. For the nodes in PL and OPL, when we extract the values from relevant tables, we also have to note that if the property is multi-valued, whether only the satisfied values are required or all values are required.

We can see that the existing algorithm can process TP+Output queries with a simple extension, and a significant benefit is gained because there is only one pass for pattern matching for queries with complex output information.

Note that, *VERT* complements pattern matching algorithms to handle values. Thus though $VERT_{ext}$ is bound to *VERT*, it is not limited to a particular pattern matching algorithm to perform a structural search. In other words, any pattern matching algorithm can be extended to process *TP+Output* queries.

Example 1. Consider the TP+Output query Q6 shown in Fig. 7(a). This query aims to find the employees who have age greater than 30, and have completed some training (thus given a grade), and output the employee's name, age, all the hobbies he/she has if one of them is 'movie', the title of the training he/she completed, and the trainers if any. In this query, all four types of query nodes are involved. If we use the original twig patterns to represent Q6, we need to match four sub-patterns, as shown in Fig. 7(b), and post-process matching results with inner and outer joins. In $VERT_{ext}$, the predicate node *grade*, as well as the predicate on *age*, are solved by table selection before pattern matching, and then removed from the twig pattern. Output nodes, optional-output nodes, predicated-output nodes and optional-predicated-output nodes are inserted into corresponding lists based on the description above. Particularly, *hobby* is a optional-predicated-output node with $\longrightarrow$, so it is inserted into *OPL* with the predicate and flag of *all*. After solving the enhanced notations, the twig pattern query is rewritten by removing optional-output node *trainer* and optional-predicated-output node *hobby*, because they are not required to qualify a result during pattern matching. The rewritten query is processed by pattern matching, and then the values for the property nodes in L, PL, OL and OPL are extracted using the relational tables. The whole process is shown in Fig. 7(c). Notice in particular that the columns *hobby* and *trainer* in the final result contain two values respectively. This is because we get answers for such multi-valued property in the object/property tables using a unique employee label. If we process this query by matching multiple original twig patterns and joining the results, we will get four tuples of answers with the same employee name and different hobby-trainer combinations in a cross product manner. Obviously the output format generated by our approach is more readable.

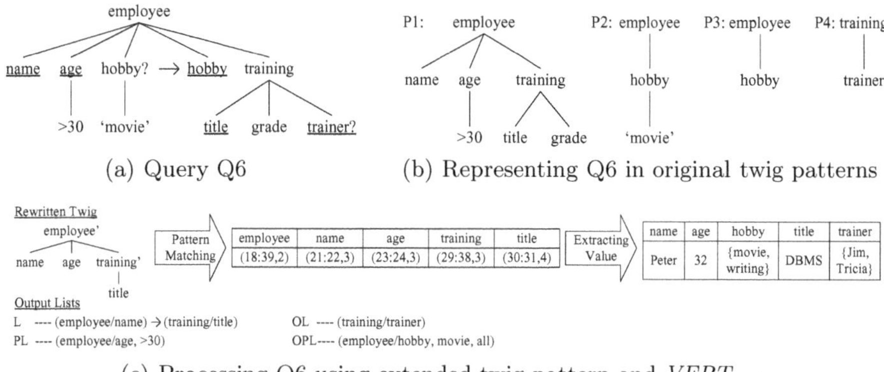

Fig. 7. Example query and query processing using original and extended twig pattern

6 Experiments

6.1 Experimental Settings

Implementation: All algorithms are implemented in Java, and executed with a dual-core 2.33GHz CPU and a 4GB RAM under Windows XP.

Data and Queries: We use two real-life data sets and one benchmark data set for our experiments: NASA [3], a 25MB real-life document with a complex schema; DBLP, a 91MB document with a simple schema and a large amount of data; and XMark, an 80MB well-known benchmark document. We randomly choose 5 queries for each data set to execute. The queries contain different types of output nodes for different query purposes. They are shown in Fig. 8, as TP+Output expressions.

6.2 Compare TP+Output with TP

We first test query processing efficiency using TP+Output and the original twig pattern (TP) to represent queries. The TP+Output representations for each query are shown in Fig. 8. We transform each query into TP representation in such a way that (1) for each optional edge, we break the TP+Output expression into two TPs with outer join, and (2) for each multi-valued (optional-)predicated-output node that outputs ALL values, we use a separate twig pattern query to get all values for the multi-valued node. Due to space limitation, we do not

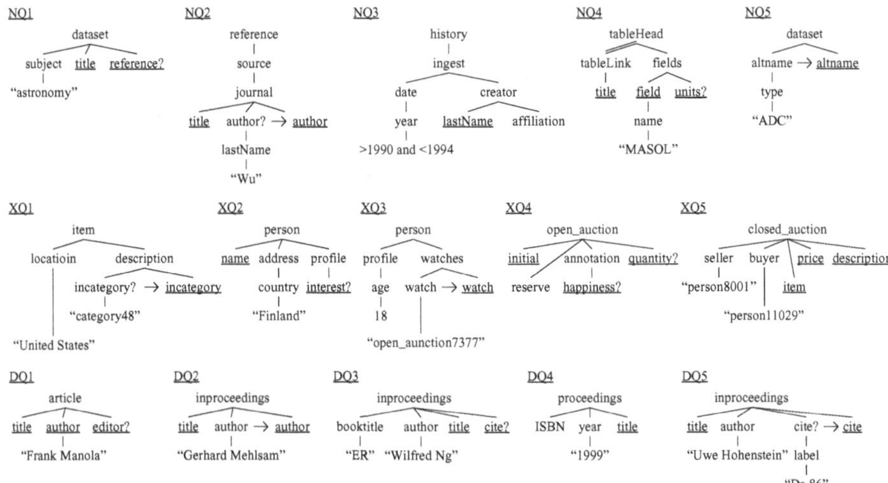

Fig. 8. Experimental queries in TP+Output expressions

show the TP expressions for the queries. We use the same pattern matching technique to match each TP+Output and TP to the corresponding document. In particular, we use *TwigStack* for structural search (joins), and use *VERT* for content search. Thus the only factor that affects the performance is the query representation, instead of the efficiency of pattern matching. The experimental results are shown in Fig. 9.

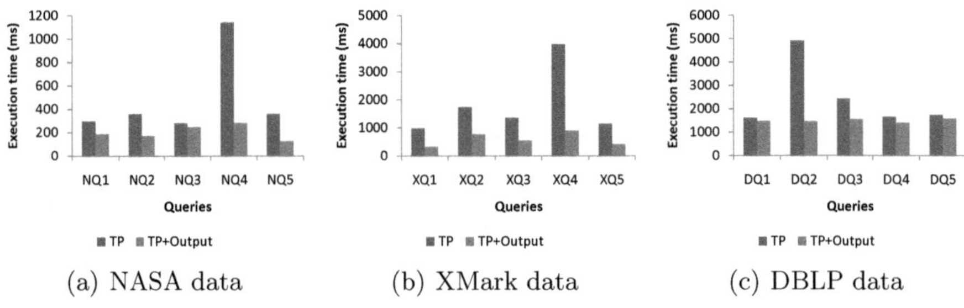

(a) NASA data (b) XMark data (c) DBLP data

Fig. 9. Performance comparison between TP and TP+Output representations

We can see that for all the queries, TP+Output has a better performance. We will look more closely at two cases. The first case is where the query involves optional output nodes, or involves multi-valued output nodes requiring all values to be output. In this case, TP cannot express the query using a single pattern. To perform such a query, we need to match more than one query pattern and outer join the results. Thus the query processing performance is seriously affected. For example, for query NQ1, we first match the pattern without *reference* to select all the satisfied *title*s, and then match all the *reference*s and outer join the results with previously selected labels. When the twig pattern for the optional output leads a large size of intermediate result, the overall performance will be significantly affected, like in NQ4 and XQ4.

In the second case, the query does not involve optional-output nodes or multi-valued nodes requiring all values to be output, so like TP+Output, TP requires only a single pattern to represent the query. Queries NQ3 and DQ4 are examples of such queries that only contain predicate nodes and output nodes. In this case, TP+Output still demonstrates better performance, though not as significant as that in the first case. The reason is $VERT_{ext}$ rewrites TP+Output expression by reducing the predicate property nodes and the inverted list size of the object nodes, instead of performing a structural join for such predicates; whereas in TP representation, every edge requires a structural join, because it cannot differentiate leaf predicate nodes from output nodes.

6.3 Scalability of $VERT_{ext}$

We test the scalability of $VERT_{ext}$ to process TP+Output queries. We execute queries XQ1-XQ5 on four XMark data sets of differing sizes. The experimental result in Fig. 10(a) shows that all queries scale well.

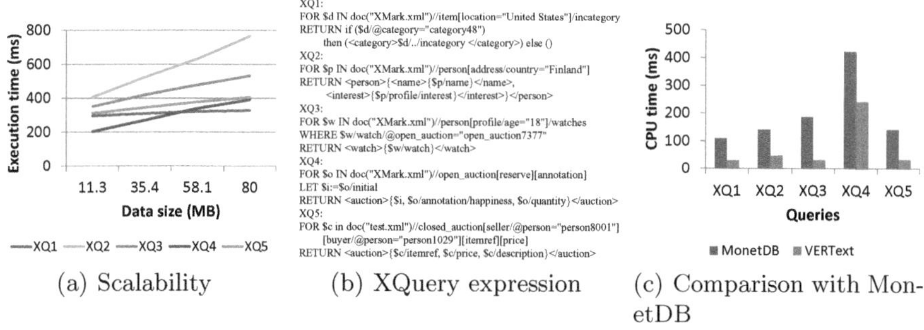

(a) Scalability (b) XQuery expression (c) Comparison with MonetDB

Fig. 10. Figures for scalability test and comparison with MonetDB

6.4 Comparison with XQuery Processors

Last, we compare $VERT_{ext}$ with two XQuery processors, to further validate the efficiency advantage of TP+Output. We use two XQuery processors: MonetDB[2] and IBM DB2[1]. MonetDB adopts relational approach to process queries, while DB2 is native based. These are two representative approaches to process XML queries. The execution time of $VERT_{ext}$ include both table accessing cost and structural join cost.

Since MonetDB is a memory-based XQuery processor which cannot accept large XML data files, we use a small XMark data set (11MB) for the queries XQ1-XQ5, and only compare CPU time in this test. We show the XQuery expressions for the tested queries as in Fig. 10(b), which are executed by MonetDB. The testing result is shown in Fig. 10(c). We can see for all the queries $VERT_{ext}$ is more efficient than MonetDB.

Next we use DB2 to execute all the queries in the three documents as mentioned in Section 6.1, to compare with $VERT_{ext}$. Due to the limited space, we do not present the XQuery expressions of all queries. In this test, the execution time in $VERT_{ext}$ includes index loading, pattern matching and result outputting, thus it is slower than the time shown in Fig. 9 in our first test. The result is shown in Fig. 11. We can see that for all queries, our approach is more efficient than DB2, which adopts a navigational approach to evaluate each XQuery expression.

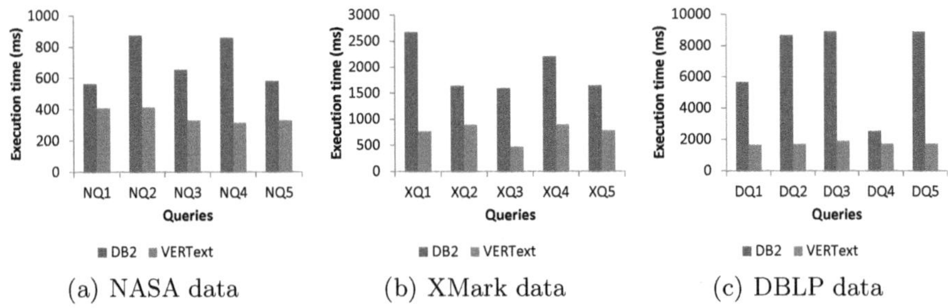

(a) NASA data (b) XMark data (c) DBLP data

Fig. 11. Performance comparison between $VERT_{ext}$ and DB2

7 Conclusion

In this paper we extend the expressive power of twig pattern queries so that queries with complex output under a single object query node can be expressed easily with a single twig pattern. We first analyze the purpose of each query node, and the optionality and the occurrence of the output information. Based on these characteristics, we define four types of query node in a twig pattern query to express output information, namely *output node*, *optional-output node*, *predicated-output node* and *optional-predicated-output node*. After that we propose a more expressive twig pattern, TP+Output, by introducing a set of notations to distinguish different types of query nodes. We also extend our previously proposed algorithm, *VERT* to efficiently process TP+Output queries, and show experimentally the advantage of our approach.

As an intermediate query pattern, how to generate TP+Output expression from XQuery or other XML query languages has yet to be investigated. Also, since TP+Output has richer semantics than other intermediate query pattern, it is potential to enrich it to be an independent graphical XML query language.

References

1. http://ibm.com/db2/xml/
2. http://monetdb.cwi.nl/

3. http://www.cs.washington.edu/research/xmldatasets/data/nasa/nasa.xml
4. Al-Khalifa, S., Jagadish, H.V., Patel, J.M., Wu, Y., Koudas, N., Srivastava, D.: Structural joins: A primitive for efficient XML query pattern matching. In: ICDE, pp. 141–154 (2002)
5. Berglund, A., Chamberlin, D., Fernandez, M.F., Kay, M., Robie, J., Simeon, J.: XML Path Language (XPath) 2.0. W3C Working Draft (2003)
6. Boag, S., Chamberlin, D., Fernandez, M.F., Florescu, D., Robie, J., Simeon, J.: XQuery 1.0: An XML Query. W3C Working Draft (2003)
7. Bruno, N., Koudas, N., Srivastava, D.: Holistic twig joins: Optimal XML pattern matching. In: SIGMOD Conference, pp. 310–321 (2002)
8. Chen, S., Li, H., Tatemura, J., Hsiung, W., Agrawal, D., Candan, K.S.: Twig^{2}Stack: bottom-up processing of generalized-tree-pattern queries over XML documents. In: VLDB, pp. 283–294 (2006)
9. Chen, T., Lu, J., Ling, T.W.: On boosting holism in XML twig pattern matching using structural indexing techniques. In: SIGMOD Conference, pp. 455–466 (2005)
10. Chen, Z., Jagadish, H.V., Lakshmanan, L.V.S., Paparizos, S.: From tree patterns to generalized tree patterns: on efficient evaluation of XQuery. In: VLDB, pp. 237–248 (2003)
11. Florescu, D., Kossmann, D.: Storing and querying XML data using an RDMBS. IEEE Data Eng. Bull., 27–34 (1999)
12. Gou, G., Chirkova, R.: Efficiently querying large XML data repositories: a survey. IEEE Trans. Knowl. Data Eng. 19(10), 1381–1403 (2007)
13. Jiang, H., Lu, H., Wang, W.: Efficient processing of XML twig queries with OR-predicates. In: SIGMOD Conference, pp. 59–70 (2004)
14. Jiang, H., Wang, W., Lu, H., Yu, J.: Holistic twig joins on indexed XML documents. In: VLDB, pp. 273–284 (2003)
15. Lu, J., Ling, T.W., Chan, C., Chen, T.: From region encoding to extended dewey: On efficient processing of XML twig pattern matching. In: VLDB, pp. 193–204 (2005)
16. Pal, S., Cseri, I., Seeliger, O., Schaller, G., Giakoumakis, L., Zolotov, V.: Indexing XML data stored in a relational database. In: VLDB, pp. 1146–1157 (2004)
17. Shanmugasundaram, J., Tufte, K., He, G., Zhang, C., Dewitt, D., Naughton, J.: Relational databases for querying XML documents: limitations and opportunities. In: VLDB, pp. 302–314 (1999)
18. Theodoratos, D., Dalamagas, T., Koufopoulos, A., Gehani, N.: Semantic querying of tree-structured data sources using partially specified tree patterns. In: CIKM, pp. 712–719 (2005)
19. Wu, H., Ling, T.W., Chen, B.: VERT: a semantic approach for content search and content extraction in XML query processing. In: Parent, C., Schewe, K.-D., Storey, V.C., Thalheim, B. (eds.) ER 2007. LNCS, vol. 4801, pp. 534–549. Springer, Heidelberg (2007)
20. Yoshikawa, M., Amagasa, T., Shimura, T., Uemura, S.: XRel: a path-based approach to storage and retrieval of XML documents using relational databases. ACM Trans. Interet Technol. 1, 110–141 (2001)
21. Zhang, C., Naughton, J., Dewitt, D., Luo, Q., Lohman, G.: On supporting containment queries in relational database management systems. In: SIGMOD Conference, pp. 425–436 (2001)

Promoting the Semantic Capability of XML Keys

Flavio Ferrarotti[1], Sven Hartmann[2], Sebastian Link[1], and Jing Wang[3]

[1] Victoria University of Wellington, New Zealand
[2] Clausthal University of Technology, Germany
[3] Massey University, New Zealand
Flavio.Ferrarotti@vuw.ac.nz

Abstract. Keys for XML data trees can uniquely identify nodes based on the data values on some of their subnodes, either in the entire tree or relatively to some selected subtrees. Such keys have an impact on several XML applications. A challenge is to identify expressive classes of keys with good computational properties. In this paper, we propose such a new class of keys. In comparison to previous work, the new class of XML keys is defined using a more expressive navigational path language that allows the specification of single-label wildcards. This provides designers with an enhanced ability to capture properties of XML data that are significant for the application at hand. We establish a sound and complete set of inference rules that characterizes all keys that are implicit in the explicit specification of XML keys. Furthermore, we establish an efficient algorithm for deciding XML key implication.

1 Introduction

The study of integrity constraints has been recognized as one of the most important yet challenging areas of XML research [5,10] The importance of XML constraints is due to a variety of applications ranging from schema design, query optimization, efficient storing and updating, data exchange and integration, to data cleaning [5]. However, for almost all classes of constraints the complex structure of XML data results in decision problems that are intractable. In particular, the consistency problem is either infeasible or intractable for several fragments of keys as defined by XML schema [2]. It is therefore a major challenge to find natural and useful classes of XML constraints that can be reasoned about efficiently [5,10]. Prime candidates of such classes are absolute and relative keys [3] that are defined on the basis of a tree model for XML as proposed by DOM [1] and XPath [4], but independently from schema specifications such as DTDs or XSDs [11]. Figures 1 and 2 show such a representation in which nodes are annotated by their type: E for element, A for attribute, and S for string (PCDATA).

Keys for XML can uniquely identify nodes based on the data values on some of their subnodes, either in the entire tree or relatively to some selected subtrees. In this context, keys are defined in terms of path expressions. Nodes are determined by (complex) values on some selected descendent nodes. In Figure 1, an example

M.L. Lee et al. (Eds.): XSym 2010, LNCS 6309, pp. 144–153, 2010.

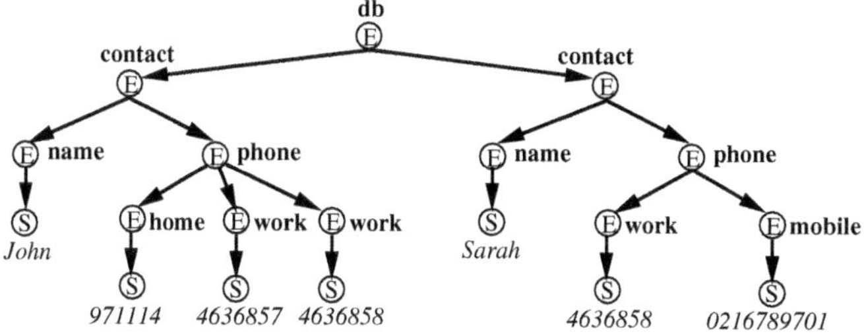

Fig. 1. Tree representation of XML data

of a reasonable absolute key is that a *contact* node can be uniquely identified in the whole document by values found on the leaves under its *name* and *phone* children. More precisely, assuming that we do not want two contacts with the same name and a phone number in common to appear in our XML agenda, our XML key should express that different *contact* nodes must differ on the values of their *name.S* descendent nodes, or otherwise their corresponding sets formed by the values of all their *phone._.S* descendent nodes must be disjoint. Here the single-label wildcard "_" is a place holder for *work*, *home*, *mobile*, and any other child of a *phone* node. Note that the XML document in Figure 1 satisfies this key because even though both contacts share the phone number 4636858, they have different names.

In order to unlock the vast amount of application domains effectively it is crucial to define expressive notions of XML keys whose associated decision problems are still tractable. As shown in [7,8], for XML keys as defined in [3], the complexity of the implication problem is influenced by the choice of a path language for defining such XML keys. On the other hand, the choice of a navigational path language for defining XML keys influences the expressiveness of these keys. For instance, the class of XML keys with non-empty sets of simple key paths proposed in [3] is quite expressive. However, those XML keys cannot express the one from the previous example. A wider range of XML keys can be expressed by the class of XML keys proposed in [3] in which variable length wildcards in key paths as well as empty sets of key paths are allowed. But, up to our knowledge, the problems of axiomatising and developing efficient algorithms that decide the implication of such class of XML keys are still open (see [7,8]). By contrast, for the class of XML keys with non-empty sets of simple key paths, a sound and complete axiomatization and an efficient algorithm for the implication problem was presented in [7,8].

It is noteworthy that there are alternative XML representations of the example presented in Figure 1 in which the use of wildcards to specify the proposed XML key can be avoided. See for instance Figure 2. Nevertheless, the ability to interchange structure (the names) with data (their values) constitutes one of the strong points of semistructured data and XML. It allows users to generate intuitive XML documents, such as the one in Figure 1. In fact, it is unrealistic and counter-productive to generate less intuitive XML documents, for example the document in Figure 2, for the sake of making restricted tools applicable.

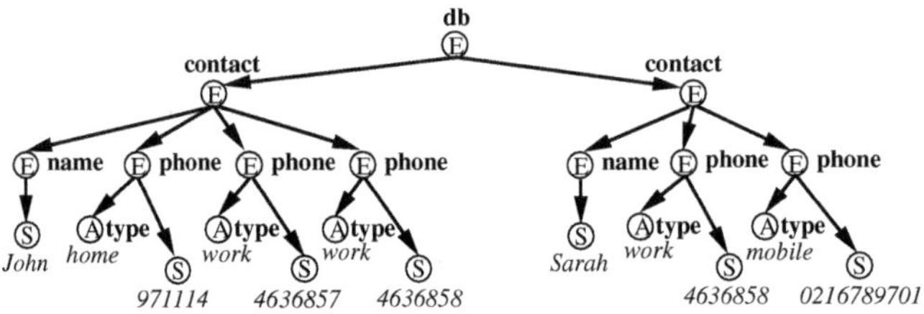

Fig. 2. Alternative tree representation of XML data in Figure 1

Thus, it is a significant challenge to identify expressive classes of XML keys that still enjoy good computational properties. In this paper, we propose such a new class of XML keys. In comparison to previous work, the new class utilizes a more expressive navigational path language that allows the specification of single-label wildcards. This provides designers with an enhanced ability to capture properties of XML data that are significant for the application at hand. In particular, the XML key (ϵ, contact, ({name.S, phone._.S})) falls into this new class of keys, and captures successfully the semantics of our example. We establish a sound and complete set of inference rules that characterizes all keys that are implicit in the explicit specification of XML keys. Furthermore, we establish an efficient algorithm for deciding XML key implication.

2 Preliminaries

The XML Tree Model. We assume that there is a countably infinite set **E** denoting element tags, a countably infinite set **A** denoting attribute names, and a singleton set $\{S\}$ denoting text (PCDATA). We further assume that these sets are pairwise disjoint. We refer to the elements of $\mathcal{L} = \mathbf{E} \cup \mathbf{A} \cup \{S\}$ as *labels*. An *XML tree* is a 6-tuple $T = (V, lab, ele, att, val, r)$ where V denotes a set of nodes, and lab is a mapping $V \to \mathcal{L}$ assigning a label to every node in V. A node $v \in V$ is called an *element node* if $lab(v) \in \mathbf{E}$, an *attribute node* if $lab(v) \in \mathbf{A}$, and a *text node* if $lab(v) = S$. Moreover, ele and att are partial mappings defining the edge relation of T: for any node $v \in V$, if v is an element node, then $ele(v)$ is a list of element and text nodes in V and $att(v)$ is a set of attribute nodes in V. If v is an attribute or text node, then $ele(v)$ and $att(v)$ are undefined. The partial mapping val assigns a string to each attribute and text node: for each node $v \in V$, $val(v)$ is a string if v is an attribute or text node, while $val(v)$ is undefined otherwise. Finally, r is the unique and distinguished root node. A *path* p of T is a finite sequence of nodes $v_0, \ldots, v_m$ in V such that (v_{i-1}, v_i) is an edge of T for $i = 1, \ldots, m$. The path p determines a word $lab(v_1). \cdots .lab(v_m)$ over the alphabet $\mathcal{L}$, denoted by $lab(p)$.

Value Equality of Nodes in XML Trees. Two nodes $u, v \in V$ are *value equal*, denoted by $u =_v v$, iff the following conditions are satisfied: (a) $lab(u) = lab(v)$, (b) if u, v are attribute or text nodes, then $val(u) = val(v)$, (c) if u, v are element nodes, then *(i)* if $att(u) = \{a_1, \ldots, a_m\}$, then $att(v) = \{a'_1, \ldots, a'_m\}$ and there is a permutation π on $\{1, \ldots, m\}$ such that $a_i =_v a'_{\pi(i)}$ for $i = 1, \ldots, m$, and *(ii)* if $ele(u) = [u_1, \ldots, u_k]$, then $ele(v) = [v_1, \ldots, v_k]$ and $u_i =_v v_i$ for $i = 1, \ldots, k$.

Path Expressions for Node Selection in XML Trees. We use the path language $PL^{\{.,\_,\_^*\}}$ consisting of expressions given by the following grammar: $Q \to \ell \mid \varepsilon \mid Q.Q \mid \_ \mid \_^*$. Here $\ell \in \mathcal{L}$ is any label, ε denotes the empty path expression, "." denotes the concatenation of two path expressions, "_" denotes the *single-label* wildcard, and "_*" denotes the *variable length don't care* wildcard. Let P, Q be words from $PL^{\{.,\_,\_^*\}}$. P is a *refinement* of Q, denoted by $P \lesssim Q$, if P is obtained from Q by replacing variable length wildcards in Q by words from $PL^{\{.,\_,\_^*\}}$ and single-label wildcards in Q by labels from $\mathcal{L}$. Let Q be a word from $PL^{\{.,\_,\_^*\}}$. A path p in the XML tree T is called a Q-path if $lab(p)$ is a refinement of Q. For nodes $v, w \in V$, we write $T \models Q(v,w)$ if w is reachable from v following a Q-path in T. For a node $v \in V$, let $v[\![Q]\!]$ denote the set of nodes in T that are reachable from v following any Q-path, that is, $v[\![Q]\!] = \{w \mid T \models Q(v,w)\}$. We use $[\![Q]\!]$ as an abbreviation for $r[\![Q]\!]$ where r is the root node of T. For S a nonempty subset of $\{.,\_,\_^*\}$, PL^S denotes the subset of $PL^{\{.,\_,\_^*\}}$ expressions restricted to the constructs in S. $Q \in PL^{\{.,\_,\_^*\}}$ is *valid* if it does not have labels $\ell \in \mathbf{A}$ or $\ell = S$ in a position other than the last one. Let P, Q be words from $PL^{\{.,\_,\_^*\}}$. P is *contained* in Q, denoted by $P \subseteq Q$, if for every XML tree T and every node v of T we have $v[\![P]\!] \subseteq v[\![Q]\!]$. It follows immediately from the definition that $P \lesssim Q$ implies $P \subseteq Q$. For nodes v and v' of an XML tree T, the *value intersection* of $v[\![Q]\!]$ and $v'[\![Q]\!]$ is given by $v[\![Q]\!] \cap_v v'[\![Q]\!] = \{(w,w') \mid w \in v[\![Q]\!], w' \in v'[\![Q]\!], w =_v w'\}$.

3 Keys for XML

Following [3], let us first define formally the concept of XML key. Let PL_1, PL_2 and PL_3 be path languages suitable for node selection in XML trees such that for some fixed $1 \leq m \leq 3$, it holds that for $1 \leq i \leq 3$, if a path expression is in PL_i, then it is also in PL_m. An *XML key* φ in a class $\mathcal{K}(PL_1, PL_2, PL_3)$ of XML keys, is an expression of the form $(Q, (Q', \{Q_1, \ldots, Q_k\}))$ where Q is a PL_1 expression, Q' is a PL_2 expression, and for $1 \leq i \leq k$, Q_i is a PL_3 expression such that $Q.Q'.Q_i$ is a valid PL_m expression. Herein, Q is called the *context path*, Q' is called the *target path*, and $Q_1, \ldots, Q_k$ are called the *key paths* of φ. An XML tree T satisfies a key $(Q, (Q', \{Q_1, \ldots, Q_k\}))$ if and only if for every node $q \in [\![Q]\!]$ and all nodes $q_1', q_2' \in q[\![Q']\!]$ such that there are nodes $x_i \in q_1'[\![Q_i]\!], y_i \in q_2'[\![Q_i]\!]$ with $x_i =_v y_i$ for all $i = 1, \ldots, k$, then $q_1' = q_2'$. Some examples of XML keys follow.

a. $(\varepsilon, (\text{contact}, \{\text{name}.S, \text{phone}.\_.S\}))$. This XML key formalizes our example from the introduction in XML trees with the form of the tree in Figure 1.
b. $(\varepsilon, (\_^*.\text{contact}, \{\text{phone}.\_.S\}))$. This key is not satisfied by the tree in Figure 1 since both contacts share the work phone number 4636858.
c. $(\varepsilon, (\text{contact}, \{\text{name}.S, \text{phone}.S\}))$. This XML key expresses the same as the key in a., but over XML trees with the form of the tree in Figure 2.
d. $(\varepsilon, (\text{contact}, \{\text{name}.S, \text{phone}.\_^*.S\}))$. Over trees with the form of the one in Figure 1, this XML key is equivalent to the key in a., and over trees with the form of the one in Figure 2, it is equivalent to the key in c.

e. $(\varepsilon, (\_^*.\text{contact}, \{\_^*.S\}))$. It roughly expresses that any two different *contact* nodes in the tree must differ in all values of all their descendent S nodes. Neither the tree in Figure 1 nor the tree in Figure 2 satisfies this key.
f. $(\varepsilon, (\text{contact}, \{\varepsilon\}))$. This key expresses that there cannot be two different *contact* nodes u and v such that both are children of the root node and the subtrees rooted at u and v are isomorphic by an isomorphism that is the identity on string values. It is satisfied by both the tree in Figure 1 and the tree in Figure 2.
g. $(\varepsilon, (\text{contact}, \emptyset))$. This is satisfied by a tree if there is at most one *contact* node that is a child of the root node.
h. $(\varepsilon, (\_, \{\_\}))$. In an XML tree that satisfies this key, one will never find two different children nodes of the root for which the value intersection of their corresponding sets of child nodes is non-empty. This key is satisfied by the tree in Figure 1 and violated by the tree in Figure 2.
i. $(\text{contact}, (\text{phone}.\_, \{S\}))$. Interpreted in a XML tree with the form of the tree in Figure 1, this key expresses that , for each individual *contact* node, different *work*, *home* and *mobile* nodes must all have different phone numbers.

Let $\Sigma \cup \{\varphi\}$ be a finite set of XML keys in a class $\mathcal{C}$. We say that Σ *(finitely) implies* φ, denoted by $\Sigma \models_{(f)} \varphi$, if and only if every (finite) XML tree T that satisfies all $\sigma \in \Sigma$ also satisfies φ. The *(finite) implication problem for* $\mathcal{C}$ is to decide, given any finite set $\Sigma \cup \{\varphi\}$ of keys in $\mathcal{C}$, whether $\Sigma \models_{(f)} \varphi$. For a set Σ of keys in $\mathcal{C}$, let $\Sigma^*_{(f)} = \{\varphi \in \mathcal{C} \mid \Sigma \models_{(f)} \varphi\}$ be its *(finite) semantic closure*, i.e., the set of all keys (finitely) implied by Σ. The notion of syntactical inference ($\vdash_{\mathfrak{R}}$) with respect to a set $\mathfrak{R}$ of inference rules can be defined analogously to the notion in the relational data model. That is, a finite sequence $\gamma = [\gamma_1, \ldots, \gamma_l]$ of XML keys is called an *inference from* Σ *by* $\mathfrak{R}$ if every γ_i is either an element of Σ or is obtained by applying one of the rules of $\mathfrak{R}$ to appropriate elements of $\{\gamma_1, \ldots, \gamma_{i-1}\}$. We say that the inference γ infers γ_l, i.e. the last element of the sequence γ, and write $\Sigma \vdash_{\mathfrak{R}} \gamma_l$. For a finite set Σ of keys in $\mathcal{C}$, let $\Sigma^+_{\mathfrak{R}} = \{\varphi \mid \Sigma \vdash_{\mathfrak{R}} \varphi\}$ be its *syntactic closure* under inferences by $\mathfrak{R}$. A set $\mathfrak{R}$ of inference rules is said to be *sound* (*complete*) for the (finite) implication of keys in $\mathcal{C}$ if for every finite set Σ of XML keys in $\mathcal{C}$ we have $\Sigma^+_{\mathfrak{R}} \subseteq \Sigma^*_{(f)}$ ($\Sigma^*_{(f)} \subseteq \Sigma^+_{\mathfrak{R}}$). The set $\mathfrak{R}$ is said to be an *axiomatisation* for the (finite) implication of keys in $\mathcal{C}$ if $\mathfrak{R}$ is both sound and complete for the (finite) implication of keys in $\mathcal{C}$. Finally, an axiomatisation $\mathfrak{R}$ is said to be *finite* if the set $\mathfrak{R}$ is finite.

A finite axiomatization for the (finite) implication of keys in the class of XML keys with non-empty sets of simple key paths $\mathcal{K}(PL^{\{.,\_^*\}}, PL^{\{.,\_^*\}}, PL^{\{.\}}_{+})$, was established in [7,8]. Here we use the "+" symbol to indicate that the finite set of key paths must not be empty. It is important to note that from a practical point of view, and as illustrated by the examples given in [3,7,8], many useful XML keys belong to the class $\mathcal{K}(PL^{\{.,\_^*\}}, PL^{\{.,\_^*\}}, PL^{\{.\}}_{+})$. Note that the XML keys in points (c) and (f) above belong to this class.

A more expressive class of XML keys was studied in [9], namely the class $\mathcal{K}(PL^{\{.,\_^*\}}, PL^{\{.,\_^*\}}, PL^{\{.\}}_{*})$. Here we use the "$*$" symbol to stress that the finite set of key paths can be empty. Note that, the key in point (g) above belongs to this class of XML keys. Also the keys in points (c) and (f) belong to this class since those keys also belong to the class $\mathcal{K}(PL^{\{\cdot,\_^*\}}, PL^{\{\cdot,\_^*\}}, PL_+^{\{\cdot\}})$ which is strictly included in it.

In this paper, we study the class $\mathcal{K}(PL^{\{\cdot,\_,\_^*\}}, PL^{\{\cdot,\_,\_^*\}}, PL_+^{\{\cdot,\_\}})$ of XML keys in which single-label wildcards are allowed in context, target and key paths. Except for the keys in points (d), (e) and (g), all other keys introduced above belong to this class. Clearly, this class of XML keys is more expressive than the class studied in [7,8] as it strictly includes all XML keys that belong to $\mathcal{K}(PL^{\{\cdot,\_^*\}}, PL^{\{\cdot,\_^*\}}, PL_+^{\{\cdot\}})$ and, at the same time, it includes keys as those in points (a), (b), (h) and (i) for which there are no equivalent XML keys in $\mathcal{K}(PL^{\{\cdot,\_^*\}}, PL^{\{\cdot,\_^*\}}, PL_+^{\{\cdot\}})$. Note that this new class is orthogonal to the class $\mathcal{K}(PL^{\{\cdot,\_^*\}}, PL^{\{\cdot,\_^*\}}, PL_*^{\{\cdot\}})$ studied in [9]. Take for instance the key in point (h), it is easy to see that there is no XML key in $\mathcal{K}(PL^{\{\cdot,\_^*\}}, PL^{\{\cdot,\_^*\}}, PL_*^{\{\cdot\}})$ that is satisfied by exactly those XML trees that satisfy $(\varepsilon, (\_, \{\_\}))$. A clear example in the other direction is given by the XML key in point (g). Also note that the set of inference rules used in [9] for the finite axiomatization of the class $\mathcal{K}(PL^{\{\cdot,\_^*\}}, PL^{\{\cdot,\_^*\}}, PL_*^{\{\cdot\}})$ is considerably different from the set of inference rules proposed in this work for the class $\mathcal{K}(PL^{\{\cdot,\_,\_^*\}}, PL^{\{\cdot,\_,\_^*\}}, PL_+^{\{\cdot,\_\}})$. Furthermore, the techniques and results used in that paper are different.

From now on, for an XML key φ, we use Q_φ to denote its context path, Q'_φ to denote its target path, and $P_1^\varphi, \ldots, P_{k_\varphi}^\varphi$ to denote its key paths, where k_φ is the number of its key paths.

4 An Axiomatisation

Theorem 1. *Let $\mathfrak{R}$ denote the set of inference rules in Table 1 together with the key-path containment rule in Equation (1). Then $\mathfrak{R}$ forms a finite axiomatisation for the implication of XML keys in $\mathcal{K}(PL^{\{\cdot,\_,\_^*\}}, PL^{\{\cdot,\_,\_^*\}}, PL_+^{\{\cdot,\_\}})$.*

$$\frac{(Q,(Q',\mathcal{S}\cup\{P\}))}{(Q,(Q',\mathcal{S}\cup\{P'\}))}\,P'\subseteq P \qquad \text{(key-path containment)} \tag{1}$$

The soundness of the *key-path containment rule* is not difficult to see. Suppose an XML tree T violates $(Q,(Q',\mathcal{S}\cup\{P'\}))$. Then there is some node $q \in [\![Q]\!]$ and some nodes $q'_1, q'_2 \in q[\![Q']\!]$ such that $q'_1 \neq q'_2$ and for all $P_i \in \mathcal{S}\cup\{P'\}$ it holds that $q'_1[\![P_i]\!] \cap_v q'_2[\![P_i]\!] \neq \emptyset$. In particular, this means that $q'_1[\![P']\!] \cap_v q'_2[\![P']\!] \neq \emptyset$. Since $P' \subseteq P$, we have that $q'_1[\![P']\!] \subseteq q'_1[\![P]\!]$ and $q'_2[\![P']\!] \subseteq q'_2[\![P]\!]$. But then, $q'_1[\![P]\!] \cap_v q'_2[\![P]\!] \neq \emptyset$. Hence, T also violates $(Q,(Q',\mathcal{S}\cup\{P\}))$. It is a simple technical task to modify the soundness proofs of the rules in Table 1, to show that they remain sound.

For the completeness proof we need to show that, for an arbitrary finite set $\Sigma \cup \{\varphi\}$ of keys in $\mathcal{K}(PL^{\{\cdot,\_,\_^*\}}, PL^{\{\cdot,\_,\_^*\}}, PL_+^{\{\cdot,\_\}})$, if $\varphi \notin \Sigma^+_{\mathfrak{R}}$, then there is some XML tree T which is a counter-example for the implication of φ by Σ.

The general proof strategy is as follows. In a first step, we represent φ in terms of a finite node-labelled tree $T_{\Sigma,\varphi}$, which we call the *mini-tree*. Then, we calculate the impact of each key in Σ on the counter-example tree T that we

Table 1. An axiomatisation of XML keys in $\mathcal{K}(PL^{\{.,\_^*\}}, PL^{\{.,\_^*\}}, PL_+^{\{.\}})$ [8]

$\overline{(Q,(\varepsilon,\mathcal{S}))}$ (epsilon)	$\dfrac{(Q,(Q',\mathcal{S}\cup\{\varepsilon,P\}))}{(Q,(Q',\mathcal{S}\cup\{\varepsilon,P.P'\}))}$ (prefix-epsilon)	$\dfrac{(Q,(Q',\mathcal{S}))}{(Q,(Q',\mathcal{S}\cup\{P\}))}$ (superkey)
$\dfrac{(Q,(Q'.P,\{P'\}))}{(Q,(Q',\{P.P'\}))}$ (subnodes)	$\dfrac{(Q,(Q',\mathcal{S}))}{(Q'',(Q',\mathcal{S}))}\, Q''\subseteq Q$ (context-path-containment)	$\dfrac{(Q,(Q',\mathcal{S}))}{(Q,(Q'',\mathcal{S}))}\, Q''\subseteq Q'$ (target-path-containment)
$\dfrac{(Q,(Q'.Q'',\mathcal{S}))}{(Q.Q',(Q'',\mathcal{S}))}$ (context-target)	$\dfrac{(Q,(Q'.P,\{\varepsilon,P'\}))}{(Q,(Q',\{\varepsilon,P.P'\}))}$ (subnodes-epsilon)	$\dfrac{(Q,(Q',\{P.P_1,\dots,P.P_k\})),\ (Q.Q',(P,\{P_1,\dots,P_k\}))}{(Q,(Q'.P,\{P_1,\dots,P_k\}))}$ (interaction)

want to build. We keep track of these impacts by inserting additional upward-directed edges into $T_{\Sigma,\varphi}$. This result in a digraph $G_{\Sigma,\varphi}$ which we call *witness graph.* Finally, we apply a reachability algorithm to $G_{\Sigma,\varphi}$ to decide which nodes to duplicate in $T_{\Sigma,\varphi}$, in order to generate the desired counter-example tree T .

Even though the strategy is similar to the strategy used in [7,8], the actual proofs required a thorough revision of the original approach and some novel ideas. Even a different construction for the mini-trees is needed to cope with the case of single-label wildcards.

Mini-trees and Witness Graphs. Let $\Sigma \cup \{\varphi\}$ be a finite set of keys in $\mathcal{K}(PL^{\{.,\_,\_^*\}}, PL^{\{.,\_,\_^*\}}, PL_+^{\{.,\_\}})$. Let $\mathcal{L}_{\Sigma,\varphi}$ denote the set of all labels $\ell \in \mathcal{L}$ that occur in path expressions of keys in $\Sigma \cup \{\varphi\}$, and fix a label $\ell_0 \in \mathbf{E} - \mathcal{L}_{\Sigma,\varphi}$. Let O_φ and O'_φ be the $PL^{\{.\}}$ expressions obtained from the $PL^{\{.,\_,\_^*\}}$ expressions Q_φ and Q'_φ, respectively, by replacing each single-label wildcard "_" by ℓ_0 and each variable length wildcard "_*" by a sequence of $l+1$ labels ℓ_0, where l is the maximum number of consecutive single-label wildcards that occur in any key in Σ. Further, for each $i = 1, \dots, k_\varphi$, let O_i^φ be the $PL^{\{.\}}$ expression obtained from the $PL^{\{.,\_\}}$ expression P_i^φ by replacing each single label wildcard "_" by ℓ_0. Let p be an O_φ-path from a node r_φ to a node q_φ, let p' be an O'_φ-path from a node r'_φ to a node q'_φ and, for each $i = 1, \dots, k_\varphi$, let p_i be a O_i^φ-path from a node r_i^φ to a node x_i^φ, such that the paths $p, p', p_1, \dots, p_{k_\varphi}$ are mutually node-disjoint. From the paths $p, p', p_1, \dots, p_{k_\varphi}$ we obtain the *mini-tree* $T_{\Sigma,\varphi}$ by identifying the node r'_φ with q_φ, and by identifying each of the nodes r_i^φ with q'_φ. The *marking* of the mini-tree $T_{\Sigma,\varphi}$ is a subset $\mathcal{M}$ of the node set of $T_{\Sigma,\varphi}$: if for all $i = 1, \dots, k_\varphi$ we have $P_i^\varphi \neq \varepsilon$, then $\mathcal{M}$ consists of the leaves of $T_{\Sigma,\varphi}$, and otherwise $\mathcal{M}$ consists of all descendant nodes of q'_φ in $T_{\Sigma,\varphi}$.

Example 1. Let Σ consist of $\sigma_1 = (\varepsilon, (\_^*.\text{contact}, \{\_.\text{name.S}, \_.\text{phone.S}\}))$ and $\sigma_2 = (\_.\text{contact}, (\_, \{\text{name.S}, \text{phone.S}\}))$. The left of Figure 3 shows the mini-tree $T_{\Sigma,\varphi}$ for the key $\varphi = (\varepsilon, (\_^*.\text{contact}.\_, \{\text{name.S}, \text{phone.S}\}))$, where $\ell_0 = \textit{diary}$ and the marking of the mini-tree consists of its leaves (emphasised by $\times$).

We use mini-trees to calculate the impact of a key in Σ on a possible counter-example tree for the implication of φ by Σ. To distinguish keys that have an

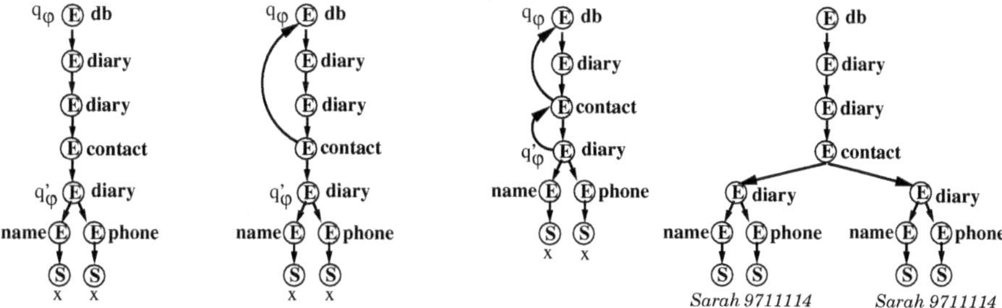

Fig. 3. A mini-tree, two witness graphs and a counter-example tree

impact from those that do not, we introduce the notion of *applicability*. Let $T_{\Sigma,\varphi}$ be the mini-tree of the key φ with respect to Σ, and let $\mathcal{M}$ be its marking. A key σ is said to be *applicable* to φ if and only if there are nodes $w_\sigma \in [\![Q_\sigma]\!]$ and $w'_\sigma \in w_\sigma[\![Q'_\sigma]\!]$ in $T_{\Sigma,\varphi}$ such that $w'_\sigma[\![P^\sigma_i]\!] \cap \mathcal{M} \neq \emptyset$ for all $i = 1, \ldots, k_\sigma$. We say that w_σ and w'_σ *witness* the applicability of σ to φ. As an example, consider Σ and φ from Example 1. While σ_1 is applicable to φ, σ_2 is not. We define the *witness graph* $G_{\Sigma,\varphi}$ as the node-labelled digraph obtained from $T_{\Sigma,\varphi}$ by inserting additional edges: for each key $\sigma \in \Sigma$ that is applicable to φ and for each pair of nodes $w_\sigma \in [\![Q_\sigma]\!]$ and $w'_\sigma \in w_\sigma[\![Q'_\sigma]\!]$ that witness the applicability of σ to φ, $G_{\Sigma,\varphi}$ contains the directed edge (w'_σ, w_σ) from w'_σ to w_σ.

Example 2. Let Σ and φ be as in Example 1. The witness graph $G_{\Sigma,\varphi}$ is shown as second picture in Figure 3. It contains a witness edge arising from σ_1.

Theorem 2. *Let $\Sigma \cup \{\varphi\}$ be a finite set of keys in $\mathcal{K}(PL^{\{.,\_,\_*\}}, PL^{\{.,\_,\_*\}}, PL^{\{.,\_\}}_+)$. We have $\Sigma \models \varphi$ if and only if q_φ is reachable from q'_φ in $G_{\Sigma,\varphi}$.*

The next example illustrates how the edges of the witness graph encode an inference by $\mathfrak{R}$.

Example 3. Let Σ consists of the two keys $\sigma_1 = (\varepsilon, (\text{diary.contact}, \{\_.\text{S}, \_\_.\_.\text{S}\})$ and $\sigma_2 = (\text{diary}, (\text{contact}.\_\_.\_, \{\_\}))$, and let $\varphi = (\varepsilon, (\text{diary.contact}.\_, \{\text{S}, \_.\text{S}\}))$. The witness graph $G_{\Sigma,\varphi}$ is shown as first picture of Figure 4. Here *detail* is the fixed label chosen from $\mathbf{E} - \mathcal{L}_{\Sigma,\varphi}$. We use the same fixed label for all cases that follow. We apply the *subnodes* rule to σ_2 to derive $\sigma'_2 = (\text{diary}, (\text{contact}.\_, \{\_.\_\}))$, the new *key-path containment* rule to σ'_2 to derive $\sigma''_2 = (\text{diary}, (\text{contact}.\_, \{\_.\text{S}\}))$ and the *superkey* rule to σ''_2 to obtain $\sigma'''_2 = (\text{diary}, (\text{contact}.\_, \{\text{S}, \_.\text{S}\}))$. Let $\Sigma' = \{\sigma_1, \sigma'''_2\}$. The witness graph $G_{\Sigma',\varphi}$ is shown as second picture in Figure 4. We apply *context-target* to σ'''_2 to derive $(\text{diary.contact}, (\_, \{\text{S}, \_.\text{S}\}))$ denoted by σ_3. Let $\Sigma'' = \{\sigma_1, \sigma_3\}$. The corresponding witness graph $G_{\Sigma'',\varphi}$ is shown as third picture in Figure 4. An application of the *interaction* rule to σ_1 and σ_3 results in φ which shows that $\varphi \in \Sigma^+_{\mathfrak{R}}$, illustrated on the right of Figure 4.

Note that, if we simply apply the construction of the mini-trees from [7,8], i.e., if we simply replace each variable length wildcard "_*" by the single label ℓ_0 instead of a sequence of $l + 1$ labels ℓ_0, then Theorem 2 does not hold. In fact,

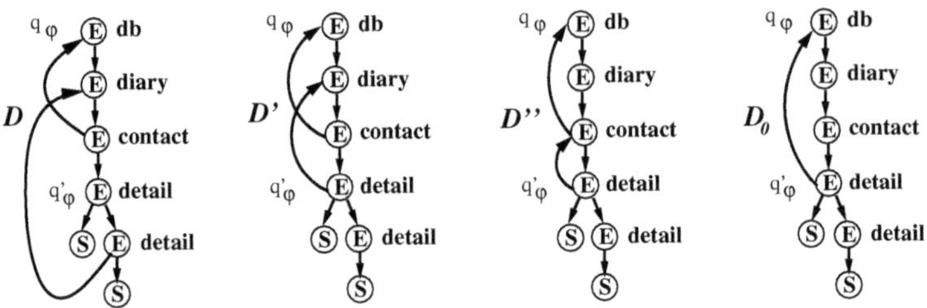

Fig. 4. Encoding the keys from Example 3 as witness edges

for the mini-tree of φ in Example 1, we would get the witness graph shown as third picture in Figure 3. Hence, q_φ would be reachable from q'_φ but $\varphi \notin \Sigma^*$ as the tree on the right of Figure 3 shows.

An Illustration of The Completeness Argument. Let $\Sigma \cup \{\varphi\}$ be an arbitrary finite set of keys in $\mathcal{K}(PL^{\{\cdot,\_,\_^*\}}, PL^{\{\cdot,\_,\_^*\}}, PL_{+}^{\{\cdot,\_\}})$ such that $\varphi \notin \Sigma_{\mathfrak{R}}^{+}$. In order to show completeness one needs to demonstrate that $\varphi \notin \Sigma^*$. Indeed, we can construct a finite XML tree T which satisfies all keys in Σ but does not satisfy φ. If $\varphi \notin \Sigma_{\mathfrak{R}}^{+}$, then one can show that there is no path from q'_φ to q_φ in $G_{\Sigma,\varphi}$. Let u denote the bottom-most descendant node of q_φ in $T_{\Sigma,\varphi}$ such that q_φ is still reachable from u in $G_{\Sigma,\varphi}$. Consequently, u is a proper ancestor of q'_φ because otherwise u and thus q_φ were reachable from q'_φ in $G_{\Sigma,\varphi}$ according to the downward edges. Let T_0 denote a copy of the path from r to u, and T_1, T_2 denote two node-disjoint copies of the subtree of $T_{\Sigma,\varphi}$ rooted at u. We want that a node of T_1 and a node of T_2 become value equal precisely when they are copies of the same marked node in $T_{\Sigma,\varphi}$. For attribute and text nodes this is achieved by choosing string values accordingly, while for element nodes we can adjoin a new child node with a label from $\mathcal{L} - (\mathcal{L}_{\Sigma,\varphi} \cup \{\ell_0\})$ to achieve this. The counter-example tree T is obtained from T_0, T_1, T_2 by identifying the leaf node u of T_0 with the root nodes of T_1 and T_2.

Example 4. Let Σ and φ be as in Example 2. Then u is the single *contact*-node in $T_{\Sigma,\varphi}$. The counter-example tree T, shown on the right of Figure 3, is the result of this construction.

5 Deciding Implication in $\mathcal{K}(PL^{\{\cdot,\_,\_^*\}}, PL^{\{\cdot,\_,\_^*\}}, PL_{+}^{\{\cdot,\_\}})$

Theorem 2 suggests to utilise the following algorithm for deciding XML key implication.

Algorithm 3 (XML Key Implication in $\mathcal{K}(PL^{\{\cdot,\_,\_^*\}}, PL^{\{\cdot,\_,\_^*\}}, PL_{+}^{\{\cdot,\_\}})$)

> **Input:** finite set $\Sigma \cup \{\varphi\}$ of XML keys in $\mathcal{K}(PL^{\{\cdot,\_,\_^*\}}, PL^{\{\cdot,\_,\_^*\}}, PL_{+}^{\{\cdot,\_\}})$
> **Output:** yes, if $\Sigma \models \varphi$; no, otherwise
> **Method:**
> (1) Construct $G_{\Sigma,\varphi}$ for Σ and φ;
> (2) **if** q_φ is reachable from q'_φ in $G_{\Sigma,\varphi}$ **then return**(yes); **else return**(no).

For the class $\mathcal{K}(PL^{\{\cdot,\_^*\}}, PL^{\{\cdot,\_^*\}}, PL_{+}^{\{\cdot\}})$, Algorithm 3 can be implemented in time quadratic in the size of the input [7,8]. Due to the different construction needed for the mini-trees, it is not clear whether Algorithm 3 can also be implemented in quadratic time for the class $\mathcal{K}(PL^{\{.,\_,\_^*\}}, PL^{\{.,\_,\_^*\}}, PL_+^{\{.,\_\}})$. However, it can still be implemented efficiently.

Theorem 4. *If $\Sigma \cup \{\varphi\}$ is a finite set of keys in $\mathcal{K}(PL^{\{.,\_,\_^*\}}, PL^{\{.,\_,\_^*\}}, PL_+^{\{.,\_\}})$, then the implication problem $\Sigma \models \varphi$ can be decided in $\mathcal{O}(|\varphi| \times l \times (||\Sigma|| + |\varphi| \times l))$ time, where $|\varphi|$ is the sum of the lengths of all path expressions in φ, $||\Sigma||$ is the sum of all sizes $|\sigma|$ for $\sigma \in \Sigma$, and l is the maximum number of consecutive single-label wildcards that occur in Σ.*

6 Future Work

When defining XML keys there are at least two factors that determine their expressiveness: i) the navigational operators for accessing nodes (e.g., path expressions for descendants/ancestors) and ii) the notion of value equal nodes (e.g., string equality on leaves, isomorphic subtrees). It is a challenging goal to identify (combinations of) such sources of expressiveness that still permit the development of tractable solutions to the associated decision problems [6].

Future research should further address the implementation of reasoning techniques in real XML applications, e.g., in schema design, data integration, exchange and cleaning, as well as query optimisation and rewriting, and consistent query answering. This may lead to the detection of further fragments of XML keys or relaxations thereof that deserve investigation.

References

1. Apparao, V., et al.: Document object model (DOM) level 1 specification, W3C recommendation (1998), http://www.w3.org/TR/REC-DOM-Level-1/
2. Arenas, M., Fan, W., Libkin, L.: On the complexity of verifying consistency of XML specifications. SIAM J. Comput. 38(3), 841–880 (2008)
3. Buneman, P., Davidson, S., Fan, W., Hara, C., Tan, W.: Keys for XML. Computer Networks 39(5), 473–487 (2002)
4. Clark, J., DeRose, S.: XML path language (XPath) version 1.0, W3C recommendation (1999), http://www.w3.org/TR/xpath
5. Fan, W.: XML constraints. In: DEXA Workshops, pp. 805–809. IEEE Computer Society, Los Alamitos (2005)
6. Hartmann, S., Koehler, H., Link, S., Trinh, T., Wang, J.: On the notion of an XML key. In: Schewe, K.-D., Thalheim, B. (eds.) SDKB 2008. LNCS, vol. 4925, pp. 103–112. Springer, Heidelberg (2008)
7. Hartmann, S., Link, S.: Unlocking keys for XML trees. In: Schwentick, T., Suciu, D. (eds.) ICDT 2007. LNCS, vol. 4353, pp. 104–118. Springer, Heidelberg (2006)
8. Hartmann, S., Link, S.: Efficient reasoning about a robust XML key fragment. ACM Trans. Database Syst. 34(2) (2009)
9. Hartmann, S., Link, S.: Expressive, yet tractable XML keys. In: EDBT. ACM Int. Conf. Proceeding Series, vol. 360, pp. 357–367. ACM, New York (2009)
10. Suciu, D.: On database theory and XML. SIGMOD Record 30(3), 39–45 (2001)
11. Thompson, H.S., Beech, D., Maloney, M., Mendelsohn, N.: XML Schema Part 1: Structures, 2nd edn., W3C Recomm (2004), http://www.w3.org/TR/xmlschema-1/

Author Index

GPSR Compliance

The European Union's (EU) General Product Safety Regulation (GPSR) is a set of rules that requires consumer products to be safe and our obligations to ensure this.

If you have any concerns about our products, you can contact us on ProductSafety@springernature.com

In case Publisher is established outside the EU, the EU authorized representative is:

Springer Nature Customer Service Center GmbH
Europaplatz 3
69115 Heidelberg, Germany

Batch number: 09474016

Printed by Printforce, the Netherlands